Science FOR THE People

Science FOR THE People

Documents from America's Movement of Radical Scientists

EDITED BY

**Sigrid Schmalzer,
Daniel S. Chard,
AND
Alyssa Botelho**

University of Massachusetts Press
Amherst and Boston

ISBN 978-1-62534-318-5 (paper); 317-8 (hardcover)

Designed by Sally Nichols
Set in Adobe Minion Pro by Scribe, Inc.
Printed and bound by Maple Press, Inc.

Library of Congress Cataloging-in-Publication Data

Names: Schmalzer, Sigrid, editor. | Chard, Daniel S., editor. | Botelho,
Alyssa, editor.
Title: Science for the people : documents from America's movement of radical
scientists / edited by Sigrid Schmalzer, Daniel S. Chard, and Alyssa
Botelho.
Description: Amherst : University of Massachusetts Press, [2018] | Includes
bibliographical references and index.
Identifiers: LCCN 2017038238| ISBN 9781625343185 (pbk.) | ISBN 9781625343178
(hardcover)
Subjects: LCSH: Science for the People (Organization)—History. |
Science—Political aspects—United States—History—20th century.
Classification: LCC Q175.5 .S36227 2017 | DDC 506/.073—dc23
LC record available at https://lccn.loc.gov/2017038238

British Library Cataloguing-in-Publication Data
A catalog record for this book is available from the British Library.

*The original Science for the People logo that appears
on the cover was designed by Alphabet.*

We dedicate this book to the members of
Science for the People (1969–1989) and to the next generation of
"science workers"—the scientists, engineers, doctors, nurses, teachers,
scholars, and students who are putting their energy and analysis
to work for a more just and sustainable society.

Contents

Chapter 8: Energy and Environment   177
Ben Allen, Alyssa Botelho, and Daniel S. Chard

Chapter 9: Science for the People and the World   199
Daniel S. Chard

Preface

This book is the first compilation of original documents on Science for the People (SftP), the most important radical science movement in U.S. history. Between 1969 and 1989, SftP mobilized American scientists, engineers, teachers, and students who yearned to practice a socially and economically just science, rather than one that served militarism and corporate profits. With a growing sense of urgency and the stakes becoming ever clearer, we are convinced that the history of SftP will inspire many more scientists and scholars in science and technology studies to embrace an activist orientation in their work.

As this book goes to press, scientists around the United States are organizing to defend science from a new presidential administration that is blatantly dismissive of scientific consensus, committed to slashing research funding, and striving to purge government agencies of data crucial to informed decision making. Within this movement, some are not just defending "science" in the abstract, but advancing a bold vision of science in the service of social justice and environmental sustainability. And some of these activists are gathering once again under the banner of Science for the People.[1] In times of political turmoil, some may be tempted to embrace science as an apolitical force of reason. Science for the People understood that while science does offer reason, it does not do so in a political vacuum. Now, as then, we have political choices to make. We have to decide what kind of science is worth making and worth fighting for. We have to make that science. And we have to fight for it.

The contributors to this volume gathered at a three-day conference hosted by the Social Thought & Political Economy Program of the University of Massachusetts Amherst in April 2014. Titled "Science for the People: The 1970s and Today," the conference brought former members of SftP together with other scientists, scholars, students, and activists in a lively exploration of SftP's historical relevance for today's struggles. About two hundred people attended, and more than sixty people offered presentations. (The conference program, abstracts, and video of all presentations are available at http://science-for-the-people.org.) Following the conference, six participants met to discuss how we could make SftP's legacy known to a greater number of people: the result is this book.

Dozens of people contributed their time and energy to make this volume a reality. First and most obviously, we thank the writers and artists who created the materials included here. Second, we thank everyone who contributed to the conference. Special thanks go to the members of the original Science for the People who presented at the conference (listed below) and who have shared the contents of their attics and basements; the conference organizing committee; the graduate students who participated in the conference, committed to this project, and contributed chapter introductions; and the dedicated people who are now spearheading an SftP "revitalization" project. Major funding for the conference was provided by the National Science Foundation; it was hosted by the Social Thought & Political Economy Program at UMass Amherst and co-sponsored by many other departments and programs at UMass and surrounding colleges. We would also like to thank Rob Cox and Danielle Kovacs at Special Collections and University Archives for their enthusiasm and assistance in creating an SftP archive at UMass; founding member of SftP Charles Schwartz for providing public access to many important SftP documents; and independent researcher Melanie McCalmont for creating the conference website and making available documents on SftP obtained through a Freedom of Information Act request. We are profoundly grateful for the thorough reading and critical feedback provided by Kelly Moore, Banu Subramaniam, and one anonymous reviewer. Jonathan Beckwith, Charles Schwartz, and Katherine Yih reviewed portions of the manuscript for errors and omissions, and Sarah Bridger provided valuable documents. UMass Press was able to lower the cost of the book substantially thanks to generous donations from Minna Barrett (in memory of Rita Barrett), Jonathan and Barbara Beckwith, Bertram and Susan Bruce, Chandler Davis and Natalie Zemon Davis, Anne Fausto-Sterling, Ross Feldberg, Britta Fischer and Herb Fox, David Kotelchuck, Ruth Moscovitch and Vinton Thompson, Richard Rosen, Charles Schwartz, Abha Sur, and Katherine Yih. We are deeply grateful for their support. Finally, we are grateful to executive editor Matt Becker, interim series editor Eric Nystrom, and their colleagues at UMass Press for supporting our vision and making this volume a reality.

Former SftP Members who participated in the 2014 Conference

Joseph Alper, Arlene Ash, Minna Barrett, Jonathan Beckwith, Doug Boucher, Frank Bove, Carol Cina, Dave Culver, Chandler Davis, Britta Fischer, Anne Fausto-Sterling, Herb Fox, Elizabeth Fox-Wolfe, Roberta Garner, Terri Goldberg, Michael Goldhaber, Ivan Handler, Mike Hansen, Jonathan King, David Kotelchuck, Richard Levins, Frank Mirer, Steve Nadel, R. D. Ogden, Ivette Perfecto, Margaret Reeves, Rich Rosen, Scott Schneider, Brian Schultz, Robert Shapiro, Sue Tafler, Lorne Taichman, Vinton Thompson, John Vandermeer, Al Weinrub, and Katherine Yih

EDITORS' NOTES

1. The "revitalized" organization's website is http://scienceforthepeople.org. See Jeffrey Mervis, "As Scientists Prepare to March, Science for the People Reboots," *Science,* April 4, 2017, http://www.sciencemag.org/news/2017/04/scientists-prepare-march-science-people -reboots.

Science FOR THE People

Science for the People, the 1970s and Today

How should we understand the problems of science in society? How does our understanding of these problems shape our course of action?

Many scientists are frustrated by climate change denial, attacks on teaching evolution in the schools, and other impediments to harnessing scientific knowledge for social benefit. Typically, "scientific illiteracy" gets the blame: if only the public received better science education, and if only scientists communicated more effectively, scientists would receive the support and autonomy they need to address the world's problems. However, not all stakeholders are willing to leave the problems of science in society to scientists alone. Many activists who care deeply about climate change, health care, and other issues of scientific importance are profoundly skeptical of the scientific establishment. They question scientists' loyalties given the funding they often receive from fossil fuel, chemical, and pharmaceutical corporations; and they ask why scientific perspectives so often promote narrow understandings of social problems. Here again, progressive scientists often suggest that better communication is needed to build the public's trust in scientists and the scientific method.

Scientists are right to call for educational reforms to improve scientific literacy and for more emphasis on public communication. But the challenges activists raise will not be resolved so simply. The education and communication paradigm dominant in discussions of science and society today fails to account for the workings of power. Not that long ago, another approach, rooted in an analysis of political, economic, and social power structures, attracted considerable attention from scientists and others committed to

1

harnessing science and technology to serve human needs. Crucially, this approach disputed the scientific establishment's claims to political neutrality.[1] While sidelined in mainstream discussions, this type of analysis continues to inform the perspectives of critical scholars and scientists today. If more widely embraced, it would greatly enrich our public discussions of energy policy, medicine, environmental conservation, agricultural technologies, and other social projects.

During the 1970s and 1980s, a movement led by the organization Science for the People (SftP) put forward such an alternative approach—one that fundamentally challenged the dominant social relations of science. While SftP members promoted science education, they did not see public ignorance as the primary constraint on science's capacity to fully benefit humanity. Rather, they critiqued the power structures—capitalism, imperialism, patriarchy, and racism—that benefited from public ignorance and impeded the production, circulation, and application of socially beneficial scientific knowledge. SftP understood that scientific practice is a political act, informed by particular understandings of power and social need. Unlike colleagues who imagined science as separate from the social sphere, SftP scientists rejected this divide and used their knowledge to question the social, political, and economic status quo. Through research, writing, protest, and grassroots organizing, they sought to demystify scientific knowledge and embolden "the people" to take science and technology into their own hands.

SftP initially emerged as part of the mass movement to end the U.S. war in Vietnam, which between 1955 and 1975 took the lives of approximately 58,000 Americans, more than 3 million Vietnamese, and more than 500,000 Cambodians and Laotians.[2] One of the first steps toward creating a movement of radical scientists occurred in 1967, when University of California–Berkeley physicist Charles Schwartz proposed that the American Physical Society (APS) amend its bylaws to enable the organization to formally oppose the war. APS members voted against the "Schwartz Amendment" in 1968, but the election only helped radicalize a growing cohort of young, dissident scientists.[3] As members of the Boston SftP collective later recalled, the vote demonstrated that "there was a *physics establishment*—and there was the rest of us."[4]

Schwartz co-founded SftP's predecessor organization, Scientists for Social and Political Action, during the January 1969 APS meeting in New York City together with Martin Perl, Mike Goldhaber, and Marc Ross. Nearly two hundred scientists attended the group's first meeting.[5] A few months later, the organization changed its name to Scientists and Engineers for Social and Political Action (SESPA). During the December 1969 annual meeting of the American Association for the Advancement of Science (AAAS) in Boston, SESPA recruited still more participants and began also referring to itself as Science for the People (the group used both names throughout the early 1970s). Soon thereafter, SftP transformed the recently created SESPA newsletter into a bi-monthly magazine called *Science for the People*. By the time of the organization's dissolution in 1989, SftP had published one hundred and nine issues of its magazine.

SftP grew quickly after its founding, as members established chapters in Ann Arbor, Berkeley, Boston, Chicago, Madison, Stony Brook, and more than a dozen other cities, most of them on or near university campuses. Prominent scientists, including Rita Arditti, Jonathan Beckwith, Stephen Jay Gould, Ruth Hubbard, Richard Lewontin, Richard Levins, and Freda Salzman joined the organization, as did many more "rank-and-file" scientists, engineers, doctors, nurses, social workers, and graduate students. SftP's membership was predominantly white and majority male. Members of the group endeavored to combat sexism, racism, and class exploitation within the scientific discipline; challenged gendered and racialized theories of biological determinism; and worked in solidarity with other activists fighting for women's liberation, racial equality, and self-determination. There were limits to these efforts, however. For example, though a strong core of feminists within SftP worked to make gender a key axis of analysis, they felt that they could not sustain interest and cohesion around feminist critiques of science due to resistance from many male colleagues.[6]

From its inception, SftP dedicated itself to intellectual intervention, political organizing, and direct action. Members of the group wrote prolifically, publishing works of political critique, journalism, and scientific research in their magazine, self-published booklets, and scientific journals. They organized both inside and outside the scientific profession, struggling to recruit fellow scientists and transform the APS, the AAAS, other professional organizations, and their universities while building working relationships with radical groups such as the Black Panther Party, Vietnam Veterans Against the War, and the Clamshell Alliance. They worked with labor organizations to fight for occupational health on farms and in factories, and sought meaningful international scientific exchange in Vietnam, China, Cuba, Nicaragua, and other countries. In the early years, SftP activists also engaged in direct action campaigns aimed at remaking scientific institutions. As the essays and documents in this volume illustrate, SftP activists participated in the March 4, 1969, Massachusetts Institute of Technology (MIT) "research stoppage" opposing the U.S. military's Anti-Ballistic Missile system; demonstrations and civil disobedience outside the weapons laboratories of Manhattan's Riverside Research Institute; and disruptions of lectures by prominent scientists and political figures during AAAS national conferences in Chicago and Philadelphia.

SftP departed from the liberal model of scientist activism adopted by the Union of Concerned Scientists and other organizations, where scientists worked within the existing political system to influence policy. With a Marxist analysis and non-hierarchical governing structure, SftP's members tackled the militarization of scientific research, the corporate control of research agendas, the political implications of sociobiology theories, environmental consequences of energy policy, inequities in health care, agricultural science and food justice, and many other issues. In addition to challenging social inequalities within science, the group sought to mobilize people working in scientific fields to agitate for a science, technology, and medicine that would serve social needs rather than military and corporate interests.

In many ways, SftP's history mirrors the broader trajectory of leftist political activism in the United States during the 1970s and '80s. After an early militant direct action phase in the early 1970s, SftP's membership shifted during the middle of the decade. Several of the group's members—including Britta Fischer, Herb Fox, Al Weinrub, and others involved in what they called the Helen Keller Collective in Boston—departed SftP amid wider burnout in U.S. radical circles resulting from factional disputes, police violence, lack of funds, and disagreements over where to focus political energy after the 1975 Communist victory in Vietnam.[7]

However, SftP endured, becoming one of the few 1960s-era radical organizations to survive into the late 1970s and 1980s. Such perseverance allowed SftP to link up with the new movements that emerged during this period. New, younger members joined SftP in the late 1970s, inspired in part by the movement to oppose nuclear energy, the period's largest direct action movement. Debates over biological determinism and genetic engineering also became pressing concerns for SftP during these years, as did agriculture and food justice, toxic pollution, and other issues stemming from a growing international energy crisis and the development of a broader environmental movement.[8] Militarism returned as a central focus for SftP after 1980, when President Ronald Reagan bankrolled right-wing regimes and paramilitaries in Central America and Southern Africa and rekindled the Cold War arms race with the Soviet Union. In response, the SftP-offshoot New World Agriculture and Ecology Group at the University of Michigan sent researchers to Nicaragua to assist the revolutionary Sandinista regime's agriculture efforts. Several SftP members—including co-founder Charles Schwartz—also played key roles in the successful movement to stop Reagan's massive Strategic Defense Initiative satellite missile system.[9]

Though SftP withstood the conservative tide of the Reagan era, the group was less of an organized leftist force within American science after the 1970s. Decentralized since its inception, it grew even more diffuse during the 1980s, serving as a set of general principles that guided various individuals' and small groups' science activism. Despite its members' participation in a number of important social justice campaigns, SftP's primary focus after 1980 was publishing the magazine. This was nevertheless an important activity, as *Science for the People* remained a vital source of leftist critique and news on science, society, and resistance movements unavailable in mainstream publications.

In 1990, SftP dissolved due to tax troubles. When the Internal Revenue Service came after the magazine's editorial collective to pay around $70,000 in back taxes, they were unable to mobilize sufficient support from their dwindling members and folded instead. Nonetheless, SftP's work lives on in other organizations, some of which grew directly from SftP and others of which significantly benefited from the vision of former SftP members—including the Committee for Responsible Genetics (Genewatch); DC Metro Science for the People; the Genetics and Society Working Group; the International Collaborative for Science, Education, and the Environment; the Local Clean Energy Alliance (San Francisco Bay Area); the New World Agriculture and Ecology Group; and the Pesticide Action Network. More broadly, SftP helped many of its members find lasting ways to use their scientific knowledge in the service of the people, especially in the areas of occupational safety, public health, agriculture, consumer protection, environmental activism, and science journalism.[10]

This volume emerges from our conviction that today's struggles for climate justice, universal health care, and sustainable agriculture, among many other causes, can benefit greatly from a deeper familiarity with the history of SftP and its radical analysis. Scientists need a more robust understanding of how social and political realities shape the problems they seek to address. Activists need a stronger grasp on the scientific dimensions of their issues and a clearer sense of who their allies are in the scientific world. Students need strategies for putting their science education to work in ways consistent with their social and political values. And historians, philosophers, and social scientists in the field of science and technology studies (STS) need a deeper knowledge of an organization that had a critical influence on their field—as well as a better appreciation of how engagement with activist scientists might enrich their own research and writing. We anticipate that this volume will be used in classes for science students as well as for students of history and social movements.[11] We hope it will also be discussed in living rooms and coffee shops by study groups of the kind SftP itself once organized.

Despite its significance, the history of SftP has not yet received its due in STS and history of science literature. Moreover, the group has been almost completely overlooked by historians of U.S. social movements.[12] One reason for this relative dearth of scholarship may be the notion that SftP—and radical politics more generally—ultimately failed to present a viable means of transforming science.[13] However, in a 1975 discussion of the significance of radical science movements (SftP included), Donna Haraway offered an important caution for those who might otherwise dismiss the continued relevance of such movements: "We must not let the utter powerlessness of dissidents in the short range in advanced capitalist conditions deter us from learning from them about the political implications of our particular way of teaching about scientific thought."[14] Indeed, one of the most important reasons to study the history of SftP is because its writings continue to challenge mainstream understandings of science and politics. Speaking to both professional and popular audiences, SftP insisted that scientific research is a fundamentally political activity. One of SftP's greatest legacies is its corpus of literature analyzing how the forces of capitalism, imperialism, racism, and patriarchy shape the production, circulation, and application of scientific knowledge. SftP's other vital legacies—which we have sought to highlight in this volume—include the organization's idealistic visions for a more just, humane, and democratic science, as well as its successes and shortcomings in creating a better world.

For academics, or those interested in joining academia, another reason to study the history of SftP is its significance in the birth and development of the field of STS. SftP was founded by scientists and engineers, some of whom had a strong background in political philosophy, and all of whom had a willingness to study the social, political, and economic contexts that inform scientific knowledge. Central to SftP's analysis was a conviction that science was not, and could never be, politically neutral. Members of SftP frequently drew from the analyses of STS scholars active in the 1970s, including David Noble, Dorothy Nelkin, Robert Young, Hilary Rose, and Evelyn Fox Keller. And from the other direction, these and other STS scholars clearly benefited from their participation in SftP and sister organizations in other countries.[15] For example, years before historian of science Robert Proctor published his path-breaking book on medicine in Nazi Germany, *Science for the People* printed his article "Nazi Science and Medicine."[16] Proctor also served on the editorial committee for the magazine in 1983. The roster of authors represented in the 1996 volume *Science Wars* (a defense against a conservative backlash bent on maintaining the view that science is politically neutral) further testifies to the tight connections between SftP and STS: Ruth Hubbard, Richard Levins, and other prominent SftP members were published alongside Sandra Harding, Emily Martin, and other influential STS scholars.[17]

However, as STS matured and became more "professional" in its orientation, some scholars grew frustrated with what they saw as a diminished commitment to engaging seriously *with* and *as* activists. In 1993, STS scholar Brian Martin published a provocative article titled "The Critique of Science Becomes Academic," in which he lambasted others in the field for their "lack of acknowledgment of [the] radical or activist origins" of their ideas. He specifically highlighted SftP in this context: "The magazine *Science for the People* published many incisive critiques of science. Yet it is a frustrating quest to attempt to find a single reference to *Science for the People* in a scholarly analysis of science. The problem is twofold: *Science for the People* was openly political and, in part as a consequence of this, it was not recognized as a scholarly publication itself, in spite of its many top-flight contributors and detailed referencing."[18]

The gauntlet Martin threw down offended many STS scholars, not surprisingly. And it must be said, his article failed to recognize the ways in which many STS scholars continued to write in politically engaged ways. However, Martin's polemic remains useful if it reminds us of the need to acknowledge our activist antecedents, guard against insularity, and, most importantly, seize opportunities to intervene in the issues that motivated many of us to enter the field in the first place. These interventions may take many forms. At the empirical level, STS scholars can analyze the misuse of science by power holders and document activist struggles to place science in the service of human needs. At the level of theory, we can advance more robust alternatives to the top-down model of "communication" found in dominant discourse on science and society. The decades since SftP's activism have provided some excellent models for such work. For example, Robert Proctor's *Golden Holocaust: Origins of the Cigarette Catastrophe and the Case for Abolition* and Naomi Oreskes and Erik Conway's *Merchants of Doubt: How a Handful of Scientists Obscured the Truth on Issues from Tobacco Smoke to Global Warming* provide incisive analysis of the power of corporations and free-market ideology to mobilize scientific resources against the public interest. Steven Epstein's landmark study *Impure Science: AIDS, Activism, and the Politics of Knowledge* documents the success of activists in shaping knowledge production and drug development during the HIV/AIDS epidemic—and offers essential insights on the dilemmas they faced as they moved from outside agitators to inside experts. In *Body and Soul: The Black Panther Party and the Fight against Medical Discrimination,* Alondra Nelson studies the Black Panthers' radical approach to health activism, which rejected the for-profit "medical-industrial complex" and began from the assumption that "therapeutic matters were inextricably articulated to social justice ones."[19] And Giovanna Di Chiro's engaged scholarship with environmental justice activists in Mexico and the United States has helped articulate an understanding of science politics that "spans borders of all kinds—national, racial, gendered, economic, linguistic, ecological, technological, spiritual, and epistemic," and offers a model for "popular knowledge" based on "shared observation, careful research, and the forging of syncretic assemblages of 'experts' of all stripes."[20] We have been inspired by the work of these and other engaged STS scholars and offer this volume as a contribution that we hope will inspire more scientists, scholars, and activists to step up the pace.

We have organized this volume's chapters thematically to highlight the key realms of science and society into which SftP members intervened with ideas, research, and direct action. In selecting the documents for inclusion, we sought materials that most clearly demonstrate core SftP arguments and positions in succinct, accessible prose. In many (though by no means all) cases, the materials that best fit these criteria were articles from *Science for the People* magazine, which throughout much of the organization's twenty-year history represented SftP's most sustained efforts and its most polished analysis. Chapter 1, "Science, Power, and Ideology," discusses SftP's analyses in relation to earlier Marxist writings on science. It also documents some of SftP's most important intellectual challenges to the ideologies undergirding science. Chapter 2, "Disrupting the 'AAA\$,'" illuminates SftP activists' early efforts to mobilize left-leaning scientists through their disruptions of American Association for the Advancement of Science conferences during the early 1970s. Chapters 3 through 8 highlight SftP's activism in the areas of "Militarism," "Biology and Medicine," "Race and Gender," "Agriculture, Ecology, and Food," "Technology," and "Energy and Environment." Finally, Chapter 9, "Science for the People and the World," documents SftP's efforts to build international movements for social revolution in partnership with scientists and activists around the globe. Each chapter opens with an introduction offering an historical overview of SftP's activities in relation to the given theme, followed by a series of excerpted SftP writings on the issues of interest. Each document excerpted in the chapters is accompanied by a brief explanation placing the selection in its historical context.

We offer this volume as a window into SftP's thoughts and actions. When possible, we highlight moments when science activists succeeded, even if only slightly, in challenging or reshaping ideology, knowledge, and the direction of scientific research. For the most part, however, this volume documents an unfinished struggle. After all, scientific institutions today remain largely undemocratic and dominated by capitalist and military interests while war, starvation, inequality, and climate change pose even greater threats than they did during the 1970s and 1980s. Therefore, rather than being a definitive history of SftP, this book is part of the organization's ongoing legacy. Using this volume to understand the past, develop political theory, and strategize for social change, we the readers will determine the future of that legacy.

EDITORS' NOTES

1. Sarah Bridger, "Anti-Militarism and the Critique of Professional Neutrality in the Origins of Science for the People," *Science as Culture* 25, no. 3 (August 2016): 373–78.
2. Christian G. Appy, *American Reckoning: The Vietnam War and our National Identity* (New York: Viking, 2015), 229.
3. For more on the "Schwartz Amendment," see Document 2.1 in this volume. Also see Sarah Bridger, *Scientists at War: The Ethics of Cold War Weapons Research* (Cambridge, MA: Harvard University Press, 2015), 196–99; and Kelly Moore, *Disrupting Science: Social Movements, American Science, and the Politics of the Military 1945–1975* (Princeton, NJ: Princeton University Press, 2008), 146–51.
4. "SESPA: A History," *Science for the People* 2, no. 4 (1970): 2.
5. Bridger, *Scientists at War,* 201; Moore, *Disrupting Science,* 151.

6. Moore, *Disrupting Science,* 183–84.
7. These individuals parted from SftP amid an internal split over ideology and political strategy, when other members rejected their efforts to unify the organization under a Marxist-Leninist party model. Britta Fischer, Herb Fox, Elizabeth Fox-Wolfe, and Al Weinrub, oral history interview with Alyssa Botelho and Daniel S. Chard, April 13, 2014, Amherst, Massachusetts; Kathy Greely and Sue Tafler, "Science for the People: A Ten Year Retrospective," *Science for the People* 11, no. 1 (January–February 1979): 24; Moore, *Disrupting Science,* 182.
8. Greely and Tafler, "Science for the People: A Ten Year Retrospective," 18–25.
9. SftP's story adds to a growing body of historical literature challenging the popular notion that progressive social movements died in the early 1970s, and that the United States in the late 1970s and 1980s was characterized exclusively by popular political apathy and the rising influence of conservatism in government. For more on activism in the United States during the 1970s and 1980s, see Michael Foley, *Front Porch Politics: The Forgotten Heyday of American Activism in the 1970s and 1980s* (New York: Hill and Wang, 2013); Roger Peace, *A Call to Conscience: The Anti-Contra War Campaign* (Amherst: University of Massachusetts Press, 2012); Dan Berger, ed., *The Hidden 1970s: Histories of Radicalism* (New Brunswick, NJ: Rutgers University Press, 2010); and Robert Surbrug Jr., *Beyond Vietnam: The Politics of Protest in Massachusetts, 1974–1990* (Amherst: University of Massachusetts Press, 2009). On the New World Agriculture and Ecology Group, see Ivette Perfecto, "New World Agriculture and Ecology Group: The Sandinista Years," conference presentation, Science for the People: The 1970s and Today, April 13, 2014, Science for the People website, http://science-for-the-people.org/sftp-in-the-world/ (accessed December 9, 2016). Also see Document 9.5 in this volume on the Science for Nicaragua project. For more on scientist opposition to Reagan's Strategic Defense Initiative, see Document 3.5 in this volume, and Bridger, *Scientists at War,* 245–69.
10. Jonathan Beckwith, "The Radical Science Movement in the United States," *Monthly Review* 38, no. 3 (1986): 119–28. Readers interested in learning more about how former members have carried on SftP's legacy should consult the videos of panel presentations from the 2014 conference, archived at http://science-for-the-people.org.
11. For ideas on teaching with primary sources from this volume, see Sigrid Schmalzer, "Teaching the History of Radical Science with Materials on Science for the People," and Daniel S. Chard, "Teaching with the FBI's Science for the People File," *Radical History Review* 127 (January 2017): 173–79 and 180–85.
12. Moore, *Disrupting Science,* and Bridger, *Scientists at War,* remain the most extensive scholarly treatments of SftP's history.
13. Rebecca Slayton, "Discursive Choices: Boycotting Star Wars between Science and Politics," *Social Studies of Science* 37, no. 1 (2007): 61n106.
14. Donna Jeanne Haraway, "The Transformation of the Left in Science: Radical Associations in Britain in the 30's and the U.S.A. in the 60's," *Soundings* 58, no. 4 (1975): 459.
15. Most important among these organizations for SftP was the group British Society for Social Responsibility in Science, whose journal took the name *Science for People.* See Jerome Ravetz, "Anti-Establishment Science in Some British Journals," in *Countermovements in the Sciences: The Sociology of the Alternatives to Big Science,* ed. Helga Nowotny and Hilary Rose, 27–37 (Boston: D. Reidel, 1979).
16. Robert Proctor, "The Road to the Holocaust: Nazi Science and Medicine," *Science for the People* 14, no. 2 (March–April 1982): 15–20.
17. Andrew Ross, ed., *Science Wars* (Durham, NC: Duke University Press, 1996).
18. Brian Martin, "The Critique of Science Becomes Academic," *Science, Technology, and Human Values* 18, no. 2 (1993): 249. See also Edward Woodhouse, David Hess, Steve Breyman, and Brian Martin, "Science Studies and Activism: Possibilities and Problems for Reconstructivist Agendas," *Social Studies of Science* 32, no. 2 (April 2002): 297–319.

19. Alondra Nelson, *Body and Soul: The Black Panther Party and the Fight against Medical Discrimination* (Minneapolis: University of Minnesota Press, 2011), 11.
20. Giovanna Di Chiro, "'Living Is for Everyone': Border Crossings for Community, Environment, and Health," *Osiris* 19 (2004): 112–29, 128–29.

FIGURE 1. Marx and Lenin in lab coats. Cover of *Science for the People* 6, no. 4 (July 1974).

CHAPTER 1

Science, Power, and Ideology

Ben Allen
and
Sigrid Schmalzer

From disrupting academic conferences to providing technological assistance to social movements, Science for the People's practical engagement with science and society rested on its radical ideology. SftP was very much a product of its time: its ideology reflected the widely articulated critiques of Western cultural and political norms in the 1960s and early 1970s, as well as the revolutionary ambitions of the period's student, antiwar, and national liberation movements.[1] However, SftP's analysis of science and society was also deeply influenced by earlier social critics, in particular 1930s Marxist scientists, philosophers, and historians of science in the United Kingdom (e.g., J. D. Bernal, J. B. S. Haldane, Julian Huxley, and Joseph Needham) and the Soviet Union (especially Boris Hessen in his highly influential treatise, "The Social and Economic Roots of Newton's 'Principia'").[2] These early thinkers wrote voluminously on the social relations of science and offered a systematic critique of science under capitalism. They argued against "internalist" histories of science that assumed new ideas emerged independently of social, political, and economic power structures, and they challenged the notion that science could be divided into separate realms of "pure" and "applied," with advances in scientific theory providing the impetus for changes in technology. Rather, Hessen argued that "science develops out of production," and thus the social relations of production operating in any historical context structured the possibilities for scientific advances and determined whom those advances would serve.[3] Dialectical materialism further provided a basis for arguing against reductionism; this was especially important in the biological sciences, where Marxist scientists highlighted the complex and dynamic character of organic processes. Finally, 1930s Marxists placed their faith in the kind of rational, centralized planning that they believed had allowed the Soviets to mobilize science on a large scale for broad social benefit. These thinkers laid an analytical foundation for the scientist-activists who in 1969 founded Scientists for Social and Political Action (later SftP) in the United States and, across the Atlantic, the British Society for Social Responsibility in Science.[4] SftP members read the writings of 1930s Marxists and made efforts to keep their work in circulation—readers of *Science for the People* magazine were invited to order copies of some of these books by mail from the Cambridge, Massachusetts, office.[5]

The four selections featured in this chapter reveal the continuities between the writings of 1930s Marxists and SftP's analysis of science, power, and ideology. As their predecessors did, and as politically engaged STS scholars have also done,[6] SftP sought to explain how social relations shaped ideology, and how ideology in turn shaped the production of scientific knowledge. They sought to pierce the façade of pure or disinterested inquiry, dismantle the notion that science could operate outside of the sway of dominant power structures, and offer in its place a critical analysis of the social, political, and economic contexts that governed the organization and orientation of scientific work. In addition, they used Marxist dialectics to attack scientific reductionism and the related, oppressive theories of biological determinism. For SftP, such a critique was necessary to liberate science from its complicity in the preservation of class, racial, and gender stratification and from its contributions to the destruction of the planet and its people. Moreover, SftP members rearticulated 1930s critiques of the supposed division between basic and applied science and drew ever-clearer connections between the results of so-called "pure" or basic research and the destructive technologies they enabled.

Of course, much had changed in forty years, and the selections included here could not be mistaken for the work of Bernal, Needham, or other 1930s Marxists. The atomic bombing of Hiroshima and Nagasaki had greatly eroded confidence in science as a force for good, heightening the stakes of the critique of "purity" in theoretical science. Still more importantly, by the 1960s the capitalist West (and the United States in particular) had established something very much resembling the large-scale state sponsorship of science that Bernal and others had called for, and which had now gained the moniker "big science."[7] Meanwhile, the Soviet model had lost much of its luster for leftists in the United States and the United Kingdom. And so, rather than imagining a future of big, state-sponsored science as the 1930s Marxists had, SftP members were more concerned with critiquing big science as developed by the "American corporate state" (see Document 1.1). SftP members, along with many STS scholars, also differed from their predecessors in their emphasis on race and gender as axes of oppression;[8] and many of the most prominent examples of people's science that SftP members cited came from health movements led by feminists and "Third World" liberation organizations like the Black Panther Party and Young Lords Organization.[9] Nonetheless, socialist states such as China, Cuba, and Nicaragua also provided inspirational models and opportunities for international solidarity (see Chapter 9, "Science for the People and the World").

Document 1.1

Bill Zimmerman, Len Radinsky, Mel Rothenberg, Bart Meyers, "Toward a Science for the People" (Science for the People Booklet, 1972).

More than any other publication, this essay captures Science for the People's Marxist analysis of science in the "American corporate state" and its vision for mobilizing scientists to pursue revolutionary alternatives. The document, first conceived in pamphlet form, was authored by a group that called itself The People's Science Collective. These writers came together at the New University Conference, a national organization of radical graduate students and faculty that emerged in Chicago during the social eruptions of 1968. SftP went on to distribute several thousand copies of the essay at the 1970 meeting of the American Association for the Advancement of Science (AAAS). The following year, the authors expanded the article and submitted it to *Science* magazine, a publication of the AAAS and one of the world's top scientific journals. According to Bill Zimmerman, *Science* editor Philip Abelson ignored favorable reviews and recommendations to publish, deciding instead to reject the submission. SftP itself published several versions of the article, including "People's Science" (published in the February 1971 issue of *Science for the People* magazine); "CENSORED" (December 1971); and "Toward a People's History of Science" (December 1972). This long and tortured history of publication speaks to SftP's sustained effort to engage the mainstream scientific press.

In the 15th century, Leonardo Da Vinci refused to publish plans for a submarine because he anticipated that it would be used as a weapon. In the 17th century, for similar reasons, Boyle kept secret a poison he had developed. In 1946, Leo Szilard, who had been one of the key developers of the atom bomb, quit physics in disillusionment over the ways in which the government had used his work. By and large, this kind of resistance on the part of scientists to the misuse of their research has been very sporadic, from isolated individuals, and generally in opposition only to particular, unusually repugnant projects. As such, it has been ineffective. If scientists want to help prevent socially destructive applications of science, they must forego acting in an ad hoc or purely moralistic fashion, and begin to respond collectively from the vantage point of a political and economic analysis of their work. This analysis must be firmly anchored in an understanding of the American corporate state.

We will argue below that science is inevitably political, and in the context of contemporary American corporate capitalism, that it largely contributes to the exploitation and oppression of most of the people both in this country and abroad. We will call for a reorientation of scientific work and will suggest ways in which scientific workers can redirect their research to further meaningful social change.

Science in Capitalist America

Concurrent with the weakening of Cold War ideology over the past 15 years has been the growing realization on the part of increasing numbers of Americans that a tiny minority of the population, through its wealth and power, controls the major decision-making institutions of our society. Research such as that of Mills (*The Power Elite*), Domhoff (*Who Rules America*), and Lundgren (*The Rich and the Superrich*) has exposed the existence of this minority to public scrutiny. Although the term "ruling class" may have an anachronistic ring to some, we still find it useful to describe that dominant minority that owns and controls the productive economic resources of our society. The means by which the American ruling class exerts control in our society and over much of the Third World has been described in such works as Baran and Sweezy's *Monopoly Capital,* Horowitz's *The Free World Colossus,* and Magdoff's *The Age of Imperialism.* These works argue that it is not a conspiracy but rather the logical outcome of corporate capitalism that a minority with wealth and power, functioning efficiently within the system to maintain its position, inevitably will oversee the oppression and exploitation of the majority of the people in this country, as well as the more extreme impoverishment and degradation of the people of the Third World. It is within the context of this political economic system, a system that has produced the Military-Industrial complex as its highest expression, and that will use all the resources at its disposal to maintain its control, that is, within the context of the American Corporate State, that we must consider the role played by scientific work.

We view the long term strategy of the U.S. capitalist class as resting on two basic pillars. The first is the maintenance and strengthening of the international domination of U.S. capital. The principal economic aspect of this lies in continually increasing the profitable opportunities for the export of capital so as to absorb the surplus constantly being generated both internally and abroad. With the growing revolt of the oppressed peoples of the world, the traditional political and military mechanisms necessary to sustain this imperialist control are disintegrating. More and more the U.S. ruling class is coming to rely openly on technological and military means of mass terrorization and repression which approach genocide: anti-personnel bombs, napalm, pacification-assassination programs, herbicides, and other attempts to induce famines, etc.

While this use of scientific resources is becoming more clearly evident (witness the crisis of conscience among increasing numbers of young scientists), the importance of scientific and technological resources for the second pillar of capitalist strategy is even more central, although less generally accorded the significance it deserves.

The second fundamental thrust of capitalist political economic strategy is to guarantee a steady and predictable increase in the productivity of domestic labor. The ability to extract an increasingly better return on the wage investment by curtailment of the necessary labor time to produce a given product is crucial to the maintenance of the profitability of domestic industry, and its ability to compete on the international market. Without this increase in labor productivity it would be impossible to maintain profits and at the same time sustain the living standard and employment of the working class, and without this it would be impossible to sustain the internal consumer market and blunt domestic class struggle so necessary to the preservation of social control by the ruling class.

The key to increasing the productivity of labor is the transformation and reorganization of our major industries through accelerated automation and rationalization of the production process (through economy of scale, the introduction of labor saving plant and machinery, doing away with the traditional craft prerogatives of the workers, etc., such as is occurring now in the construction industry). This reorganization will depend on programmed advances in technology.

There are basically two reasons why these advances and new developments cannot be left to the 'natural' progress of scientific-technological knowledge, why they must be foreseen and included in the social-economic planning of the ruling class. First is the mammoth investment in the present day plant, equipment and organizational apparatus of the major monopolies. The sudden obsolescence of a significant part of their apparatus would be an economic disaster which could very well endanger their market position. (One sees the results of this lack of planning in the airline industry.) Secondly, the transformation of the process of production entails major reorganization of education, transportation, and communication. This has far-reaching social and political consequences which cause profound strains in traditional class, race, and sex relationships, which have already generated and will continue to generate political and social crises. For the ruling class to deal with these crises it is necessary to be able to plan ahead, to anticipate new developments so that they do not get out of hand.

In our view, because planned and programmed advances in technology are absolutely central to ruling class strategy, an entirely new relationship is required between the ruling and the technical-scientific sectors of society, a relationship which has been emerging since the Second World War, and which, rooted deeply in social-economic developments, cannot be reversed. If one looks at the new sciences which have developed in this period—cybernetics, systems analysis, management science, linear programming, game theory, as well as the direction of development in the social sciences, one sees an enormous development in the techniques of gathering, processing, organizing, and utilizing information, exactly the type of technological advance most needed by the rulers. . . .

The ruling class, through government, big corporations, and tax-exempt foundations, funds most of our research. In the case of industrial research, the control and direction of research are obvious. With government or private foundation supported research, controls are somewhat less obvious but nonetheless effective. Major areas of research may be preferentially funded by direction of Congress or foundation trustees. For example, billions of dollars are spent on space research while pressing domestic needs are given lower priority. We believe implications of space research for the military and the profits of the influential aerospace industries are clearly the decisive factors. Within specific areas of research, ruling class bias is also evident in selection of priorities. For example, in medicine money has been poured into research on heart disease, cancer and stroke, major killers of the middle and upper class, rather than into research on sickle cell anemia, the broad range of effects of malnutrition (higher incidences of most diseases), etc., which effect mainly the lower classes. Large sums of money are provided for study of ghetto populations but nothing is available to support studies of how the powerful operate. . . .

The same government-corporate axis that funds applied research that is narrowly beneficial to ruling class interests also supports almost all our basic, or to use the euphemism "pure," research; it is called pure because it is ostensibly performed not for specific applications but only to seek the truth. Many scientific workers engaged in some form of basic research do not envision any applications of their work and thus believe themselves absolved of any responsibility for applications. Others perform basic research in hopes that it will lead to the betterment of mankind. In either case these workers have failed to understand the contemporary situation.

Today basic research is closely followed by those in a position to reap the benefits of its application—the government and the corporations. Only rich institutions have the resources and staff to keep abreast of current research and to mount the technology necessary for its application. As the attention paid by government corporations to scientific research has increased, the amount of time required to apply it has decreased. In the last century, fifty years elapsed between Faraday's demonstration that an electric current could be generated by moving a magnet near a piece of wire and Edison's construction of the first central power station. Only seven years passed between the recognition that the atomic bomb was theoretically possible and its detonation over Hiroshima and Nagasaki. The transistor went from invention to sales in a mere three years. More recently, research on lasers was barely completed when engineers began using it to design new weapons for the government and new long distance transmission systems for the telephone company.

The result is that in many ways discovery and application, scientific research and engineering, can no longer be distinguished from each other. Our technological society has brought them so close together that today they can only be considered part of the same process. Consequently, while most scientific workers are motivated by humane considerations, or a detached pursuit of truth for truth's sake, their discoveries cannot be separated from applications which all too frequently destroy or debase human life.

Theoretical and experimental physicists, working on problems of esoteric intellectual interest, provided the knowledge that eventually was pulled together to make the H-bomb, while mathematicians, geophysicists, and metallurgists, wittingly or unwittingly, made the discoveries necessary to construct intercontinental ballistic missiles. Physicists doing basic work in optics and infrared spectroscopy may have been shocked to find that their research would help government and corporate engineers build detection and surveillance devices for use in Indochina. . . .

[T]he potentially beneficial achievements of scientific technology do not escape the political and economic context. Rather, they emerge as products which are systematically distributed in an inequitable way to become another means of further defining and producing the desired political or economic ends of those in power. New knowledge capable of application in ways which would alleviate the many injustices of capitalism and imperialism is either not created in the first place or is made worthless by the limited resources of the victims.

If we are to take seriously the observation that discovery and application are practically inseparable, it follows that basic researchers have more than a casual responsibility for the applications of their work. The possible consequences of research in progress or planned for the future must be subjected to careful scrutiny. . . .

An analysis of scientific research merely begins with a description of how it is misapplied and maldistributed. The next step must be an unequivocal statement that scientific activity in a technological society is not, and cannot be, politically neutral or value-free. Some people, particularly after Hiroshima and Nuremberg, have accepted this. Others still argue that science should be an unbridled search for truth, not subject to a political or a moral critique. J. Robert Oppenheimer, the man in charge of the Los Alamos project which built and tested the first atomic bombs, said in 1967 that, "our work has changed the conditions in which men live, but the use made of these changes is the problem of governments, not of scientists." . . .

What Is To Be Done?

In this society, at this time, it is not possible to escape the political implications of scientific work. The American ruling class has long had a commitment to science, not merely limited to short range practical applications, but based on the belief that science was good for the long term welfare of American capitalism, and that what was good for American capitalism was good for humanity. This outlook is shared by the trustees of universities, the official leaders of U.S. science, the administrators of government and private funding agencies. Further, they see this viewpoint as representing a mature social responsibility, morally superior to the 'pure search for truth' attitudes of some of the scientists. But they tolerate that ideology since it furthers their own aims and does not challenge their uses of science.

We find the alternatives of 'science for science's sake' and 'science for progress and capitalism' equally unacceptable. We can no longer identify the cause of humanity with that of U.S. capitalism. We don't have two governments, one which beneficently funds research and another which represses and kills in the ghetto, in Latin America, and in Indochina. Nor do we have two corporate structures, manipulating for profit on the one hand while desiring social equity and justice on the other. Rather there is a single government-corporate axis which supports research with the intention of acquiring powerful tools, of both the hard- and software varieties, for the pursuit of exploitive and imperial goals.

Recognizing the political implications of their work, some scientists in recent years have sought to organize, as scientists, to oppose the more noxious or potentially catastrophic schemes of the government, such as atmospheric nuclear testing, chemical and biological warfare development, and the antiballistic missile system. Others shifted fields to find less "controversial" disciplines: Leo Szilard, who had been wartime codirector of the University of Chicago experiments which led to the first self-sustaining chain reaction, quit physics in disillusionment over the manner in which the government had used his work, and devoted the rest of his life to research in molecular biology and public affairs. In subsequent years other physicists followed Szilard's lead into biology, including Donald Glaser, the 1960 recipient of the Nobel Prize in physics. Yet in 1969, James Shapiro, one of the group of microbiologists who first isolated a pure gene, announced that for political reasons he was going to stop doing any research. Shapiro's decision points up the inadequacy of Szilard's, but is no less inadequate itself.

Traditional attempts to reform scientific activity, to disentangle it from its more malevolent and vicious applications, have failed. Actions designed to preserve the moral integrity of individuals without addressing themselves to the political and economic system which is at the root of the problem have been ineffective. The ruling class can always replace a Leo Szilard with an Edward Teller. What is needed now is not liberal reform or withdrawal, but a radical attack, a strategy of opposition. Scientific workers must develop ways to put their skills at the service of the people and against the oppressors.

How to do this is perhaps best exemplified in the area of health care. It is not by accident that the groups now most seriously dealing with the problem of people's health needs are political organizations. The Black Panther Party recently initiated a series of free health clinics to provide sorely needed medical services that should be, but are not, available to the poor, and the idea has been picked up by other community groups, such as the Young Lords, an organization of revolutionary Latins and Puerto Ricans. Health and scientific workers, organized by political groups like the Medical Committee for Human Rights and the Student Health Organization have helped provide the necessary professional support, and in the past few years literally hundreds of free people's health centers have sprung up across the country.

Health workers, organized into political groups, can provide more than just diagnosis and treatment. They can begin to redefine some medical problems as social problems, and through medical education begin to loosen the dependency of people on the medical profession. They can provide basic biological information, demystify medical sciences, and help give people more control over their own bodies. For example, recently in New York, health workers provided a simple way of detecting lead poisoning to the Young Lords Organization. This enabled the Young Lords to directly serve their people through a door to door testing campaign in the Barrio, and also to organize them against the landlords who refused to cover lead painted walls, often with the tacit complicity of the city housing officials.

It is this kind of scientific practice that most clearly characterizes Science for the People. It serves the oppressed and impoverished classes and strengthens their ability to struggle. The development of People's Science must entail these and other characteristics. For example, any discoveries or new techniques should be such that all people have reasonably easy access to them, both physically and financially. This would also mitigate against their use as a means of generating individual or corporate profit. Scientific developments, whether in the natural or social sciences, that could conceivably be employed as weapons against the people must be carefully evaluated before the work is carried out. Such decisions will always be difficult. They demand a consideration of factors like the relative accessibility of these developments to each side, the relative ease and certainty of use, which will of course depend on the demand, the extent to which the power balance in a specific situation could be shifted and at what risk, and so forth. Finally, scientific or technological programs posing as meeting the needs of the people, but which in fact strengthen the existing political system and defuse the ability to struggle, are the opposite of People's Science.

There is a wide range of activities that might constitute a Science for the People. This work can be described in six broad areas:

1. Technical assistance to movement organizations and oppressed people . . .

2. Foreign technical help to revolutionary movements . . .

3. People's research. Unlike the technical assistance projects described above, which are directly tied in with ongoing struggles, there are areas in which scientists should take the initiative and begin developing projects that will aid struggles that are just beginning to develop. For example, workers in the medical and social sciences and in education could help design a program for client-controlled day care centers which would both free women from the necessity of continual child care and provide a thoroughly socialist educational experience for the children . . .

4. Exposés and power structure research. Most of the important political, military, and economic decisions in this country are made behind closed doors, outside of the public arena . . .

5. Ideological struggle. The ruling class ideology is effectively disseminated by educational institutions and the mass media, resulting in misinformation that clouds people's understanding of their own oppression and limits their ability to resist it. This ruling class ideology must be exposed as the self-serving manipulation that it is. There are many areas where this needs to be accomplished. Arguments of biological determinism are used to help keep Blacks and other Third World people in lower educational tracks, and these racist arguments have recently been bolstered by Jensen's focusing on supposed racial differences in intelligence. Virtually every school of psychopathology and psychotherapy defines homosexuals as sick or "maladjusted" (to a presumably "sane" society). These definitions are used to excuse this society's discriminatory laws and practices with respect to its large homosexual population, and have only recently been actively opposed by the Gay Liberation Movement . . .

6. Demystification of science and technology. No one would deny that science and technology have become major influences in the shaping of peoples' lives. Yet most people lack the information necessary to understand how they are affected by technological manipulation and control. As a result they are physically and intellectually incapable of performing many operations that they are dependent upon, and control over these operations has been relinquished to various experts. Furthermore, these same people undergo an incapacitating

emotional change which results in the feeling that everything is too complicated to cope with (whether technological or not), and that only the various experts should participate in decision making which often directly affects their own lives. Clearly, these two factors are mutually enhancing.

In the interest of democracy and people's control, the false mystery surrounding science and technology must be removed and the hold of experts on decision making must be destroyed. Understandable information can be made available to all those for whom it is pertinent. . . .

Scientists must succeed in redirecting their professional activities away from services to the forces and institutions they oppose and toward a movement they wish to build. Short of this, no matter how much they desire to contribute to the solution, they remain part of the problem.

Document 1.2

Norman Diamond, "The Politics of Scientific Conceptualization," *Science for the People* 8, no. 3 (May 1976): 14–17, 40.

This essay offers a Marxist analysis of the historical and material forces at play in the development of scientific knowledge. Diamond articulated the relationship between scientific knowledge and social context, and on that basis called upon scientists to transform their consciousness and realize their role in developing scientific concepts that support radical social change. Five years after its publication in *Science for the People* magazine, this piece was republished in a volume edited by Les Levidow and Robert Young titled *Science, Technology, and the Labour Process: Marxist Studies* (London: CSE Books, 1981). The compilation and Diamond's contribution received praise and critical reviews from outlets like *New Scientist* and *The Scientist*, suggesting an impact beyond SftP's usual readers. Diamond was the president of Pacific Northwest Labor College and in 1988 the co-author of *The Power in Our Hands: A Curriculum on the History of Work and Workers in the United States,* a high school history curriculum.

In its most basic aspects, the concepts with which scientists organize data and formulate theories, science is inherently political. Scientific concepts are not simply asymptotic approaches to underlying truth. They are products of a particular social structure and may in turn either reinforce of challenge the social status quo. Not only the daily practice and social use, but also the content of science would be different in a differently organized society. No one interested in building a more humane society can unquestioningly accept present-day science as if it were a given, unable to be radically different.

Origin of New Concepts

Philosophers of science and even some science textbooks increasingly recognize that factors extrinsic to science influence the formulation of scientific concepts. I shall argue that these extrinsic factors are primarily social, though of course expressed by individuals, and that, far from detracting from science, they are the factors potentially most under human control. Thus there is the possibility of a science in which scientists can take responsibility for their concepts, as a product of and contributor toward a society which is controlled and intentionally shaped by all the people in it.

Scientists who recognize that concepts do not simply derive from raw data and even that there may be social influences on the formation of concepts, nevertheless mainly continue to believe that their conclusions are responsive only to the correspondence test—whether or not predicted results are verified by experimentation, whether or not they correspond to external reality. No experiment can be designed, however, to test a proposition outside of a conceptual context or in isolation from all other propositions. Rather all experiments test complex theories with multiple components, many of them simply assumed as commonsensical by the experimenter. There is a large margin of choice in evaluating which component to regard as falsified by any experiment. In the history of science there are many instances of scientists from different historical periods observing the same phenomenon or conducting what would seem to an observer to be the same experiment, but interpreting the results quite differently. Scientists really use two different tests of any hypothesis: one is the correspondence test, the other is whether the hypothesis makes sense in terms of how the scientist is used to interpreting reality as a whole. This latter interpretative framework derives mainly from the scientist's existence in a particular society. . . .

All our ideas, whether in science, politics or music, are conditioned by our world-view. They are thus indirectly shaped by our society and our position in it. We develop or accept ideas as they seem to make sense to us in terms of our general explanatory framework. Life in any particular society thus shapes the range of understandings and approaches in any particular realm of thought. As societies change, as world-views change, new ranges of conceptual possibility are opened in every sphere of thought. . . .

New World-Views and the Copernican Revolution

. . . How we organize data in science as in every sphere of consciousness embodies an over-all outlook which derives from our social existence. Underlying and structuring all our thoughts is our understanding of our society and our reactions and adaptations to it. Scientific concepts are thus inherently political, continuing to express and reaffirm socially based world-views. Einstein's reluctance to accept probabilistic quantum theory, to take one modern realization, stemmed explicitly from his rejection of the discordant outlook of which he saw it a product. An excellent recent study (of sexism in the history of biology) in *Science for the People* provides a further illustration of how scientific concepts, in part socially based, in turn reinforces the social status quo.[3] To 'serve the people' with existing science is insufficient.

Practicing Politics and Science

For a worker in science who recognizes the need for fundamental social change, the more familiar respects in which science is political lead to relatively limited ways of combining jobs with political activity. Many indeed choose to separate professional from political lives, working with other people after job hours and outside job roles. Others publicize political abuses in connection with science or take advantage of respected positions based on work in science to speak out on social issues. Some scientists or science workers who are radicals organize their co-workers to rearrange or diminish hierarchies in the work situation. And yet all of these approaches leave the science itself, the content of research and formulation of results, untouched. Considered in those terms, science seems to offer fulfillment mainly in ways that are apolitical. For someone who is politically committed, there are constant qualms about whether and how much even to be working on science. Some people become science dropouts to expend energy on efforts more directly political. For others who need to hold a job in science and yet are unable to reconcile science and politics, the tension may result in lessening political commitment.

There is another important political option which derives from the above discussion. It is possible to use one's scientific knowledge to oppose specialization or overcome some of its deleterious effects. Often what passes for narrow technical decisions really contain disguised political decisions which can be extricated and pointed out. *Science for the People* has been full of examples.[4] The aura of technical expertise shelters what are political decisions from question and criticism. There is a political point too in attempting to enhance not only the scientific understanding of non-scientists but also their sense of their own ability to understand. Effective "popularization" has negative connections only to people who accept the elitist premises of modern science. And yet, integrating the concepts with which scientists work for presentation to a lay audience, still accepts those concepts as given. *It is through recognizing that scientific concepts themselves are political that it is primarily possible not only to be a radical and a scientist, but to be a radical scientist.*

Every society rests on the consciousness of its members. Their adherence to, or at least acceptance of, its structure is ultimately what holds the society together. The major obstacles we face in doing political organizing in our own society are a widespread lack of ability to conceive of a better society, or more commonly a sense that it is impossible fundamentally to change what we've got. Corporations, the state, etc., all of them clearly opponents, are obstacles primarily because too many people continue to believe them legitimate. . . .

A crucial objective of organizing is the fundamental transformation of outlook. Through their struggles, people must learn to understand our society, what maintains it and what will be required to change it. There are important answers that will elude us until we have a mass movement with the capacity to shake and test the society. People must see themselves as capable, if united, of effecting basic change and increasingly able themselves to decide which tactics will further our growing knowledge and ability to transform. It is insufficient to be only anti-capitalist, anti-ruling class, anti-racist, etc. More than an abstract idea of the kind of egalitarian, genuinely democratic society toward which we aim is necessary. That society must be seen as a real prospect and legitimate objective. Unfortunately even many radicals deep down do not believe that a better society is anything more than a theoretical possibility. Their actions and the ways they work with others manifest their acceptance of the prevailing order.

Going Beyond: Doing Radical Science

Knowing that science concepts would and will be different in a qualitatively different society* enables science workers in their daily practice now to call into question this society and the consciousness that sustains it. This can be done in two basic ways. The first is by learning to identify the hidden, seemingly commonsensical and thus hard to see, premises that underlie accepted concepts, and by learning to recognize how these premises reflect a world-view which is socially based and socially restricted. Showing their connection to the structure of our society, teaching others to understand all ideas and cultural products in social terms, aids people in recognizing that this society is not eternal and cannot be simply accepted as a given.

This first possibility for political practice within science leads to a second. Having discerned the kinds of premises and perspectives promoted by life in this society, radical scientists may begin to be able to develop alternative science concepts based on empathy with a qualitatively better society; to attempt the new possibilities for organizing data which arise out of a different world-view. The difficulties in undertaking this science/political option are formidable, for it requires identifying with a society not yet existent. We are of course fortunate in the availability of socialist societies to present us with alternative models. These can serve, however, to indicate only the barest outlines, the most abstract hopes, for what we could create here. Undoubtedly it is impossible to put oneself entirely outside of one's society. To step back from it, to delegitimate it at its roots within oneself and others is immensely difficult. Yet this is a fundamental goal of radical practice and the precondition of radical science.

A word is necessary regarding validity in science. Concepts are not arbitrary, nor are they plastic. There is an external reality to which they must correspond.

Most of the concepts in present-day science have a definite operational validity (this is not the place to explore other possible tests for validity); they are not, however, the exclusive ways to organize data. Modern science recognizes the tentativeness and incompleteness of any particular concept, the possibility that it will be transformed through further discovery. What is not readily acknowledged is that its supersession, at the level of fundamental conceptual change, is tied to social developments. In addition, scientific concepts are partial not only because they correspond to a particular social structure, as we have seen, but also because most scientists, as a relatively privileged social group, have a stake in only a partial view of their social reality. The world-view which the concepts manifest is thus that of a group barred from an over-all perspective. As partial, the concepts in present-day science have been functional both in controlling natural reality (the operational test) and in not questioning social reality. . . .

There has been a tendency among radicals to reject the usual posing of issues in terms of the scientist's personal or social responsibility, and rightly so.[5] Abuses of science are endemic to an oppressive social order. There is, however, a higher level of individual responsibility which comes with the awareness that concepts do not automatically derive from raw data and are socially influenced. Recognizing that there are choices behind concepts and that these choices have political implications, radical scientists are able to take responsibility for the concepts they use. By doing so they act as precursors of a society in which consciousness is no longer subordinate to social conditions. Through their science now, they can contribute to fundamental social change.

—Norman Diamond

*Again, there is no implication that ideas change automatically in one-to-one correspondence with social change. Elements of ideas from previous world-views, from previous social structures, are retained long after the context that gave rise to them or permitted them has been altered. They are retained selectively, however, according to what continues to make sense in terms of people's new social experience and setting. A modern reader of Newton, for example, is struck by the distortion of his intentions and of the interconnection of his thoughts represented in the selective culling his ideas receive in secondary accounts today. It is not so much that each generation rewrites the past as that each social configuration understands the same past differently because it has something different to understand about itself.

References

3. Rita Arditti, "Women as Objects: Science and Sexual Politics," *Science for the People*, September 1973.
4. On the choice between nuclear fission and fusion, see "Energy Crisis," *Science for the People*, January 1974, especially pp. 12–15. On the "green revolution," see

K. R. Bhattacharya, "Soyabeans in India?" *Science for the People*, January 1974. On priorities in cancer research, see Michele Fluck, "Cancer Prevention," *Science for the People*, November 1974.
5. See, e.g., Hilary Rose and Steven Rose, "The Radicalisation of Science," *Socialist Register*, 1972.

Document 1.3

Steven Rose, "The Limits to Science," *Science for the People* 16, no. 6 (November–December 1984): 16, 24–26.

This article appeared in an issue of *Science for the People* magazine titled "Setting Our Priorities." It was adapted from a debate that took place the same year that the author published his famous book *Not in Our Genes* with Richard Lewontin and Leon Kamin. The article reveals both the continuities with 1930s Marxist critiques of science (e.g., with respect to reductionism and the supposed "purity" of basic research) and SftP's departures from that tradition (e.g., in the emphasis on race and gender and in the critique of what Rose calls "technoenthusiasm"). Steven and Hilary Rose were among the most important figures bridging Science for the People with its British counterpart, and bridging SftP-style activism with the academic field of science and technology studies (STS). They remain regular contributors to *The Guardian* newspaper and other publications on subjects ranging from science, technology, and society to the liberation of Palestine.

For the great ideological "spokesmen" of science, from Francis Bacon onward, science has always been without limits, about "the effecting of all things possible." Human curiosity, after all, is boundless. There seems to be an infinity of questions one can ask about nature. At the end of his long scientific career Isaac Newton felt, he said, as if he had merely stood at the edge of a vast sea, playing with the pebbles on the beach. What is more, because science is not merely about the passive knowledge of nature but about the development of ways of changing it, of transforming the world through technology, these same apologists offer us a breathtaking vision of the prospect of a world, a nature—including human nature—made over in humanity's image to serve human needs.

It is only when one looks a little more closely at these visions that one sees that a science which claims to speak for the universality of the human condition, and to seek disinterestedly to make over the world for human need, is in fact speaking for a very precise group. Its universalism turns out to be a projection of the needs, curiosity, and ways of appreciating the world not of some classless, raceless, genderless humanity, but of a particular class, race, and gender who have been the makers of science and the framers of its questions indeed since Francis Bacon's time.

The ideology is powerful, and in the second half of this century it has been of endless fascination to politicians as well as scientists.

Towards the end of the second world war, in the U.S., Vannevar Bush, whose life had been spent with "Pieces of the Action"* of science, offered Presidents Roosevelt and Truman "Science, the Endless Frontier" as a vision of how the greatness and power of the U.S. could be indefinitely extended. In Britain the visionary Marxist tradition of J. D. Bernal inspired Harold Wilson in 1964 to speak of the "building of socialism in the white heat of the scientific and technological revolution" which has, rather than politics and class struggle, become the motor of the growth of Soviet society.

Against such claims for the limitless nature of human curiosity and the techno-enthusiasms of the politicians, the anti-science movement of the last decades has cried a series of halts: halts to the "tampering with nature" of the nuclear industry and militarism; halts to the possibility of knowledge by the endless dissection of animals into molecules and molecules into elementary particles; halts to the restless experimentation implied by the very scientific method itself as a way of knowing the universe, as opposed to the contemplative knowledge offered by alternative philosophical systems.

I am not an anti-scientist in this, or indeed in any sense that I would accept. I want to argue, however, that we cannot understand science or speak of its limits or boundlessness in the abstract. To speak of "science for science's sake"—as if, to paraphrase Samuel Butler on art, science had a "sake," is to mystify what science is and what scientists do. This mystification, still often on the lips of the ideologues of science, serves to justify specific interests and privileges. Instead, we have to consider this science in this society. I shall argue that it is indeed limited, and that its limits are provided by a combination of two major factors. The first is material, the second ideological. I will consider each in turn.

Material Limits

Apologists for the purity of science (although it is the purest of high energy physics that gave us the bomb) may argue that this is all technology—real science is unaffected by such directive processes. They are on shaky ground making this science/technology distinction, of course. The distinguished American organic chemist Louis Fieser invented that nastiest of conventional weapons, napalm, experimenting on it in the playing fields of Harvard during the 1939–45 war. He wrote about his discovery afterwards in a fascinating book called simply *The Scientific Method*. The argument that pure science is divorced from direction can't be sustained for a moment.

Take the triumphant progress of molecular biology these past decades. There have always been two broadly contrasting traditions in biology, a reductionist, or analytic and atomising one; and a holistic or more synthetic one. This latter tradition was strongly represented in the 1930s by such developmental and theoretical biologists as Needham, Woodger, and Waddington. There was a proposal to set up a major institute of theoretical biology in Cambridge which would have brought the field together. But the funding was to come from Rockefeller, and Rockefeller, under the guidance of Warren Weaver, decided that the future was to be chemical. They backed biochemistry and molecular biology instead. The double helix and all that followed from it from 1953 on was a direct result of that funding decision. Many people would argue it was a correct one, and I might well agree. The fact is that it changed the direction of biology by a deliberate act of policy. Rockefeller's decision is thus comparable to those being made routinely by government and charitable funding agencies as they decide which are high priority areas to back, and which should not be supported. One of the things that is clear from that fact and from the combined efforts of Richard Nixon and Jim Watson in the 1970s to "cure" cancer by the end of the decade is that the most exquisite molecular biology has brought us no nearer to controlling cancer, a disease many of whose precipitating causes are located in the chemical environment of our industrial society. The vast funds Nixon allocated have given us more and more molecular biology, though.

Ideological Limits

Let me move from the material to the ideological limits to science. The point I want to make here is not just that we get the science we pay for, but that at a deeper level, what science we do, what questions scientists consider important and worth asking at any time—indeed, the very way they frame the questions—are profoundly shaped by the historical and social context in which we frame our hypotheses and realise our experiments. Let me spell this out at three levels.

First, we can only ask questions we can begin to frame; the role of chromosomes in cell replication and genetic transmission was unaskable until there were microscopes powerful enough to see the chromosomes, as well as a genetic theory to be tested—the technology and the theory came together at the beginning of the present century.

Second, not all scientific facts are of equal value. There is an infinity—in the strict sense of the term—of questions one can ask about the material world; which ones are relevant at all is strictly historically contingent. . . .

Third, and at a much deeper level than either of the two previous points, there is the issue of reductionism and its alternatives. The mode of thinking which has characterised the period of the rise of science from the 17th-century minds is a reductionist one. Reductionism holds that to understand the world requires disassembling it into its component parts, and that these parts are in some way more fundamental than the wholes they compose. To understand societies, you study individuals, to understand individuals you study their organs; for the organs, their cells; for the cells, their molecules; for the molecules, their atoms . . . right down to the most "fundamental" physical particles. Reductionism is committed to the claim that this is the scientific method, that ultimately the knowledge of the laws of motion of particles will enable us to understand the rise of capitalism, the nature of love, or even the winner of the next [Kentucky] Derby.

The fallacies of such reductionism should be apparent. We cannot understand the music a tape recorder generates simply by analyzing the chemical and magnetic properties of the tape or the nature of the recording and playing heads—though these are part of any such explanation. Yet reductionism runs deep. For Richard Dawkins the well-springs of human motivation are to be interpreted by analysis of human DNA; for Jim Watson, 'What else is there but atoms?' The answer is: the organizing relations between the atoms, which are not strictly deducible from the properties of the atoms themselves. After all, quantum physics can't even deal with the interactions of more than two particles simultaneously or predict the properties of a molecule as simple as water from the properties of its constituents. Beginning as a way of acquiring new and real knowledge about the world—from the structure of molecules to the motions of the planets—it has become an obstacle to scientific progress.

So long as science—in the questions it asks, and the answers it accepts—is couched in reductionist and determinist terms, understanding of complex phenomena is frustrated. A reductionist science, I believe, cannot advance knowledge of brain functions, or solve the riddle of the relationship between levels of description of phenomena such as the "mind-brain problem," which Western science is almost incapable even of conceiving except in Cartesian dualist or mechanical materialist terms. Reductionism cannot cope with the open, richly interconnected systems of ecology, or with integrating its scientific understanding of the present frozen moment in time with the dynamic recognition that the present is part of an historical flux, be it of development of the individual or of evolution of the species.

Failing to approach the complexity of such systems, reductionism resorts to more or less vulgar simplifications which, in the prevailing social climate become refracted into defenses of the status quo in the form of biological determinism, which claims that the present social order, with all its inequalities in status, wealth and power, between individuals, classes, genders and races, is 'given' inevitably by our genes. . . .

*This is the title of one of Bush's books, as is "Science, The Endless Frontier."

Document 1.4

Richard Levins, "One Foot In, One Foot Out," presentation in panel titled "Science and Ideology" at the conference *Science for the People: The 1970s and Today,* held April 11–13, 2014, at the University of Massachusetts, Amherst (archived at http://science-for-the-people.org/science-and-ideology-with-video/).

Richard (Dick) Levins was a founding member of the Chicago chapter of Science for the People and of the group Science for Vietnam, and an influential member of the Boston chapter of SftP after his move to Harvard University. Along with his colleague Richard Lewontin (with whom he co-authored two books on biology and Marxist dialectics), Levins modeled the use of Marxist theory to effect sustained political criticism of scientific knowledge and policy under capitalism and imperialism. His talk "One Foot In, One Foot Out" was widely regarded as one of the highlights of the 2014 conference on the history and legacy of Science for the People because it resonated so deeply with the analysis that informed SftP's 1970s–1980s organizing while demonstrating the continued relevance of that analysis for activist scientists today.

. . . We are professionals in the sciences in one way or another, but professionals are also workers. . . . We are workers in the knowledge industry. The products of our industry are commodities: knowledge, ideas, theories, and so on, and increasingly these can be owned, sold, marketed, invested in, claimed. As a result of this, scientific labor is increasingly carried on by a working class of scientists, people whose employment is temporary, adjunct, part-time, and they hop around from one job to the next. . . .

At the opposite end of the hierarchy of the class structure in science are the owners of science. And we might borrow a term from Soviet days, the *nomenklatura*. The *nomenklatura* is the pool of respectables: the people eligible to be named to advisory commissions, invited to give graduation addresses, elected to the leadership of the National Academy of Sciences, run for political office. In general, as C. Wright Mills pointed out a few generations back, there's a rotation among these various ruling positions, which gives us a population who are running science, appreciate each other enormously, and from that appreciation develop the sense of what is obviously true.

So that is what we are contending with. We have a class structure of people who are increasingly becoming forced into a scientific proletariat, and on the other hand . . . the owners of science, the ones who develop rationalizations for science, make the investments, turn universities into businesses. So one of the things I would like to propose . . . is that . . . we take on the analysis of the *nomenklatura,* the ownership of science and knowledge.

As workers, we share concerns with other workers. We have the problems of salaries, job security, conditions of employment. . . . So the first general milieu in which we operate is as workers. The second is that we're activists. . . . But our activism is not limited to the correction of today's abuses. The training that we get in the sciences and in academia in general allows us to stand back from the immediate, to theorize, analyze, contemplate—to ask how our present struggles contribute to or detract from the long haul. Theorizing is a vital task and is one of the things that is lacking particularly in the American political movements. . . . One of the tasks of scientists within the Left is to fight for the legitimacy of intellectual labor, but intellectual labor directed toward other goals than the dominant communities of intellectual labor in our society.

Now this places us in a situation of partial conflict and partial cooperation in our institutions. And it's what I meant by the title "One Foot In, One Foot Out." Or, paraphrasing St. Paul, we are "in this world but not of this world." We are there because we have to be. We don't own it, we don't control it, but we are going to make the most of being there and of acknowledging the labyrinths in which we have to move. . . .

One of the things we can do is to recapture the spirit of earlier socialist movements, where it was realized that knowledge about the world is something that has been ripped off of the surplus created by working people, and we have the right to demand it back. . . .

Being both workers and activists separates us from the caricature of scientists as being disinterested and detached and objective. The term "objective," like the term "efficient," is part of a whole vocabulary developed by the ruling class to feel satisfied about what they're doing. Yes, there are objectivities, but there is objectivity from different points of view. There is the objectivity of the working class; on the other hand there is the objectivity of social scientists in the United States who don't mention class. . . . Erasing knowledge that is inconvenient is one of the major intellectual tasks of the rulers. . . .

The fact that science is owned sets its agenda. We started out in Science for the People denouncing the misuse of science. We talked about use and misuse, and we thought there was a correct way of using science and there was a bad way that we have to purify the system from. But that's not the case. The people who own science determine the agenda, and part of that is the economy of producing scientific workers. . . . What does a pharmaceutical researcher have to know about the ways in which the different chemicals within the plants, the so-called "secondary compounds," all form a consortium of molecules that jointly have the beneficial effects from plants—the herbs they use in alternative medicine? Instead, the reason we look for the active ingredient is that it's more patent-able. . . . So that even on questions which seem to be several steps away from political struggle, our recognition that science is owned is one of the ways in which we not only have a different orientation toward scientific questions, but also a more exciting one. And I have found examples of people whose radical-ization came about through the critique of the content of the science, through recognizing reductionism. . . .

Consider a model of the regulation of blood sugar. We know that if you have more blood sugar circulating, this brings out insulin from the pancreas. . . . Furthermore, that the adrenals can bring out sugar from the liver. And this will happen if you're anxious: the anxiety can activate your adrenals and bring out sugar, and this might calm the anxiety in a negative feedback loop. But . . . the greater the metabolic rate, the more you're burning up the sugar, the more you need some outside source. And that outside source might be taking a work break or taking a snack. Except that there's a foreman lurking around the edges. The foreman sees when you're goofing off and begins to move in. Except that this place has a good union, and the shop steward moves in to intercept the foreman, preventing the stimulation of the anxiety, allowing the metabolic rate to go down. When we present this kind of diagram, the conclusion we reach is that all people share more or less the same network of physiological relations, but they are all embedded in very different social ones, and that good medicine must include people in their social context. So that it's legitimate to ask . . . What can we say about the pancreas under neo-colonialism? The adrenals under deficient housing? And it may be that the best therapy for a diabetic is to go in there and organize a union. . . .

One of our critiques of the existing way of doing science is its reductionism down to a narrow pattern of acceptable variables along with acceptable people to study them and acceptable answers to questions. Determining acceptability is one of the tasks of the *nomenklatura*.

Finally, I'd like to come to the question of what do we do about it. We're in different situations, each of us, within the hierarchical structure, and that gives different degrees of freedom. But a rule that's been learned in political struggles throughout the world is that every system, no matter how oppressive, has a domain of the permitted and a domain of the forbidden. . . . Part of the task of a revolutionary movement is to push the boundary of the permissible, to be able to say things that are not allowed to be said. . . . One option is to struggle within the intellectual community to change the boundaries. A second one is to work semi-clandestinely: that is, write your term papers but have a missing chapter, the kind that says the things that you're not supposed to refer to, using forbidden words like class, and so on. Another is to step outside of academia and work for people's organizations, the organizations which taught the women of Woburn to look at the water for pollution and finally pin it down on the W. R. Grace company. . . . There are community-based people who don't trust the authorities anymore and who learn how to do assays of water. . . . Or you can leave employment in the sciences, drive a cab, and do your agitation in your spare time. That's another option if your health permits it and if your social relations require it.

I'd like to end up with three hypotheses that can guide some of our work. The first one is the hypothesis of complexity, which says that if two very good arguments supported by data lead to opposing conclusions, the problem has been posed badly . . . usually too narrowly. . . . Where is the rest of the world? Where does it come into the system? The second is when two movements for social justice come in conflict, it means that they're both asking for too little. They're accepting boundary conditions. So for instance, if people want to chop down the forests in order to preserve jobs, our task becomes to show that there is a rational, ecological forestry that can serve the people even if it is not as profitable as the other kind. And then the third one is that all theories are wrong which promote, justify, or tolerate injustice.

EDITORS' NOTES

1. See Kelly Moore, *Disrupting Science: Social Movements, American Scientists, and the Politics of the Military, 1945–1975* (Princeton, NJ: Princeton University Press, 2008).
2. See Donna Jeanne Haraway, "The Transformation of the Left in Science: Radical Associations in Britain in the 30's and the U.S.A. in the 60's," *Soundings* 58, no. 4 (1975): 441–62; Gary Werskey, *The Visible College: The Collective Biography of British Scientific Socialists of the 1930's* (New York: Holt, Rinehart, and Winston, 1979); Nikolai Bukharin, *Science at the Cross Roads* (London: F. Cass, 1971).
3. Boris Hessen, "The Social and Economic Roots of Newton's 'Principia,'" in Bukharin, *Science at the Cross Roads,* 210.
4. The BSSRS had its own magazine titled *Science for People.*
5. "Resources," *Science for the People* 9, no. 6 (1977): 18.
6. Helen Longino, *Science as Social Knowledge: Values and Objectivity in Scientific Inquiry* (Princeton, NJ: Princeton University Press, 1990), 194–96; Joseph Rouse, *Knowledge and Power: Toward a Political Philosophy of Science* (Ithaca, NY: Cornell University Press, 1987).
7. Peter Louis Galison and Bruce Hevly, eds., *Big Science: The Growth of Large-Scale Research* (Stanford, CA: Stanford University Press, 1992).
8. See, for example, Sandra Harding, *The Science Question in Feminism* (Ithaca, NY: Cornell University Press, 1986); Donna Haraway, *Primate Visions: Gender, Race, and Nature in the World of Modern Science* (New York: Routledge, 1989).
9. Despite these important sources of inspiration, and despite the efforts of a strong core of feminist activists and allies within SftP who worked to make gender and race important axes of analysis, the organization was unable to sustain cohesion around these issues to the same extent as on other issues. This is discussed further in Chapter 5, "Race and Gender."

FIGURE 2. Cartoon by Tony Auth depicting Science for the People's disruption of the 1971 meeting of the American Association for the Advancement of Science. The cartoon was originally published in the *Philadelphia Inquirer* and was reprinted in *Science for the People,* 4, no. 2 (March 1972): 3.

CHAPTER 2

Disrupting the "AAA$"

Colin Garvey

and

Daniel S. Chard

From 1969 to 1973, Science for the People gained notoriety throughout the U.S. scientific community by disrupting the annual meetings of the American Association for the Advancement of Science (AAAS), the world's largest scientific society. As part of the era's broader upsurge of direct action against war, racism, sexism, and capitalism, SftP members descended upon AAAS meetings to challenge the scientific establishment's complicity in these matters. SftP was particularly concerned with scientists' involvement in research critical to the U.S. war in Vietnam and the nuclear arms race. The young radicals took staid conference halls by storm with an innovative repertoire of disruptive tactics, from impromptu speeches, demonstrations, confrontational interruptions, and picketing to outright takeovers of scientific symposia. In their publications and flyers, SftP irreverently referred to the AAAS as the "AAA$," denoting the body's alignment with capitalist imperatives.

Throughout its disruptions of the AAAS, SftP contested the widely held notion that scientific inquiry is inherently disinterested, neutral, and unaffected by the social and political contexts in which it is conducted. While Chapter 1 ("Science, Power, and Ideology") highlighted SftP's intellectual efforts to challenge the ideologies undergirding the mainstream scientific discipline, this chapter documents how SftP activists translated their beliefs into direct action and political organizing, and how these, in turn, affected their beliefs. During the first four years of its existence, SftP coupled ongoing direct action and organizing with critical reflection and theorizing, a dialectic of praxis that was critical to the organization's political evolution.

SftP engaged the AAAS most fiercely from 1970 to 1972, when its protests ruptured the annual meetings' traditional atmosphere of supposedly dispassionate inquiry and elite, male-dominated discussion.[1] However, this was not the first time that 1960s-era protest movements had spilled into America's scientific professional organizations. Indeed, in 1967 and 1968, when Charles Schwartz led an attempt to amend the constitution of the American Physical Society (APS) to allow its membership to take a public stand on the Vietnam War and other political issues (Document 2.1), he paved the way for the founding of SftP. By challenging the purported political neutrality of professional organizations, Schwartz and his comrades compelled other scientists to reckon with how institutions like the APS and AAAS contributed to war, economic inequality, and other forces detrimental to humanity. As Schwartz put it, "Professional societies are, almost by definition, tightly structured to promote and preserve some narrow set of self-interests. . . . Therefore, it should not be surprising that the pursuits of social responsibility and the pursuits of professional societies come into conflict."[2]

SftP also proposed resolutions, staffed literature tables, and organized sessions at the meetings of other professional organizations during the 1970s, including National Science Teachers Conference and the American Chemical Society.[3] The AAAS, however, was undoubtedly SftP's primary target. Ahead of the December 1970 meeting in Chicago, SftP members outlined a critical historical analysis of the AAAS in *Science for the People* magazine titled "A History of the AAAS" (Document 2.2). According to the members of the editorial collective who authored the piece, the AAAS's alignment with industry and government since its founding in 1848 put it at odds with the Association's purported aim of improving human welfare. In SftP's analysis, the AAAS was fundamentally invested not in expanding knowledge and human potential, but in deploying scientific authority and expertise to maintain an exploitative, patriarchal, and capitalist status quo.

SftP did not entirely abandon traditional venues of scientific communication and governance. They did, however, push such spaces beyond their normal limits. In "SESPA Tells It Like It Is: Opening Statement AAA$ '70" (Document 2.3), an address given before the first major event of the 1970 AAAS meeting in Chicago, activists from the local SftP chapter made clear that while they embraced radical protest strategies, they still saw themselves as scientists—scientists who consciously worked *for* the people and *against* capitalism and U.S. imperialism. At the conference, SftP members interrupted panels, shouted down speakers, and staged guerrilla theater, but also held a two-day symposium on "The Sorry State of Science" that incorporated rock music and antiwar slideshows. In addition, they formally engaged the governing council of the AAAS with a draft of resolutions from SftP's AAA$ Action '70 Resolutions Committee (Document 2.4), beseeching the professional organization to take a stand against political repression, the Vietnam War, and the inequalities women faced in science.[4] Furthermore, SftP activists reached out to fellow scientists with a barrage of pamphlets and other literature that encouraged readers to critically consider the role of science and scientists in a racist, patriarchal, and capitalist society. Productions like the "Leaflet Handed Out at One AAAS Session" (Document 2.7) targeted specific AAAS panels (in this case, a session called *Technology and the Humanization of Work*), and aimed to provide attendees alternative perspectives on the speakers' topics.

Still, no efforts garnered publicity or earned the ire of their adversaries quite like SftP's theatrical attacks on high-profile elites. SftP's satirical presentation of the "Second Annual Dr. Strangelove Award" to nuclear physicist Edward Teller (Document 2.5) was a pivotal moment for the group, as was their indictment of the director of the United States Atomic Energy Commission, Glenn Seaborg, "for the Crime of Science against the People."[5] However, the limited effectiveness of these tactics invited collective reflection, as a group of Boston SftP activists offered in "1970 Chicago AAAS Actions: Review and Critique" (Document 2.6). The authors did not disavow direct action; instead, they sought to improve their effectiveness in enacting social change though a commitment to constructive self-criticism. Reflecting on their actions, the Boston SftP members observed that while their theatrical disruption of Teller's speech "served the function of ridicule," it had "little analytic content" and did not help the audience "understand Teller as a product of society." The authors also recalled a notorious incident of backlash toward SftP's raucous antics: during one SftP disruption, the wife of a scientist on the stalled panel snuck up behind activist Frank Rosenthal and jabbed him with a knitting needle.[6] According to the Boston SftP members, mainstream media accounts focused more on this incident than on the content of SftP's critique of the panel's treatment of the topic, "Crime, Violence, and Social Control."

SftP's direct action tactics attracted attention from law enforcement and provoked resistance from the scientific establishment. The Federal Bureau of Investigation (FBI)—the primary state agency charged with the United

States' "internal security"—began investigating SftP in 1970. Excerpts from a 1972 FBI surveillance report (Document 2.8) reveal that although the Bureau monitored the organization's members in order to prevent their potential involvement in disruptive "revolutionary activity," agents made genuine efforts to understand the organization's political message. The document provided a detailed account of SftP activities at the December 1971 AAAS meeting in Philadelphia, including SftP members' protests of speeches by Hubert Humphrey, the former U.S. vice president and Minnesota senator who was the 1968 Democratic presidential nominee, and former National Security Advisor McGeorge Bundy, both of whom had played key roles in the Johnson administration's escalation of the Vietnam War. The FBI report noted that protesters heckled loudly during Humphrey's address, tossing paper airplanes and tomatoes at the speaker (though the author of the document acknowledged SftP's claims that their members were not responsible for the projectiles).

FBI agents gained their information through informants recruited from within either SftP or allied groups whose identities remain unknown today. Accordingly, the December 1972 FBI teletype included here (Document 2.9) provides a detailed account of SftP's plans for actions at the 1972 Washington, DC, AAAS meeting days before it was to take place. Coincidence or not, Washington police arrested eight SftP members at the conference for allegedly refusing to take down their literature table. That same year, the AAAS's journal *Science* broke with peer-review protocol and refused to publish a co-authored piece by SftP members (Document 1.1).

Despite these setbacks, in January 1973 SftP issued a "Call to AAAS Actions" (Document 2.10), encouraging members to return to protest once more at the AAAS. An account of SftP protests at the 1973 AAAS meeting in Mexico City is available in Chapter 9, "Science for the People and the World" (Document 9.2). Although SftP members would shift their focus away from disrupting AAAS meetings in later years, SftP's annual presence at the Association's meetings from 1969 to 1973 nevertheless established a basis for the group's struggles for social and scientific change throughout the remainder of the 1970s and the 1980s.

Document 2.1

Charles Schwartz, "Should APS Discuss Public Issues? For the Schwartz Amendment," *Physics Today* 21, no. 1 (January 1968): 9, 11.

In this letter to the editors of *Physics Today*, University of California physicist Charles Schwartz explained his efforts to amend the constitution of the American Physical Society (APS) to allow members to vote on formal public resolutions regarding matters of social consequence. Schwartz initially proposed what would become known as the "Schwartz Amendment" in 1967 in an effort to adopt an APS resolution opposing the U.S. war in Vietnam. Of the more than 24,000 APS members, 248 signed a petition supporting the "Schwartz Amendment," which stated "the members may express their opinion, will, or intent on any matter of concern to the Society by voting on one or several resolutions formally presented for their consideration."[7] In his letter, Schwartz explained why he believed the amendment was necessary and, more broadly, why he believed it was necessary for the APS to shed its façade of political neutrality and "involve itself in public issues." Though the "Schwartz Amendment" was ultimately defeated, the struggle over its adoption led to the formation of Science for the People during the January 1969 APS meeting in New York City.

As the author of the constitutional amendment now before members of the American Physical Society I would like to present arguments in favor of its adoption. There are two questions to be considered. The larger one is, Should the American Physical Society involve itself in public issues?; and the specific one is, Why is this constitutional amendment needed? Let me start by answering the second, more technical, question.

One individual physicist may talk to another about any subject at all, but if he wishes to address the entire membership of his professional organization he must have the approval of those officers of APS and the American Institute of Physics who control the publication facilities. While I agree that some controls are needed, recent experience has shown me that the present manner in which these decisions are made is seriously out of balance. I believe that there operates today a censorship completely alien to the principles of free discourse upon which a scientific community is built. The correctness of this opinion is most clearly demonstrated by the manner in which the debate on this amendment has been handled. The editors of the *Bulletin* of APS and of PHYSICS TODAY have rejected publication of both a summary statement and a thorough expository article, by means of which I had hoped to explain to the society membership at the outset of the debate just what had motivated 248 members to sign the original petition. Instead, and against repeated objections, they have chosen to present this whole debate in their own terms, as if they could play the role of an impartial mediator, when in fact they represent the chief target of my complaints. By the time this letter appears in print—at least two months after the first announcement of the proposed amendment—I fear the issues may have become badly confused.

The change we hope to achieve should lead to a more open-minded attitude on the part of the society towards new situations now and in the future. In the opening sentence of the proposed amendment, "The members may express their opinion," etc., the emphasis is on "members." The basic idea is that the members retain for themselves the right to decide which issues they wish to consider and which they choose to ignore. Specifically, upon petition by 1% of the membership any question, in the form of a proposed resolution, would be placed before the society for formal consideration and voting in a mail ballot. This critical measure, 1%, should make it not too easy for any extreme faction to coerce the majority, but not too hard for a respectable minority to get its views presented.

Further discussion of the procedural details of the proposed amendment is, I understand, the subject of other items in PHYSICS TODAY and so I shall not dwell on these here. However, one crucial point deserves comment: the interpretation of the phrase "on any matter of concern to the society," which defines the scope of resolutions that members may vote upon. The editorial in the December PHYSICS TODAY says that presumably the APS council will decide how to read this. While I agree that the council might concern itself with this question, I point out that the whole intent of this amendment is to create motive power for the members outside of the council. Thus I claim the view should be that any matter meeting the formal requirements (1% support) was ipso facto of concern to the society.

Now I turn to the major question of society policy: the appropriateness of discussing public issues. Certainly one of the easiest ways to destroy the integrity of the society would be to turn it into a debating club open to every political issue of the day; and the proposed amendment is carefully designed to protect against such excesses. At the other extreme we must recognize the absurdity of complete political innocence. Such statements as, "We are concerned only with physics as physics," are simply nonsense. There exists a whole range of issues where the technical activity of physicists gets tied up with political decision making. Our individual requests for government funds and the scientific appraisal of others' proposals are the most obvious examples. Each reader, and each letter writer, will doubtless have his own list of priorities in this regard. The choice in these cases of whether to take a position—as a professional group—and when to stand aloof should always be an open question, to be decided by the members as a whole once some threshold of community concern has been passed. At present it too often happens that the "public opinion of physicists" emerges from sources quite remote from the actual majority of our colleagues. (For this we have only our own lassitude to blame.)

There is one other situation when, I believe, my professional society should concern itself with a public issue: when there exists an external crisis of such magnitude that we fear a general catastrophe of a political, military or cultural nature. In my view the Vietnam War in all its ramifications does now pose such a crisis; and I would like to see the Physical Society face up to this issue, not because we have any unique competence in this matter, but because we share an equal concern and responsibility along with all other segments of American social structure.

In closing I return to the immediate question of the proposed constitutional amendment and remark that it refers to no particular issue or class of issues. It simply seeks to establish the means whereby the members can take it upon themselves to consider when some issue may be pertinent to their professional future. That is to say we are individually and cooperatively willing to be responsive to external realities, while retaining concern for our internal integrity as scientists. Such a commitment is neither easy nor guaranteed safe from criticism, but I believe it is a responsibility we should assume. If not, then we shall continue to be judged according to the dictum, "silence implies consent."

Document 2.2

"A History of the AAA$," *Science for the People* 2, no. 5 (December 1970): 15–19.

This article by the editorial committee then in charge of *Science for the People* magazine outlined an analysis of the history of the American Association for the Advancement of Science in time for distribution at that year's annual meeting in Chicago. The piece argued that the AAAS's long history of alignment with industry and government put it at odds with its purported mission of advancing human welfare.

Philadelphia was the site, in September 1848, of the first meeting of the American Association for the Promotion of Science—or so it was called in the notice appearing in the *American Journal of Science*. The organization, an outgrowth of the more limited Association of American Geologists and Naturalists, was intended by its founders to be a broad, national society of scientists which would encompass all fields of scientific endeavor. For at that time the scientific community was highly fragmented and dispersed, consisting of a few small elite societies on the one hand, and many independent researchers on the other. . . .

But of considerably more importance to scientists at that time was the need they felt to establish the social legitimacy of science, to win public recognition and support for their work . . . [For] gentleman science to prosper it became paramount that its practitioners establish themselves on a firm professional level. That task required the formation of an organization of national scope, one which could speak not only in the name of science, but also on behalf of science. Thus the objects of the new Association as formulated in 1848 were:

> . . . to promote intercourse between those who are cultivating science in different parts of the United States; to give a stronger and more general impulse, and a more systematic direction to scientific research in our country, and to procure for the labours of scientific men, increased facilities and a wider usefulness.

Except when interrupted by cholera or war, the Association met annually in different cities throughout the United States, predominantly in the East. The gatherings were held during the summer, when travel required the least hardship and when many outings and recreational activities could add to the pleasure and attraction of the meeting. After all, the membership of the AAAS was small enough (originally 460, climbing to 2000 by 1900) so that the meeting could be quite enjoyable. . . .

At the turn of the century, the AAAS established itself as the uncontested spokesman for the American scientific community. In this capacity, it has expended much energy in creating and cultivating a favorable public image for science. It has struggled hard to attract increasing numbers of young people into research and to develop better educational programs for students. It has unceasingly proclaimed the great value of scientific research to society and stressed the necessity of long term financial support for continued technical advance. In short it has been, with unflagging zeal, the great champion of American science!

These activities are the trademarks not of a scientific organization, but of a political self-interest organization for science. The Association's purpose has been to attain for the scientific community a maximum of growth and institutional stability . . . Of course, there is nothing new in the scientists' use of most any expedient for obtaining research funds, and therefore it is not surprising that the AAAS has bent over backwards to maintain congenial ties with the federal government. Surprise comes in comparing such unprincipled behavior to the high-flown declarations of the Association. In 1952, for example, the AAAS drew up a new set of purposes—the ones which appear in every issue of *Science* magazine. The new objects of the Association are:

> to further the work of scientists, to facilitate cooperation among them, to improve
> the effectiveness of science in the promotion of human welfare, and to increase
> public understanding and appreciation of the importance and promise of the meth-
> ods of science in human progress.

In addition to its traditional commitment to the promotion of science, the AAAS now appears to show great concern also for human welfare and human progress.

The change in the objects of the AAAS reflected changes which had taken place during the century of the Association's existence. Scientists by 1952 had won public recognition and support, largely due to their contributions to industry, government and war. As a result, many scientists occupied high ranking positions and enjoyed considerable prestige and respect. The National Science Foundation was soon to cater directly to scientists' research needs. However, the development of the atomic bomb had introduced an element of doubt about the blessing of scientific advance, and adverse reaction was developing to the unchecked growth of technology. It was to counter these currents and project the name of science that the AAA$ formulated new objectives. New times required new tactics, and the Association was prepared to enter the arena of social action. How successful has it been? . . .

The record . . . shows the failure of the AAA$ to develop any substantial program of social action. Rather, its energy has been consumed in enlarging the Association, in attempting to stimulate the growth of science, and in creating an image of social concern favorable to the public. Thus its self-serving pronouncements must be carefully weighed against its long history of promotional activity. In 1969 for example, the AAA$ Board of Directors (the administrative body) announced bold "new" plans for the next decade. These included an expansion of the Association's membership and "a major increase in the scale and effectiveness of its work on the chief contemporary problems concerning the mutual relations of science, technology, and social change, including the uses of science and technology in the promotion of human welfare." There seems to be no end to empty rhetoric.

It is important to realize at this point that the failure of the AAA$ to develop any meaningful program of social action lies in the direct conflict of such an undertaking with the basic interests and purposes of the Association, as presently constituted. The leadership of the 120,000 member organization, the Council and Board of Directors, consists of scientists whose important positions in industry, the university and government bind them to the dominant institutions in our society. They are the scientific elite—the consultants, the administrators, and the research directors. Their prestige and financial security depends upon the maintenance of present institutional forms. Moreover, the ability of the AAA$ to obtain recognition and support for research depends on the usefulness of science in rationalizing and strengthening the government and corporate enterprise. Thus, in every respect, from the composition of its leadership to the attainment of its promotional objectives, the AAA$ maintains a tremendous vested interest in the status quo.

But the essence of meaningful social action is the alteration of that status quo. For only by fundamental change in the social and economic structure of society can the misuse of science and technology be prevented. So long as control over technology rests in the hands of corporate enterprise, and a government which functions on its behalf, scientific advance will be used to further corporate interests at the expense of the people. The technology of death, destruction, despoliation, waste, and mass manipulation will continue, for these are the devices by which the domination of the oppressive social institutions of society are maintained. Such institutions must be replaced by democratic ones in which science is applied to meeting the collective needs of the people, instead of being used for their subjugation. However, the material and political ties of the AAA$ leadership to the established social order and economic order insures that meaningful social action would undermine the Association's stance. Under these circumstances, it is extremely unlikely that significant action can be forthcoming.

In 1848 the AAA$ was formed to respond to definite needs felt by the scientific community. In 1970, however, the AAA$ is incapable of responding to the new needs of scientists living in a very different society. The Association's Board of Directors is chosen by the Council, which, in turn, represents the affiliated societies. Thus the leadership does not represent the working scientist, and in fact has self-interests, as described, which are very different from those of the scientific community at large. Thus the AAA$ does not address the important questions of job security or retraining for technically obsolete scientific workers. It can do nothing to alleviate the growing malaise of many scientists over the inevitable misuse of their work. At a time when technical personnel are in tremendous surplus, the AAA$ continues to encourage more people into science. Moreover, the activities of the Association are altogether irrelevant to the special problems of young scientists: overspecialized education, their subordination to research directors, the rat race of publish or perish, stultifying teaching experiences, and political impotence in the scientific hierarchy.

Thus, in addition to its failure to serve any valuable function to society, the AAA$ also fails to be of any significant value to its own constituency, the scientific community. Nor can it be looked to as the source of progressive programs for social action—adopting the expedients of the present is hardly the way to a brighter future. The social action of scientists must be aimed rather at resisting the authoritarian, technocratic, elitist, and manipulative designs of the ruling classes in this country. It must be aimed at the demystification of science and scientific expertise and at providing an understanding of the social liabilities of a technology under domination of anti-social forces. It must be aimed at forging new instruments for the collective control of technology. It must be aimed at creating new forms of social organizations within which people can determine and respond to their common social needs. It must be aimed at forming the alliances which will transform a fragmented, competitive, stratified, undemocratic order into a cooperative, egalitarian society. It must be aimed at creating a social and economic system which will set free the productive and creative capacities of all men and women, so they may join together to build a new world.

Science for the People!

Document 2.3

Chicago SESPA, "SESPA Tells It Like It Is: Opening Statement AAA$ '70," *Science for the People* 3, no. 1 (February 1971): 6–7.

Shortly before the National Academy of Sciences president Dr. Philip Handler was to open the December 1970 American Association for the Advancement of Science meeting in Chicago with a special lecture on "Obligations of the Scientific Community," members of Science for the People gained permission to address the audience. In this pointed speech, SftP members called upon fellow "science workers" to use their skills in the service of "a movement for revolutionary change," and announced their plans to make their voices heard throughout the conference.

. . . But what is to be done? Huey Newton said, "The spirit of the people is greater than the man's technology." Too many of us have been involuntarily recruited into creating the man's technology. Our job now must be to shift our services away from the man and align ourselves with the spirit of the people. . . .

This is what we are about, and this is why we are in attendance at this convention. There are perhaps many people here whom we would consider our brothers and sisters and with whom we wish to communicate and develop that strategy of opposition for scientific workers. . . .

Finally, one brief word about free speech and the necessity for our insisting on this opportunity to address you. Men at the top of the scientific establishment can command at will the enormous audience the mass media provide access to, because their interests are congruent with those of the people who control the media. Similarly, scientists working within the accepted bounds of the AAA$ establishment have easy access to the audience this organization can provide. We who are challenging the role science is playing in the United States today—that of serving ruling class interests—have to struggle for our supposed right of free speech. Speech, like the products of science, is freer for some than for others in a capitalist society. Of course the granting of equal time to opposition viewpoints does not create a climate of freedom when the two sides are not equally capable of putting what they have to say into effect. Nevertheless, during the remainder of this convention, we will be insisting on some of your time and we intend to get it.

You still have the opportunity to work constructively with the movement for revolutionary change. There is still time to stop working for the man and start serving the people. But if scientists continue to provide the ruling class with more tools of oppression, people like us won't be standing here trying to communicate our ideas to you. Out of desperation and urgency, and because no other solution is available, we will be out in the streets, with all of those excluded from ruling-class privilege, doing everything we can to tear this racist, imperialist system to shreds.

Document 2.4

AAA$ Action '70 Resolutions Committee, "Resolutions for the AAA$,"
Science for the People 2, no. 4 (December 1970): 26–27.

In 1970 Science for the People proposed resolutions to the American Association for the Advancement of Science governing board based on similar ones the
body had rejected in 1969. SftP members submitted the resolutions included
here one month in advance of the annual meeting, as per regulation. Although
the governing board voted them down, SftP members used the resolutions as an
organizing tool to mobilize scientists for political action.

On Political Repression

Whereas many Americans are exercising their privilege as free citizens in working together to change the oppressive social and economic system in which we live;

and whereas the institutional powers react to this by mobilizing public opinion
through appeals to fear and prejudice by proposing yet more repressive legislation,
by jailing political dissenters and by killing blacks, Chicanos and students;

and whereas the scientific community—through its leaders, administrators and
spokesmen, under the banner "science is neutral"—is courted, menaced and/or
bought off by the large corporations, the U.S. government and its thousand agencies into serving the cause of the privileged and the oppressors;

and whereas in particular scientific workers have been among those arrested,
black-listed, fired, discriminated against in hiring and promotion and otherwise
harassed for exercising their rights to the free expression of their political beliefs;

It is time for the AAAS to act to the best of its ability, in accordance with its
stated goals, to promote human welfare and further the work of scientists.

Therefore be it resolved:

1. That the AAAS establish a committee of scientists and victims of repression
   to look into the activities of scientists in connection with the police, military,
   intelligence, and other repressive agencies in such areas as wiretaps, surveillance, data banks, riot control and weapons development. This committee will
   report to the public facts and figures concerning contracts, development and
   specific uses of these instruments of political and social repression.

2. That the AAAS establish a fund to help, protect and secure the liberties of the
   victims of such repression. In particular, the committee should consider immediately the cases of scientists and academics, . . . as well as non-scientists . . . and
   the many black and white victims of repression presently illegitimately incar-
   cerated or threatened.

3. That the AAAS take a public stand condemning the pending Defense Facilities
   and Industrial Securities Act and similar legislation, not only because of the
   threat it represents to the scientific world, but because it is an integral part
   of the larger repression against which the AAAS commits itself to struggling in
   this resolution.

On the Indochina War

Whereas one of the purposes of the AAAS is "to improve the effectiveness of science in the promotion of human welfare";

and whereas the government of the United States exerts great effort toward improving the effectiveness of science in the suppression of struggles for liberation at home and abroad;

and whereas the current policy of the government of the United States is a formula for the indefinite prolongation of the war and the continuing destruction of the people of Indochina.

Therefore be it resolved that the AAAS demonstrate its commitment to human welfare by communicating to the President of the United States a demand for the immediate withdrawal of all U.S. men, women, and material from Indochina.

On Women in Science

Whereas the objectives of the AAAS cannot be realized while women in science are relegated to second-class status;

Therefore be it resolved that the AAAS demonstrate its commitment to its own objectives by endorsing the eight demands incorporated in the statement on equality for women in science. [See Document 5.1—eds.]

Document 2.5

"Second Annual Dr. Strangelove Award for Edward Teller," *Science for the People* 3, no. 1 (February 1971): 10.

During a panel discussion at the 1970 American Association for the Advancement of Science annual meeting in Chicago, SftP members confronted renowned nuclear scientist Edward Teller, a key figure in the development of the hydrogen bomb. While Teller spoke, activists mocked him from the side of the stage, holding up signs meant to discredit his statements. Afterward, co-panelist Richard Novick presented Teller with SftP's "Second Annual Dr. Strangelove Award." (Earlier that year, Berkeley SESPA members presented the first Dr. Strangelove Award to Dr. Michael May, head of the Lawrence Radiation Laboratory [later called Lawrence Livermore National Laboratory], one of the Atomic Energy Commission's two nuclear labs.) The award was satirical, named after Stanley Kubrick's 1964 black comedy film *Dr. Strangelove*, about a paranoid general who sets the U.S. military on a path toward nuclear war with the Soviet Union. The film's title character, a deranged nuclear scientist and former Nazi, was partially modeled on Teller himself.

S.E.S.P.A. is Nauseated to Present Its Second Annual Dr. Strangelove Award to Edward Teller

In recognition of his ceaseless efforts to follow in the footsteps of the great Peter Sellers, Dr. Teller, not content to rest on his laurels as "Father of the H-Bomb," has ceaselessly promoted the rapid development of all feasible systems of nuclear destruction.

He has argued for the indefinite continuation of atmospheric nuclear tests.

He has fought for the development and production of the ABM and MIRV weapons systems.

He has consistently espoused the practical use of nuclear weapons, most strikingly in his contention that "we must prepare for limited warfare—limited in scope, limited in objectives, but not limited in weapons. A localized limited nuclear war."

He has sought to create an atmosphere in which nuclear war would be possible by publicly belittling the effects of such weapons, as for example, in his statement, "The great majority of our citizens could survive a nuclear attack."

The name Edward Teller is recognized everywhere as a symbol of science in the service of warmakers. Nothing better exemplifies the absurdity of a "disinterested search for truth" funded by the DoD than his own philosophy:

> The duty of scientists, specifically, is to explore and to explain. This duty led to the invention of the principles that made the hydrogen bomb a practical reality. In the whole development I claim credit in one respect only: I believed in the possibility of developing the thermonuclear bomb. My scientific duty demanded exploration of that possibility.

Document 2.6

The Boston Travellers, "1970 Chicago AAAS Actions: Review and Critique," *Science for the People* 3, no. 1 (February 1971): 8–11.

This report highlights how Science for the People engaged in organizational self-reflection in order to advance political effectiveness. The authors reflected on SftP actions and activities at the December 1970 annual meeting of the American Association for the Advancement of Science in Chicago. They evaluated the strengths and weaknesses of SftP's confrontation with Edward Teller and Glenn Seaborg and of SftP's efforts to increase audience participation in a panel discussion on "Crime, Violence, and Social Control."

Our major purpose was both critical and assertive—critical of the technical and scientific obfuscation of the essentially political nature of the use, content, financial support and motivation of science in America and assertive of the need of a positive program of "people's science." . . . We tried to sharpen our own critique and to raise critical awareness among our fellow scientific workers and we tried to elaborate the concept of people's science as a means for scientific workers to become part of liberation struggles and by organizing at the work place contribute to the revolutionary change which is the precondition for science that can truly serve the people. There were other secondary objectives; improving working relationships among ourselves, gathering new friends throughout the country, widening distribution of the magazine, etc. By a few examples we want to give an impression of the extent to which the major objectives were achieved.

Sharpening the critique and raising consciousness requires a situation which breaks down the silent compliance with the power structure that dominates the thinking of so many of our fellow scientists. The system depends on prohibiting dialogue on the most fundamental issues. Therefore, a setting had to be created in which scientific workers who have not adopted the competitive, aggressive "leadership" roles set up as the pattern for "success" are encouraged to express themselves. Their shared experience must be reinforced as the basis for an understanding of their role, the role of science and of the science establishment. This cannot happen in the usual structure of scientific meetings. So we had to change the structure.

If groups are to struggle against nonparticipatory, undemocratic structure, it is necessary that they don't replicate such structure in their own organizing. Hence, we were very sensitive to the need for exemplary behavior on our own part. In this we succeeded well. Rather than providing structure we provided the means for persons and groups to generate critical activities of all types in a participatory and democratic way. Chicago SESPA, with major support from University of Chicago New University Conference (NUC) People's Science Collective provided a logistic framework—an activity center, meeting rooms, projector, typewriter, mimeograph machine, signup lists, literature tables and breakdown of the AAAS program. Individuals could sell *Science for the People* magazine (1,200 sold), buttons or tend literature tables. Groups could put out leaflets, organize actions, guerilla theater, run workshops, show films. Workshops on radical ecology, unemployment, teaching science and people's science were organized by groups of persons from all over the country who had never met before. Coordinating meetings were scheduled every night, each was attended by 250–300 people. Responsibility was shared in a conscious effort to involve and encourage everyone in decision-making. Everyday there was a different group of persons to represent the coalition to the press. The press' usual practice of inventing leaders was thus largely thwarted. Many people found the comradeliness and little services (free accommodations, messages, rider/driver matching, etc.) a refreshing contrast to the usual AAAS atmosphere. In this atmosphere great creativity and imagination was stimulated. We all learned.

AAAS meetings consist primarily of panels of 5 or so speakers delivering prepared talks of from 20 to 40 minutes on subjects that usually are stated in such a way as to establish premises that are not subjected to criticism. Passive audiences of 50–300 scientific workers and academics sit through the talks intimidated by the "expertise" of the speakers. Given the opportunity to raise questions after the speakers, they are, of course, unable to question premises or in any meaningful way participate—an insidious spectator sport that sends them back to the work place or school primed full of the latest version of what the problems are, what science is about, and the whole mind-rotting bag of ideology that is needed to keep scientific workers, teachers and their students integrated into the system.

We will describe two panels at which we took action and thus illustrate the wide variety of techniques with which we experimented. At one of these, at which Edward Teller "the father of the H-bomb" appeared, we don't believe we were as successful as at the other, a panel on violence. The final event, the indictment of Glenn Seaborg, has been widely publicized, but nowhere described fully. Since it is a good example of an action that combined elements of guerilla theater, confrontation, open discussion and a good analytical base, we will describe that also.

"Is there a Generation Gap in Science" is an example of how to frame a problem in such a way as to obscure the real issues. Margaret Mead chaired this panel of Albert Szent Gyorgi, Edward Teller, Richard Novick, and Fred Commoner with commentators Nancy Hicks and Stuart Newman. There was a gap alright—a gap between the attitudes of everyone on the panel and most of the audience on the one side and Teller and his clique on the other.

As Teller began to speak two persons appeared on the platform with placards keyed to Teller's absurdities. They judicially selected from among the placards to display quotes and descriptions that fit Teller's improvisations. Teller stopped speaking; the placards distracted him. Someone yelled from the audience that the 10 bodyguards in the room distracted us all. Mead acknowledged the bodyguards with some inane comment, "a lot of Americans have guns too." Teller gave in and continued his talk while the placards continued to be displayed and the displayers pantomimed accusatory gestures at critical moments.

Szent Gyorgi, several years Teller's senior, had preceded him taking a critical and moralistic stand that acknowledged the widespread misuse of science. Novick, Commoner, Hicks and Newman followed; they were also critical. (Novick's and Newman's talks are excerpted in "Majority View" in this issue.) The press quoted Teller extensively and virtually ignored the fact of the panel's overwhelming disagreement with Teller. In addition to the placards and the accusatory pantomime, there were two other actions. Novick followed his talk by presenting the second annual Dr. Strangelove Award to Teller in the name of SESPA (Document 2.5—eds.). The presence of the bodyguards was ridiculed by a man with BODYGUARD printed across his T-shirt standing in mock guard behind Novick after the presentation. Both actions were in good fun and served the function of ridicule. But there was negligible audience participation and little analytic content to our actions. The moralistic tone of the Strangelove award helps us not at all to understand Teller as a product of society, as an exaggerated example of what so many of us and our colleagues are in part or might be. It provides no basis for scientists to immunize themselves against the appeal of Teller's attractive personality or his obvious capability as a physicist or his intelligence.

The Teller clique, evident at the beginning, remained loyal. The largely hostile audience remained hostile. Teller substituted the facade of a warm personality, of a dedicated and concerned citizen, for an honest discussion of his political role and the role of his science. We substituted moralistic rhetoric and ridicule for a critical discussion of how and why our society makes men like Teller tools of a moribund and destructive capitalist system.

The panels on "Crime, Violence and Social Control" were another story. There we succeeded in changing the structure and stimulating participation. The press made much of "disruption" and violence with a knitting needle (see *N. Y. Times,* Dec. 30) by a person whom, in its characteristic male-chauvinist way, it identifies only by her husband Garrett Hardin, P.P.P. . . . but of the real content and positive effect of our actions nothing was reported.

At one of these panels, that on "The Community and Violence" we undertook to restructure the sessions as follows: (1) Each panelist would be given up to 5 minutes to summarize his presentation insofar as mimeographed reprints were available. (2) Anyone (audience or panel) could interrupt the speaker at any time to question a statement or premise. (3) Anyone in the audience could also speak up to 5 minutes only. (4) The primary subject was to be "institutionalized violence" since that is the most prevalent form of violence in America. To accomplish this it was necessary to prevent the chairman from running the meeting in the usual way. We decided to replace him.

The chairman hung around, apparently feeling some loss of status in our attempt to replace him, but eventually felt compelled by the audience and panel participation to ineffectually punctuate everything that seemed to go on quite well without him. One panelist, a criminal judge, left; the others were cooperative.

At first those who spoke up from the audience were our people, but soon a beautiful thing happened: persons, obviously unaccustomed to speaking up, rose to speak. One man, perhaps in his seventies, spoke of the violence of Chicago housing conditions first explaining how he had never before spoken up. Women spoke of institutionalized violence to them. The panelists were challenged; there was every evidence that having a response was more meaningful to them than the usual sterile reading of a paper. Issues were dealt with as they came up. A black man disagreed with a woman's statement that tended to identify them by a common bond of similar oppression and violence. The issue was joined. Many spoke. The meeting room filled to capacity. To emphasize the necessary relationship between thought and action if science is to be relevant, a member of the Panther defense committee spoke of needs in Chicago and asked the audience to participate in counteracting the violence of inadequate medical care to poor people and blacks by contributing to a Panther-sponsored health clinic. Money was collected. Films were then shown followed by heated discussion with wide participation. The whole experience made it ever so clear how institutional forms are the instruments of the suppression of critical discussion—a change in structure, some exemplary participation and long-constrained ordinary people full of life experience and the pent-up need to participate, to express themselves and to change the world opened up. Watch out mother country! We're going to talk to one another, analyze our experience together and that's downright subversive. For, who knows, we may figure out what's wrong together and together change it all.

Seaborg's indictment . . . was described by most of the nation's newspapers as a "disruption" and an attempt to "prevent Seaborg from speaking." The truth is that Seaborg chose not to speak rather than hear his indictment. In this he was true to form; according to *Time* of Jan. 4, p.49 ". . . he has become something of a legend in Washington for his ability to duck controversy." At the AAAS, he ducked out the side door. But the indictment stands. Unlike the Teller Panel, this time we had done our homework. Neither Seaborg's presence nor personality were relevant.

A most boring panel, a small room, television and film lights all contributed to the sighing, restless atmosphere of boredom as the speakers preceding Seaborg mouthed on. Seaborg's turn came, he split. Science for the People moved to the front and the indictment was intoned through a bullhorn in semi-legalistic irony holding Seaborg up as the paradigm of ruling-class science coordinator. A group of women read a statement pointing out the duplicity in the council's failure to pass the resolutions . . . and the meaninglessness of the token resolution they did pass. Then it happened again. The room was alive. An old and a young woman sitting a few short minutes before in non-communication and bored now spoke animatedly. The newspaper said "bedlam"—yes, bedlam, the kind that occurs in a room full of people engaged in conversation.

AAAS 1970 was an important experience for a lot of people. For us, for politically conscious activist scientific workers it was important both for the opportunities it presented and for what we learned. We learned how essential the given structures are to the maintenance of the uncritical thinking in which our brother and sister scientific workers (and ourselves) are imprisoned; we shall never again permit such structures to constrain us. We learned that moralistic *ad hominem* attacks are self-defeating; we must do our homework and analyze the institutional framework of science and the dynamics of integration and submission of scientists into capitalism. The enemy is the system, the complex interlocking social, economic and political structure that, having evolved, is reproduced, extended and adapted every day by most of us. This is the general schizophrenia: that we are extremely discontent in the very system in which we must participate to survive and to whose functioning we contribute by participating. Such a widespread ambiguity can only be resolved either by permanent self-hatred and cynicism or by a serious commitment to revolution. As revolutionary scientific workers we can empathize with our brothers and sisters standing confused in the wilderness. All of us can and must become aware through collective struggles of the contradictions of a system that breeds competition and hatred and which suppresses solidarity and love. This leads us of necessity to despise the grotesque exaggerations of the ugliest potential of the human spirit on the part of those who consciously identify with the system and who are at the same time its most dehumanized products.

The lines are clearly drawn. The polarization into those who unqualifiedly support this system and those who fight it at all levels progresses as more and more people become conscious of the inherent contradictions of capitalism.

We shall in time, make, by any means necessary, a world in which the noblest potential of the human spirit prevails.

—The Boston Travellers

Document 2.7

"Leaflet Handed Out at One AAAS Session," *Science for the People* 4, no. 2 (March 1972): 5.

This is a reprint of a leaflet distributed prior to a session on *Technology and the Humanization of Work* at the December 1971 annual meeting of the American Association for the Advancement of Science in Philadelphia. Authored anonymously (and probably by more than one activist), the document is an exemplar of the kind of literature SftP used to intervene in the conferences. See also Figure 2.

You are about to attend a session on *Technology and the Humanization of Work.*

Yet, though there are technologists and managers on the panel, there are no workers (there is an union official). That a panel should exclude rank and file workers is itself indicative of the basic problem. For technologists do not confer with the object of their experiments, nor do managers confer with the machines in their plants—and for these persons, that is just what workers are, objects. There can be no meaningful discussions of the humanization of work that does not begin with an explanation of the root of the problem—an economic system that treats labor as a commodity and creates or improves technology for the maximization of profit.

In fact, what does it mean to speak of the humanization of work in a system where the workers themselves are reduced to mere objects, bought, sold and traded like all other goods according to the demands of capital, not according to human considerations? For the workers, their creativity, humanity, and desire to be socially productive are drowned in the competitive struggle for economic security. They do not control the conditions of work nor the use made of the products of their labor.

The basic assumption underlying this symposium is that workers will remain a commodity. The effect of a session such as this is therefore not the humanization of work but the use of more sophisticated technologies and devices for controlling and manipulating workers in order to "maximize production and improve labor relations." The function of such studies is to attempt to make commodities feel like human beings and in so doing to prevent antagonism to an economic-political system which perpetuates the dehumanization of work by its institutionalization of labor as a commodity.

However, no one should think that the dehumanization and alienation so evident in the daily activity of production personnel and lower echelon white-collar workers is limited to these groups. The managers of the corporation or organization which harnesses human labor for the purposes of profit apparently have greater control over their own lives and work. Though they consciously exercise power, they are both objectively and subjectively dehumanized by their roles. Their job is to manipulate other human beings, to treat them as commodities, as things. Thus the managers' relatively increased freedom has been bought at the expense of the freedom of others. There is only one human species—the exploitation of one human by another dehumanizes both.

What will be critical to the actual humanization of work, is not only a fundamental analysis of the present forms of institutionalized dehumanization but action to change these institutions; workers' control of their work and of their lives is essential. Managers and industrial-relations technocrats serve only a destructive function. The proper topic for this session would be strategies for gaining workers' control and elimination of the managerial positions and technocratic functions of the present panelists.

Science for the People!

Document 2.8

FBI Report on Science for the People, December 6, 1972, 39–40.

The following excerpt comes from a forty-seven-page declassified Federal Bureau of Investigation (FBI) surveillance report on Science for the People (referred to here by the organization's other name SESPA, or Scientists and Engineers for Social and Political Action). This document provides a detailed outside perspective on SftP members' activities at the December 1971 annual meeting of the American Association for the Advancement of Science in Philadelphia. In particular, the document attests to SftP's disruptive impact on the conference, including at an address by the former vice president and 1968 Democratic presidential candidate Hubert Humphrey, who had supported President Lyndon B. Johnson's war in Vietnam and endured a rowdy SftP-led protest while attempting to address his audience.

The SESPA group that participated in the AAAS Convention in December, 1971, was smaller than the contingent that participated in Chicago in 1970. In Philadelphia, 50–100 persons participated with SESPA at various times throughout the convention. SESPA leaders succeeded in their objective—"polarizing the convention." By this they made both friends and enemies. They were concerned about "bad press" which stressed such things as the HUBERT HUMPHREY incident. They purposely act on two (2) levels—"destruction when necessary and being polite when unexpected," to keep the press off guard. Their intention was not to alienate the left liberals who would see a hint of good behavior and be able to comment, "They aren't bad people after all." The ultimate objective, however, was to remain a threat to the power establishment of the AAAS, and thus get SESPA's way in controlling key decisions. SESPA formed what they called "Flying Squads" of two (2) or three (3) people to each workshop session to announce a peace vigil being held. In doing so, they interrupt the session with which they disagreed, but they did so primarily without too much hatred demonstrated.

The HUBERT HUMPHREY incident mentioned above was an occurrence at the AAAS Convention, which received front page coverage in daily newspapers throughout the country. A photograph of HUBERT HUMPHREY standing at the podium with paper airplanes and tomatoes being thrown at him was printed in most newspapers throughout the United States. Signs in front of and behind HUBERT HUMPHREY indicated a desire for peace, and a slogan "Science for the People" was in plain view. SESPA received the bad publicity for this activity, although SESPA leaders claim the persons actually throwing the planes and tomatoes were not SESPA people. . . .

SESPA's policy since the 1971 AAAS disruption has remained the same. Members from various chapters throughout the United States have attended professional meetings, . . . and the regional meetings of various teaching groups throughout the country. Depending on the strength of SESPA members at meetings, they either leaflet and picket, or if insufficient numbers are in attendance, openly attempt to take over meetings. At big meetings, there is a mixture of disruptive tactics designed to destroy the existing organizational structure of the meeting and also provide positive image building for the SESPA group. The latter takes the form of "open" discussion meetings called by SESPA "The Peoples' Convention of Professional Organizations." These are meant to contrast with the structured, old-fashioned format used by those in power. The call is to change the thinking of participants in these conventions so that the participants turn away from the existing authorities and format in favor of the SESPA's way [*sic*] . . .

Document 2.9

FBI teletype, Boston Field Office to Acting FBI Director L. Patrick Gray, December 22, 1972.

This selection, from a declassified Federal Bureau of Investigation (FBI) surveillance document reporting on Science for the People activists' plans for the December 1972 annual meeting of the American Association for the Advancement of Science in Washington, DC, sheds light on FBI efforts to manage disruptive and violent political protest during the early 1970s. Boston FBI agents gleaned their "intelligence" from one of several unidentified informants close to the Boston SftP chapter and sent the information to both FBI headquarters' Domestic Security Division (DOMINTEL) and the Washington field office (WFO). In a practice common with declassified documents, the FBI redacted the name of their informant, whom agents referred to as "a source who has provided reliable information in the past." The document refers to SftP by its other name, Scientists and Engineers for Social and Political Action (SESPA).

NR 007 BS CODE

5:00 PM URGENT 12-22-72   DAB

TO: ACTING DIRECTOR (100-459865)   (ATTN: DOMINTEL)

WFO (100-55265)

FROM: BOSTON (100-42304)   P

SCIENTISTS AND ENGINEERS FOR SOCIAL AND POLITICAL ACTION (SESPA)

INTERNAL SECURITY—REVOLUTIONARY ACTIVITIES (AKA IS-REVACT)

. . . A source who has furnished reliable information in the past advised captioned organization, also known as Science for the People, intend to demonstrate in protest at the American Association for the Advancement of Science (AAAS) annual convention in WDC 12/26–31/72. SESPA has protested in these annual conventions for three years and has succeeded in taking over parts of the convention's meetings.

The same source advised that Boston Headquarters of SESPA is not aware of total SESPA membership who will attend convention. Boston chapter expects to send 20 persons to the AAAS convention. Numbers from other chapters throughout the U.S. are unknown. SESPA's general tactics have been outlined as "designed to encourage communication with the majority of the people attending the meetings and to accentuate the basis for political differences between this large group (the total AAAS membership) and those who conscientiously work for the power structure that controls science and technology. The theme of SESPA's action will be three-fold:

"1. Imperialism—the relationship between science/technology and imperialism including special focus on anti-war activities, exploits of third-world resources counter-insurgency [*sic*].

"2. Social control—the use of science to contain the social response to our repressive social system including control of behavior. One session of the convention will be run by doctors [REDACTED] concerning public policy and social science. SESPA intends to disrupt this session and completely take it over without violence.

"3. Science for survival—Alternatives to present practice in science geared to our survival at both global level and community level." Science for survival is synonymous with the ever-present theme of SESPA to make science serve the people (mankind). . . .

[NAME REDACTED] has stated that SESPA plans no violence; and in source's opinion it would be doubtful that SESPA would have any violent demonstrations at the AAAS convention.

Document 2.10

"Call to AAAS Actions," *Science for the People* 5, no. 1 (January 1973): 24–25.

In January 1973, just after the December 1972 annual meeting of the American Association for the Advancement of Science in Washington, *Science for the People* magazine ran this "Call to Action" to invite participation in disruptions at the July 1973 AAAS conference scheduled for Mexico City. The piece called on radical scientists to develop structural rather than individualistic analyses to explain why scientists with good intentions participated in institutions that perpetuated inequality and violence.

The road to Hell is paved with good intentions.

Not a strikingly original thought, of course, but one suggested by the AAAS meeting this December in Washington and its significance for SESPA/Science for the People. Our experience over the last several years tells us that the majority of scientists who attend the AAAS meeting and partake in its sessions are motivated by deeply felt social concerns. They see the genocide in Indochina, environmental destruction, and massive social unrest as clear indicators of social decay, and true to a tradition in science which goes back to the 17th century, they want to apply their knowledge and expertise to the improvement of human welfare—in this case to the resolution of the present social problems.

But the question for us all is how such good intentions can be translated into action. For it is in action, in day to day practice, where we observe whether these good intensions don't in fact become self defeating. Why is it that the work of well meaning scientists and technologists has in many cases served only to *worsen* social conditions? Why does social alienation mount with the ever increasing technological advance of our society?

Simply this: that the energy of most scientists is directed towards strengthening the archaic, dehumanizing system in which we live. The endeavor of scientists to be socially productive has been within the context of a socially unproductive (read oppressive) political and economic system. The well intentioned attempts on the part of scientists to deal with social problems is nearly always within an ideological framework bound to frustrate such efforts.

Of course these rather general statements must be clarified and expanded upon, and that's our job as radical scientists. We have to examine in detail the nature of the system and how it affects people's lives. We must explain its imperative for expansion and consumption of resources, its need for a hierarchical and oppressive class structure, its systematic dehumanization of men and women through the productive relations of capitalism, its institutional forms of violence and destruction.

And as radical scientists our job also is to understand our own role in the perpetuation of that system. Not only in the direct sense of how our technological achievements are the tools for its maintenance, but also in how the structure and ideology of science itself serve to perpetuate the present social and economic order. How the specialization and professionalism within science lead to fragmented and myopic thinking. How the competition and hierarchy reinforce individualism and non-collective attitudes. How the myth of scientific neutrality makes scientists the unwitting instruments of political power. How the technocratic mentality (that of scientific, nonpolitical decision making) is at best undemocratic and at worst fascistic. How the propagation of elitism and elitist attitudes serve only to deny the people power over their own lives. How the philosophy and methodology of a positivistic science, when applied to the social sciences, means only social manipulation and control.

While each of these points requires careful elaboration, it is sufficient for us now simply to realize that in their totality they amount to the critical re-examination of the premises of society and the premises of science. Those who fail to make this critical re-examination serve only to strengthen the present destructive social order. In their practice, they thus make science a tool of the status quo, in direct opposition to the many peoples struggling for their liberation. Good intentions serve reactionary ends.

This brings us back to the AAAS meeting. While the actions of SESPA/Science for the People at the Washington meeting have many purposes, one of them should be to bring (by our own exemplary actions) the concerned and well intentioned scientists there over to a more radical perspective. Our most important activity in this regard is to raise fundamental and probing questions within the

AAAS sessions, and in so doing, bring to light the basic political issues involved in the present practice of science. We must thus demonstrate the critical attitudes we want to impart to others. Of course, to vigorously challenge ideas and ideology often requires that the very structure of the meeting or its sessions also be challenged. Part of the political message is the search for democratic, participatory forms to replace the elitist, authoritarian structures which pervade the AAAS meeting (and society as a whole). . . .

EDITORS' NOTES

1. On SftP's founding and disruptions of AAAS meetings, see Kelly Moore, *Disrupting Science: Social Movements, American Science, and the Politics of the Military 1945–1975* (Princeton, NJ: Princeton University Press, 2008), 158–69. On SftP's disruptions of AAAS meetings, see also Bill Zimmerman, *Troublemaker: A Memoir from the Front Lines of the Sixties* (New York: Knopf Doubleday, 2012), 190–95.
2. Charles Schwartz, "Professional Organization," in *The Social Responsibility of the Scientist,* ed. Martin Brown (New York: Free Press, 1971), 19.
3. Moore, *Disrupting Science,* 176.
4. See Document 5.1 in this volume for SftP's attempt to have the AAAS adopt a more extensive resolution on women's equality.
5. On the Edward Teller disruption, see Sarah Bridger, *Scientists at War: The Ethics of Cold War Weapons Research* (Cambridge, MA: Harvard University Press, 2015), 207–9. On the Glenn T. Seaborg disruption, see Moore, *Disrupting Science,* 166–68.
6. Also see Moore, *Disrupting Science,* 166.
7. "Schwartz Amendment," quoted in Schwartz, "Professional Organization," 20.

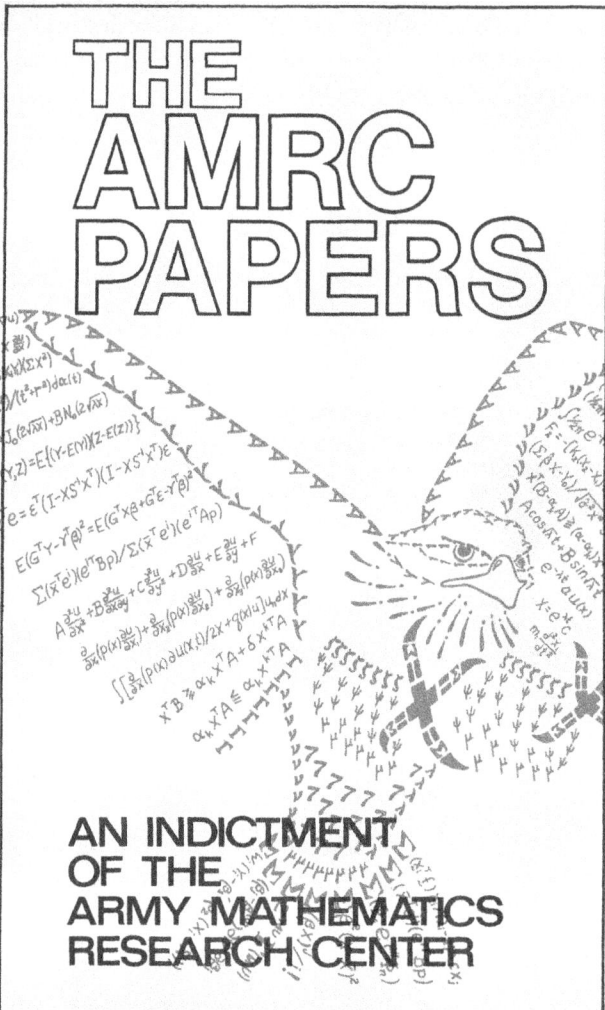

FIGURE 3. Cover of SftP's exposé of the Army Math Research Center, which supported U.S. military operations in Vietnam and which had been bombed by leftist militants in 1970. Science for the People, Madison Wisconsin Collective, *The AMRC Papers: An Indictment of the Army Math Research Center* (1973).

CHAPTER 3

Militarism

Daniel S. Chard

Anti-militarism was always at the core of Science for the People's politics. SftP first emerged as part of the antiwar movement, and its members' early efforts to reshape the American Physical Society and the American Association for the Advancement of Science (AAAS) challenged the notion that scientists could be politically neutral in the face of the U.S. war in Vietnam. SftP radicals also directly confronted federal weapons research programs and scientists whose work benefited the war and the nuclear arms race.[1] Moreover, SftP activists organized mutual aid projects to support Vietnamese and Nicaraguan Communist resistance to the United States, published exposés of other scientists' secret research on behalf of the U.S. military, and opposed the revanchist military policies of President Ronald Reagan during the 1980s.[2] Though they did not fundamentally transform the scientific establishment and its relationship with the military, SftP played important roles in larger movements that limited American leaders' war-making capacities.

At the time of SftP's founding in January 1969, a number of scientists had begun to mobilize against Congress' anti-ballistic missile (ABM) program. Opponents argued that the $1.2 billion project to build missile silos outside major U.S. cities to defend against Chinese intercontinental ballistic missile attacks was technologically infeasible, and that federal funding would be better spent on basic research. On March 4, 1969, researchers at the Massachusetts Institute of Technology (MIT) organized a walkout to protest the ABM program. The action was a key component of a broader mobilization of scientists that pushed Nixon to sign the Anti-Ballistic Missile Treaty with the Soviet Union in 1972, limiting U.S. and Soviet ABM complexes and thereby diminishing each country's incentive to expand its nuclear arsenal to defeat a rival missile shield.[3] The MIT walkout also generated further interest in SftP within a burgeoning movement of scientists opposed to U.S. militarism.[4]

In addition to disrupting AAAS meetings (see Chapter 2, "Disrupting the 'AAA$'"), SftP's earliest activities included protesting weapons laboratories and organizing fellow scientists to formally refuse participation in war-related research. Surveillance notes from a declassified 1970 Federal Bureau of Investigation (FBI) report (Document 3.1) detail some of these efforts. Citing an informant with ties to SftP, the report noted that activists in the San Francisco Bay area held a gathering in June 1969 in which more than 80 scientists and engineers signed a SftP-sponsored pledge: "I pledge that I will not participate in war research or weapons production. I further pledge to counsel my students and urge my colleagues to do the same."[5] The report also detailed SftP demonstrations and civil disobedience outside the Riverside Research Institute, a Manhattan laboratory that conducted research critical to the U.S. ABM and nuclear weapons programs.

Another way SftP members sought to end the war in Vietnam was by exposing the activities of scientific institutions that conducted research for the U.S. military. In 1972, the Berkeley SftP collective, led by the organization's co-founder Charles Schwartz, published *Science against the People: The Story of Jason* (Document 3.2). Based on meticulous research, the fifty-page booklet introduced readers to the Jason Group, a secretive consortium of physicists from elite American universities who provided the Defense Department with strategic advice, including information used to enhance the aerial bombardment of Vietnam with computer technology and a proposal for an electronic "anti-infiltration" barrier of sensors and automated weapons designed to prevent National Liberation Front guerrillas in Communist North Vietnam from entering U.S.-backed South Vietnam. The booklet also offered a powerful institutional critique of the Jason Group, arguing that even liberal members of the consortium with professed antiwar views were as responsible for the death and suffering in Vietnam as their pro-war colleagues.[6]

Similarly, the Madison SftP collective published *The AMRC Papers,* a 119-page book exposing the activities of the University of Wisconsin-Madison's Army Math Research Center (AMRC) (Document 3.3). The AMRC first gained national attention in August 24, 1970, after a group of young radicals (not members of SftP) accidentally killed physicist Robert Fassnacht in an adjacent laboratory when they detonated a truck bomb outside Sterling Hall, the campus building that housed the facility. The bombing traumatized the local community, including many of Madison's leftists, who grieved both Fassnacht's death and increased police surveillance of their movement. Published three years later, *The AMRC Papers* documented the role of the AMRC's computerized mathematical modeling research in aiding the U.S. military's development of numerous weapons and warfare strategies. The authors wrote the book as part of their ongoing efforts to close the AMRC. *The AMRC Papers* barely mentioned the explosion, though several Madison SftP members organized support for bomber Karl Armstong, whom federal authorities had recently extradited from Canada following the young radical's stint on the FBI's list of Most Wanted Fugitives. In a 1974 *Science for the People* magazine article on the AMRC and local organizing to support Armstrong's legal battles, members of the Madison SftP collective noted, "The people who defended Armstrong had different attitudes toward the bombing of the AMRC and the resulting death, but everyone was united by the idea that the American government, the murderer of more than a million in Indochina, had no right to try Armstrong for a single death."[7]

SftP moved away from its focus on militarism in the mid-1970s. Many of SftP's original, direct action-oriented members left the organization during this period, as U.S. officials wound down military involvement in Vietnam and as the larger antiwar movement shifted away from mass protest (President Nixon ended U.S. military activity in Vietnam after signing the January 15, 1973, Paris Peace Accords, and Communist forces reunited the country on April 30, 1975). Ronald Reagan's election to the presidency in 1980, however, renewed grassroots opposition to U.S. militarism. Activists organized opposition to Reagan's revival of the arms race as well as his administration's secret backing of right-wing regimes and paramilitaries in Central America and throughout the global South (see Chapter 9, "Science for the People and the World"). Though SftP ceased to be an organized force beyond the magazine during the 1980s, the magazine editors, former SftP members, and other activists inspired by the Science for the People ethos all participated in these efforts.

Recognizing a need to oppose the Reagan administration's resurrection of an arms race with the Soviet Union, *Science for the People* magazine published a special issue on "Militarism and Science" in August 1981. The editors conveyed their desire to "refocus attention on the extent to which science and technology have been pressed into the military service of U.S. capitalism."[8] The special issue, like most editions of *Science for the People* magazine after 1974, contained mostly news and analysis rather than updates on grassroots organizing or direct action. A pair of articles, for example, documented increased collaboration between academia and the military since the decline of the antiwar movement in the mid-1970s, while other pieces critiqued Reagan's invocation of a "Soviet threat" to justify a new U.S. military build-up. One article in this special issue, however, shed light on activism. An interview with members of the University of California Nuclear Weapons Labs Conversion Project (Document 3.4)— a group Charles Schwartz helped organize—described the group's five-year campaign to transition the Livermore and Los Alamos nuclear weapons laboratories toward research beneficial to humanity.

The most significant grassroots mobilization of American scientists during the 1980s was the successful campaign to stop Reagan's Strategic Defense Initiative (SDI). Popularly known as "Star Wars"—a reference to George Lucas's hit science fiction film series—SDI was the largest, most expensive military project in U.S. history.[9] The initiative sought to construct a system of satellite lasers capable of intercepting Soviet intercontinental ballistic missiles. Scientists opposed SDI for the same reasons they opposed ABM a decade earlier: they viewed it as scientifically unfeasible, a waste of tax dollars, and likely to reignite the arms race. An article by Steve Nadis in a January 1988 *Science for the People* magazine special issue on "Science and the Military" analyzed the campaign (Document 3.5), which counted the ubiquitous Charles Schwartz among its organizers. As Nadis explained, the campaign's boycott of federal military research grants was critical in pressuring Congress to block Reagan's efforts.

Despite President Nixon's reescalation of the Vietnam War and President Reagan's covert operations and arms build-up, SftP's opposition to U.S. militarism had an impact. For one, SftP was part of the larger antiwar movement that aided the Vietnamese Communists' eventual triumph over U.S. aggression and prevented American leaders from launching another full-scale foreign military intervention for the next twenty-five years.[10] Secondly, in blocking SDI, science activists inspired by SftP helped curtail the Reagan administration's efforts to revive U.S. global military power in the wake of America's defeat in Vietnam.

Document 3.1

FBI, Letterhead Memorandum on Scientists and Engineers for Social and Political Action, September 29, 1970.

This selection comes from a declassified surveillance report on Science for the People (referred to here by their other name, Scientists and Engineers for Social and Political Action, or SESPA), that the Federal Bureau of Investigation (FBI) distributed to fellow police agencies. This "Letterhead Memorandum" (as such documents were known in FBI jargon) provided details on SftP efforts to organize scientists' resistance to war research and to protest the Riverside Research Institute, a Manhattan laboratory that utilized Defense Department grants to conduct research critical to the U.S. anti-ballistic missile and nuclear weapons programs. The "sources" mentioned here refer to paid FBI informants inside or close to SftP who provided Bureau agents with "intelligence" on the organization. The names of these informants are redacted in the declassified FBI documents; their true identities remain unknown.

. . . The first source also furnished a pamphlet containing a "personal Pledge for students, teachers, and professionals in science and engineering," produced by SESPA, which reads as follows:

"I pledge that I will not participate in war research or weapons production."

"I further pledge to counsel my students and urge my colleagues to do the same."

The above pamphlet stated that on July 14, 1969, 80 scientists and engineers from the San Francisco Bay area gathered to affirm the above pledge in a small public ceremony. . . .

On August 12, 1970, the second source advised he was aware of an organization at CU [Columbia University] called SESPA. He stated that SESPA is quite persistent in picketing RRI [Riverside Research Institute], 632 West 125 Street, NYC, and is against war research and production of any type. He stated SESPA aims to encourage employees of RRI (formerly the Electronics Research Laboratory of CU, but is now a private organization) to find work elsewhere. . . .

On August 13, 1970, a third source, who has furnished reliable information in the past . . . stated that the objective of SESPA was to do anything to break down the offensive/defensive capability of the United States, by trying to get people who work at places like RRI to get jobs in non-defense work. . . .

The above source furnished a leaflet which announced a demonstration that was held at the RRI . . . on August 6, 1970. The leaflet was headed "Stop ABM on Hiroshima Day" and contained in part as follows:

"RRI employs 400 and spends $600 million a year on ABM and other weapons research."

"They are helping to carry on where the Manhattan Project left off."

"There will be opportunities for non-violent direct action. Those wishing to participate in such action should provide their own bail." . . .

On August 6, 1970, Special Agents of the FBI observed approximately 75 persons conduct a picket line demonstration at RRI . . . from 12:00 noon until 1:00 pm, which was sponsored by SESPA. Members of the Committee of Returned Volunteers performed a guerrilla theater skit which opposed the use of Dow Chemical Company and Monsanto Chemical Company defoliating agents. The guerrilla group consisted of ten individuals, four wearing sampans wearing names of Vietnam, Cambodia, Laos and Thailand. Three individuals wore skull masks while two wore costumes bearing names of "Dow" and "Monsanto." Demonstrators chanted, "Rip off Riverside," "Shut Down Riverside, Science for the People."

[NAME REDACTED] and [NAME REDACTED], both identified as SESPA members, spoke briefly at the demonstration, condemning the United States for bombing Hiroshima and for the "War Think Tank" research being conducted at RRI. Mary Kochiyama of Asian Americans for Action also spoke in condemnation of the bombing of Hiroshima and the activities at RRI. [NAME REDACTED] stated that SESPA has approximately 1,000 members in various "caucus" groups throughout the country. He indicated that they were all autonomous with only one officer in the national organization, namely the secretary, whose primary responsibility was the newsletter. He claimed that SESPA was currently active at Los Alamos, NM, Livermore, California, and RRI, NYC.

During the above demonstration, three individuals were arrested and charged with disorderly conduct by the New York City Police Department (NYCPD) when they attempted to block the entrance at RRI. . . .

On September 22, 1970, a fifth source, who has furnished reliable information in the past, furnished a leaflet headed, "SESPA is for scientists." . . . The leaflet stated as follows:

"Our projects include:

"Circulating a scientists' pledge not to participate in war research and to pressure colleges who do.

"Continuous demonstrations at RRI . . . the largest anti-ballistic missile and nuclear war think tank in New York City. We've been able to slow their research program and have convinced over a dozen employees to quit.

"Vigils at the homes of weapons scientists. These demonstrations have brought public pressure on men for whom anonymity is a crucial working condition.

"Demonstrations at technical meetings against weapons scientists who use legitimate science as a smokescreen for weapons activities.

"A national scientists' boycott of Los Alamos and Livermore weapons facilities."

Document 3.2

Jan Brown, Martin Brown, Chandler Davis, Charlie Schwartz, Jeff Stokes, Honey Well, and Joe Woodward, *Science against the People: The Story of Jason* (Berkeley SESPA Collective, 1972), 1–43.

In 1972 the Berkeley Science and Engineers for Social and Political Action collective published *Science against the People: The Story of Jason—the Elite Group of Academic Scientists who, as Technical Consultants to the Pentagon, have Developed the Latest Weapon against Peoples' Liberation Struggles: "Automated Warfare."* The nearly 50-page booklet introduced readers to the Jason Group, a secretive consortium of physicists from elite American universities who provided the Defense Department with strategic advice related to computer technology and warfare, including for the development of an "electronic barrier" of sensors and automated weapons for the U.S. military's use in Vietnam. This excerpt includes passages from the booklet's introduction, as well as a segment critiquing liberal Jason scientists' complicity in U.S. militarism despite their professed opposition to the U.S. war in Vietnam. The excerpt also includes a segment from the conclusion, which called on fellow scientists to actively oppose and resist the use of scientific research for military purposes.

[From the Introduction—eds.]

The overall involvement of scientists with government is an enormous subject. The issue is posed perhaps most sharply by the Jason group, an elite panel within the Institute for Defense Analyses (IDA). The President's Science Advisory Committee (PSAC), which works directly for the President, is still more select than Jason and presumably more influential. But in Jason, we see long-range strategic advice to the Department of Defense associated with the symbols of academic science. The forty-odd members of Jason include some of the very best known physicists in America, working at the most prestigious universities. While maintaining their public personalities as esteemed professors, they have been quietly helping the Department of Defense with—with what? They are not "free to answer."

The first aim of this study is to assemble some of the story of this classified work. An especially significant contribution of Jason to the Vietnam War was revealed in the Pentagon Papers.[11] In a 1966 report, a Jason group drew up general outlines for a system of sensors, communications links, aircraft, mines and bombs intended to stop transport of soldiers and supplies into South Vietnam. This system, adapted and expanded by the Pentagon, has become what is now known as the automated battlefield. It has made possible the policy of minimizing American casualties while continuing to devastate Indochina and its people through technological warfare; it has made possible Nixon's plan to prosecute the war indefinitely or until he can achieve "peace with honor"; it is being readied for other, future wars.

Thus, everyone concerned with anti-democratic forces in our society should be vitally interested in the nature of Jason and its activities. In this report, we present the best information available to us on this important issue. . . .

While this report focuses on the activities of the Jason group, Jason is by no means an isolated or unique phenomena. This case study of Jason serves to illustrate the nature of relationships which exist generally between elite academic scientists and government, military, and business agencies. These relationships facilitate the routine implementation of policy decisions of sweeping social consequences without the knowledge or consent of the people or their elected representatives.

[From Chapter 3, "Why They Do It"—eds.]

There is nothing new about great scientists working at new weapons: Archimedes, Leonardo, Kelvin all served their princely masters well in warfare. In our time this service has become endemic, with regiments of scientists in every advanced nation working at new generations of weapons. And it should not be thought that these scientists work only at the instigation of the military; quite the contrary, the most novel weapons cannot be anticipated by non-scientists and are often resisted by a conservative majority of career soldiers. The atom bomb, the hydrogen bomb, intercontinental missiles, nuclear submarines, chemical and biological agents, the automated battlefield—all of these had, and needed, first-rate scientists to champion them, not just to supply them to the Pentagon's order.

It is tempting to classify scientists, as other people concerned with political and military affairs, according to the labels Hawk and Dove. Indeed there are a number of scientists who show extreme xenophobia or bellicose anticommunism, and may fairly be called hawks. Such was the late John von Neumann, and such, of course, is Edward Teller. But doves have been responsible for some of the most lethal innovations in modern warfare. One thinks of the gentle and socially conscious J. Robert Oppenheimer.

Many of the Jason people fall in the second group. Some of them will speak clearly against the Vietnam War; a number of them have done so publicly. Some of them have given Congressional testimony critical of some Pentagon project. Some of them have done good work on some environmental problems. They are all creative scientists and often admired teachers. In the interviews they commonly expressed concern about working for the good of humanity, and hope that Jason gave them a way to do so.

[From the Conclusion—eds.]

    . . . We have a right, indeed a duty, to *demand from the Jasons full accountability for their service to the military.*

Just what this accounting should encompass and just what political processes should be employed to attain this end is something that needs to be widely discussed. The first step should be to circulate the information in this booklet so that the people on each campus can confront the Jason-types who reside or visit in their midst. The second step should be to undertake intensive research in order to uncover the full extent of outside consulting by faculty: then the people in each location can decide the best ways for them to move on these issues.

We will present, below, a few of our own thoughts on this subject.

1. Many of us, like the authors of this booklet, are already convinced that the U.S. military establishment, as it is now, constitutes the dominant force for death, destruction and the suppression of popular movements for Liberation throughout the capitalist-ruled world. What we say to the Jason scientists is, cease all your services for the Pentagon; repudiate the U.S. militaristic policies and the corruptions of science in that service; reveal whatever inside information you have about the military. Ellsberg did.

Those scientists who continue to work actively in support of imperialistic and warlike policies must be viewed, in some sense, as our enemies; we shall oppose them politically, as we have opposed Lyndon Johnson, Richard Nixon and their many henchmen, both in and out of uniform, who have been their willing agents in prosecuting the war.

2. To members of the scientific profession as a whole, we speak as follows. Silence, acquiescence, laissez-faire attitudes towards the military involvements of a few scientists cannot be a sufficient reply to the questions of social responsibility in science. If we are to maintain our own hopes that science can really amount to more good than evil, if we are to keep—or to regain—the respect of the non-scientific public, then we must take some actions to offset the desecrations that our profession has incurred through the Vietnam atrocity. We call on all scientists to follow, not the highest bidder or the biggest dealer but the worthiest uses of science and technology. The call for a more humane re-orientation of scientific efforts has been heard before; perhaps the story of Jason, because it is such a clear and odious example of the misuse of science, can serve as a pivot for a new turning. We ask all our fellow scientists to adopt these minimum habits:

a. Gather, and publicize information on the misuses of science;
b. Reject the rule of secrecy, insist on public accountability for all scientific endeavors;
c. Maintain dialogue on these issues with your colleagues, both in and out of government service, and do not shy from letting the Jason-types know what you think of them and their work . . .

Document 3.3

Science for the People Madison Wisconsin Collective, *The AMRC Papers: An Indictment of the Army Mathematics Research Center* (1973): 1–118.

The University of Wisconsin's Army Math Research Center first gained notoriety on August 24, 1970, when a group of young antiwar radicals (not affiliated with SftP) bombed the building housing the facility and accidentally killed a postdoc physicist. Three years later, as accused bomber Karl Armstrong faced federal murder charges, the Madison SftP Collective published *The AMRC Papers*, a 119-page book documenting the Army Math Research Center's use of computerized mathematical modeling research crucial to the U.S. military's war in Vietnam and other overseas conflicts. The book provided detailed explanation of the AMRC's history, relationship to the University of Wisconsin, and involvement in the development of counterinsurgency tactics, chemical and biological warfare, missiles, and other weapons. This excerpt features segments of the book's introduction, which provided an overview of the authors' findings, as well as portions of the report's most far-reaching section: a proposal for a state-funded "People's Math Research Center" that would replace the AMRC and conduct computerized mathematical research beneficial to community organizations.

[From the Introduction—eds.]

The Army Mathematics Research Center has helped the Army in many ways: by holding mathematics conferences at the University of Wisconsin on problems which interest the Army and by consulting directly with Army scientists to determine exactly what uses the Army has found for this mathematical technology. We have studied in detail the consulting between AMRC and the Army which is recorded in Army Math's Annual, Semi-Annual, and Quarterly Reports.

Our report emphasizes AMRC consulting because it is through such consulting that the Center transforms "pure" mathematics into information useful to the Army. The Army also profits from AMRC's conferences, Technical Reports, and the informal conversations which are not often recorded.

Consulting on Guerrilla Warfare

Alone, consulting reports reveal little, as an example from AMRC's 26 April 1968 Quarterly Report indicates:

In response to a detailed request for assistance with a problem concerning measures of effectiveness which was received from Dr. David R. Howes, U.S. STAG, Bethesda, Maryland, on March 6, 1968, Prof. Rosser wrote to Dr. Howes to suggest a meeting between STAG personnel and Prof. Bernard Harris.[12]

(26 April 1968 Quarterly Report)

To understand the reality behind this bureaucratic prose, we had to place together information on Professor Harris (a statistician), US-STAG, Dr. Howes (a creator of a computer model for guerrilla warfare), and US military policy at the time of the consultation (President Johnson's phase in the Indochina War). All this data, described in our section on STAG, demonstrates that the "measures of effectiveness" mentioned in the AMRC Report are the death and destruction by gunfire, as represented statistically in Howe's computer model of guerrilla combat.

STAG has been using such mathematical models to develop Army tactics for Indochina and the other guerrilla wars in the Third World where the US is involved.

Models for the Army

Through its mathematical modeling AMRC has helped the Army in three important areas. First, they have helped design new weapons and the technological components of new weapons systems. Second, they have aided in the testing of weapons. Third, AMRC has helped analyze and plan strategies for future warfare systems. Again, the real situation is simulated as a game in mathematical terms. The player of the game is the Army strategist, who tries out various strategies to determine which best attain the Army's goal. The assumption is then made that the strategy working best in the game will work when the situation is faced in actual combat.

Army Research Bases

The Army transforms AMRC's mathematical tools into military hardware and strategy at a number of research bases, such as the STAG operation in Maryland. These bases are a crucial step in the process which pipes "pure" University research into the American military machine. Gathered there are the scientists and engineers who apply AMRC's work to strategies and weaponry. Providing these bases with the latest mathematical techniques has been AMRC's primary purpose since its birth.

In tracing the results of AMRC's consulting, we have divided the numerous consulting reports first according to the Army base involved. By studying AMRC's descriptions of their consulting, together with the individual bases' research publications, we have often identified the exact Army project for which the AMRC mathematicians were summoned. From our discoveries, it is clear that AMRC has contributed to Army projects which have been hidden from the public. One of these, as we will demonstrate, is STAG's guerrilla warfare modeling. The extent and importance of AMRC's work can be judged far more clearly from this evidence than from the partial glimpses which AMRC spokesmen allow.

We are presenting our evidence of AMRC's consulting with the ten Army bases for which we obtained the most evidence. These ten bases are grouped according to the kinds of weapons they produce: counter-insurgency weapons, conventional weapons, chemical and biological weapons, and missiles.

The research on each group of weapons is first placed in its political context. Then, the bases working on those weapons are described, beginning with an overview of the bases' research, and concluding with the details of AMRC's consultations there. A table of AMRC's contacts with additional bases follows this analysis.

In the next sections we provide a framework for understanding the political climate in which this research began and is now carried on. Included is a short history of post–Korean War US military strategy, recent trends in this strategy, and university complicity in these developments. The research method we used to study AMRC's consulting is explained at the end of our report.

[From Part IV: An Alternative: People's Math Research Center—eds.]

In the past decade, concentrated scientific resources have gone into putting men on the moon and setting the world record in Indochina for tons of bombs dropped in a single war, while only sporadic attempts have been devoted to eradicating hunger, acute poverty and pollution. And now, crucial programs for food, education and housing are being terminated.

Most people now regard science and technology either as a pointless spectacle or as an oppressive tool in the hands of the military, government, and big business. The only way most of us can benefit from science is to purchase its products, both goods and services, at inflated and unjust prices.

In facing the reality of the Army Mathematics Research Center, we confront this central dilemma: how can powerful technology be transformed from a means of oppression into a force for molding society and our environments as people really wish?

Removing AMRC will solve only a small part of the problem. As Louis Rall of AMRC told another mathematician, "If your research was funded by NSF instead of AMRC, the Army would still get your work, perhaps a bit more slowly." As long as giant government and corporate institutions maintain their monopoly over the distribution of science in our society, the face of technology will not change.

Breaking this monopoly requires major surgery to destroy the coercive control these institutions hold over the world's technological and human resources and the creation of a new system of science which people control in order to fulfill their needs. Two essential steps in this process are the abolition of the Army Mathematics Research Center, and the creation of a People's Mathematics Research Center.

This Center will function as a coordinating point for people who wish to organize against repressive government and corporate policies; for people wholly neglected by any research developments who want to begin to implement programs towards significant improvements in their lives and who now have no access to any useful research facilities; and for mathematicians who are dedicated to creating a categorically different breed of science which will challenge the existing nature of research and those who control it.

A PMRC would use many of the same mathematical techniques as AMRC does. But the ends of this research would serve the majority of the people in this country rather than the Army. It would make mathematical resources available to everyone, rather than solely to the scientific establishment. And above all, it would begin to bring segments of today's research under popular control. These principles would guide the development and operation of a PMRC. There are several more specific questions which are more difficult to answer:

1. For whom will the Center work?
2. What will the Center do?
3. How will the Center be controlled?
4. Who will staff the Center?
5. How will the Center be funded?

For whom will the Center work?

First, it must work for the general public, giving priority to those who do not now have access to mathematical technology . . .

Secondly, PMRC would concentrate on the problems of those citizens' groups which are able to articulate the needs of a large constituency: cooperatives, neighborhood organizations, civil rights and farmers' coalitions, and rank-and-file labor groups . . .

What will the Center do?

The personnel at the Center would have two primary jobs: to carry out projects, and to recruit new projects by conducting educational programs explaining the capabilities of the Center. . . .

A central function of the Center will be to inspire confidence in science. The bitterness and disillusionment many people feel today is entirely justified, given the predominant brand of research which threatens and invades our daily lives. A wholly new and responsive research Center would begin to break down the myth that all science, all planning, all technological innovations are ultimately harmful, and would reduce the suspicion and ignorance which so many of us have toward science in general . . .

How will the Center be controlled?

If the Center is to serve the people, then the policies of the Center must reflect the will of the public. Also, workers need control over their work to ensure that it has meaning. These two requirements imply that the Center must be directed by the public as well as by the people who work there. . . .

Who will staff the Center?

The full-time participant staff in the Center would be responsible for explaining the potential benefits from mathematical modeling, its ability to predict future social, economic and political events, to those persons who have never had any contact with scientific research and to those who are bitter and skeptical about planning and science in general. . . .

How will the Center be funded?

Money is the crucial factor for anyone opposing the structure of science in America because funding is the ultimate control over the direction of science. Since the military, other branches of government, corporations, and private foundations are the only institutions with enough wealth to fund scientific research over the long run, any large scale science project must depend on these groups for funds and unfortunately accept some degree of control along with the money. . . .

Given current political realities, we feel that the State of Wisconsin is the least objectionable source of funding: it is more susceptible to popular control than federal government, and has access to funds. . . .

Document 3.4

"Challenging the Weapons Labs: An Interview with the University of California Nuclear Weapons Labs Conversion Project," *Science for the People* 13, no. 4 (July–August 1981): 21–23.

After neglecting the topic of militarism throughout the late 1970s, Science for the People magazine published a special issue on "Militarism and Science" in 1981. Included in this issue was the following interview with organizers of the University of California Nuclear Weapons Labs Conversion Project. The Project was a coalition of peace activists and scientists who worked for more than five years to research, publicize, and protest the University of California's critical role in the development of America's nuclear weapons arsenal. They also sought to convert UC Berkeley's laboratories in Livermore, California, and Los Alamos, New Mexico—where researchers developed all of the country's nuclear weapons under a contract from the Federal Department of Energy—into facilities that would produce scientific research beneficial to humanity. Though unsuccessful in their latter objective, the Project offers an example of scientists effectively utilizing their expertise in the service of grassroots movements for peace and social justice.

SftP: How did the Labs Conversion Project come into being?

Project: The founders of the Project were a few people with some years of experience at anti-war organizing. They thought the focus on these labs was a good tactic because it provided a local handle, giving people in the nearby communities some connection to the nuclear arms business, which is usually viewed as something out of sight and far away.

They also saw the university connection as providing a provocative set of contradictions, as well as access to a number of intermediate officials who could be challenged directly—UC Regents and administrators. While participation and support for the project came from a large number of students and a few UC staff members, the core organizers came from long established peace groups (the War Resisters League, the American Friends Service Committee, etc.). Staying power provided by this relatively stable base had been essential to our progress; the other necessary ingredient has been our ability to inform, excite and mobilize a much larger number of concerned people outside of these circles.

SftP: Your efforts have been widely publicized. How did that come about?

Project: The media have been very responsive to our actions. Our first public event was a letter, circulated in October 1976, only a few months after our founding, asking the UC Regents to include the public in its meetings to review the University's contracts with the weapons labs. The letter was co-signed by over a hundred people and was the focus of a local TV news spot. David Saxon, President of the University, agreed to meet with us, and promised to appoint a committee "in a month or so," but indicated that he intended to push ahead with the contracts. The controversy was now public, and in January 1977, when the Project held its first demonstration calling for public participation in the review process, we got a good press response. The Bulletin of Atomic Scientists editorialized that we had "put a good question to the public" and were "potentially . . . something to be reckoned with." We've also made an effort to be newsworthy and furnish the press with useful data. We have been largely successful in getting the University to hold public meetings on the contract issue, and the press was of course interested. After one of these meetings the *San Francisco Examiner* ran a banner headline about UC scientists at Los Alamos aggressively lobbying for the development of the neutron bomb. The Weapons Project had uncovered that story.

SftP: So you do investigations. Is that the main focus of your work?

Project: Our main efforts are directed at mustering the research that we and others have done, and publicizing the results so that people will understand the dangers posed by the labs. During the spring of 1979, for example, we worked with Friends of the Earth to stage a large public hearing on the Draft Environmental Impact Statement for the Lawrence Livermore Laboratory (LLL). We brought in expert testimony on seismic instability of the Livermore area, on the potential hazards of plutonium leaks (and the inadequate methods used for testing for leaks), on genetic implications of nuclear power, and so on. Dr. Carl Johnson testified, Dr. John Gorman spoke, Daniel Ellsberg spoke, Charles Schwartz spoke[1]—each one focusing on another aspect of the dangers posed by the labs. The original research we do is on the operation of the labs themselves. By attending virtually all meetings and reading all printed materials made available to the University's Committee, we made ourselves experts on the labs' activities, and when the Committee issued its report, we issued an Alternative Report. On several occasions, we've been able to upstage UC officials by knowing their business better than they do. They testified during a UC budget review by the California Legislature's Ways and Means Committee that they have no figures for the actual cost of operating the two labs. The Project was able to produce the figures, and thereby to impress Governor Brown's top aide for Science and Technology, who complimented us on the amount of data the Project had uncovered and presented. . . .

SftP: What are the Project's basic goals and strategies, and how have they changed?

Project: In the first months of the Project we collectively arrived at three fundamental goals, with the broad intention of involving large numbers of citizens in our work. We sought to convert the weapons-related work at Livermore and Los Alamos to useful, non-polluting work, to force the University to open up a public review of its relationship to the labs, and to obtain an independent environmental review of the dangers to health and public safety posed by the plutonium and other radioactive materials at the labs. Soon, however, it was apparent that the University was not an effective force in reforming the labs nor even in providing a forum for debating the issues. Rather, by resisting debates inside the labs, by refusing unclassified information to Project members, by resisting a feasibility study of conversion possibilities, and by allowing lab (UC) officials to use their influence to further the work of the arms race, the University gives a "mantle of legitimacy" to the nuclear arms effort. It is this mantle of legitimacy that must be challenged. We therefore revised our statement of goals to include a call for the severance of all UC ties to the two weapons labs. Our goals today are pretty much the same, but energy for the issues has subsided over the past six months. Several of the most active people have been taken away by family matters (babies, etc.), and several of those who saw the Conversion Project as a vehicle for organizing have grown tired of the issue and gone off in other directions. Our major effort now is outreach—to other campuses in an effort to mobilize student groups, and to communities in the San Francisco Bay Area.

SftP: What would you say have been the main achievements of the Project to date?

Project: The main achievements of the Project lie in the wealth of public education about the labs and the nuclear arms race which has resulted from our activities—directly, through teach-ins, literature, etc. which we and our supporters organized, and also indirectly, through the large amount of media coverage we have received. Challenging the authorities—those inside UC, those at the labs, and those sent out from Washington—has been an important step in that it shows how the global threat of nuclear war is in part rooted in the local power structure and therefore vulnerable to local demands. Getting a fair number of elected officials (as well as a few UC Regents) to speak out in partial, or sometimes full, support of our demands is important not only in showing the legitimacy of our views to doubtful members of the public, but also in confirming to us the large latent sentiment against present nuclear policies. When six Project members staged a sit-in at the office of David Saxon, President of the University, they were arrested and charged with trespass. After a week of testimony, including two hours by Saxon, the jury deliberated and found all six defendants not guilty. One of the jurors was so impressed by the protestors that she later joined the Project.

Particular efforts have been made to get the anti-nuclear power movement more aware and active in opposition to nuclear weapons. This meant opening political dialogue with environmentalists who at first did not want to touch the hot potato of "national defense" or risk being thought slightly pink. There has been real progress in this outreach.

Obviously, we have failed to achieve any of our stated goals: to end the nuclear arms race, to convert the weapons laboratories to peaceful pursuits, to get UC out of the nuclear weapons business or even to make it take some constructive responsibility for overseeing the labs. Right now the labs are rolling in money and expanding their weapons work, thanks to Reagan, and they may even be feeling cocky at having survived the challenges (and improved their PR capabilities).

Certainly we are dissatisfied that our efforts have not led to a much larger organization and a much larger base of supporters who can be mobilized. There is plenty of work to do and there are plenty of ideas about which directions to take. This much seems fair to say: we have succeeded in bringing the "unthinkable" issue of nuclear war and the "unthinkable" possibility of people challenging the

U.S. nuclear weapons establishment farther out of the closet and into local public awareness than it has been for a long time.

References

1. Johnson, the Director of Public Health in Jefferson County, Colorado (home of the Rocky Flats nuclear weapons plant) challenged the safety of the physical plant and the methodology for checking plutonium leaks; Gofman, ex-director of LLL's biomedical division, analyzed the threat to the genetic integrity of the population; Ellsberg [former policy analyst and *Pentagon Papers* whistleblower—eds.] spoke on the use of nuclear weapons to threaten other nations; and Schwartz, professor of physics at UC [and SftP co-founder—eds.], discussed nuclear strategies.

Document 3.5

Steve Nadis, "After the Boycott: How Scientists Are Stopping SDI," *Science for the People* **20, no. 1 (January–February 1988): 21–26.**

Science writer Steve Nadis's January 1988 *Science for the People* magazine article recalled the successful campaign to stop President Reagan's Strategic Defense Initiative (SDI), the largest, most expensive military project in U.S. history. Popularly known as the "Star Wars" program, SDI was Reagan's attempt to construct an elaborate network of satellite-based lasers and missiles capable of defending a nuclear attack on the United States. Critics, including scientists who opposed the measure, argued that the program was scientifically unfeasible and would exacerbate America's arms race with the Soviet Union, moving the world dangerously closer to nuclear war. Nadis explained how scientists helped thwart SDI by organizing a boycott of federal military research grants.

On March 23, 1983, President Reagan called on the nation's scientists and engineers to devise a defensive shield that would "give us the means of rendering these (nuclear) weapons impotent and obsolete." The "Star Wars" program, officially known as the Strategic Defense Initiative, or SDI, was to be the centerpiece of the Reagan military buildup—the largest peacetime effort in the nation's history. SDI, in turn, would be the most expensive military project in U.S. history, with a $26-billion, five-year budget and an overall price tag estimated between 100 billion and a trillion dollars.

Star Wars research, of course, was not new. It had been going on quietly for decades. What was new, however, was the crash effort to deploy such a system. To this end, research and development grew from 50 to 72 percent of total U.S. scientific research. The Star Wars budget correspondingly grew from $980 million in 1983 to a proposed $5.7 billion in 1988, making it the largest federal research program—exceeding the proposed research budgets of NASA ($4.7 billion), the National Science Foundation ($ 1.7 billion), or federal energy research ($2.9 billion).

"People go where the bucks are. There is a lot of money involved here," said

James Ionson, director of SDI's Office of Innovative Science and Technology (IST), set up in the fall of 1984 to lure universities and small businesses with Star Wars research grants.

"The response from the academic, business, and government laboratory communities was immediate and overwhelming as everyone tried to find out . . . how they could become involved in the research programs of this new office," IST boasted in a briefing document distributed in 1985 to potential SDI researchers.

The response from scientists was indeed "immediate and overwhelming," but not exactly what IST had hoped for. In the summer of 1985, physicists John Kogut and Michael Weissman from the University of Illinois and Lisbeth Gronlund and David Wright from Cornell University began circulating a petition against soliciting or accepting money for Star Wars research. Since then, more than 7,000 U.S. scientists and engineers have signed the "pledge." Over 12,000 scientists have signed it worldwide, including more than 3,000 from Japan, 1,000 from Canada, and 750 from England.

U.S. signers include 57 percent of the faculties at the 20 highest-rated physics departments in the country, 50 percent or more of the faculty in each of 112 physical science and engineering departments at 71 schools, and 19 Nobel laureates in physics and chemistry (23 internationally). The pledge has been endorsed throughout the U.S. by scientists and engineers at more than 110 research institutions in 41 states.

Tearing Away the Veil of Hype

Many signed the petition because they doubted the technical feasibility of the kind of leakproof defense advertised by President Reagan. These scientists did not want to be used by the administration to enhance the credibility of the new system. They also believed the Star Wars program would accelerate the arms race, jeopardize arms treaties, and lead to a less stable nuclear balance. Some, such as MIT physicist Vera Kistiakowsky (who circulated the pledge in her department), feared the Star Wars program would distort national R&D priorities away from basic research. Another concern, expressed in the pledge, was "the likelihood that SDI funding will restrict academic freedom and blur the distinction between classified and unclassified research."

For whatever reasons, scientists signed up in record numbers, making the Star Wars boycott one of the largest mass movements by scientists in history. "I know of no recent program that evoked such a massive outpouring of concern from the nation's scientists and engineers at all levels as did SDI," commented Senator J. Bennett Johnston of Louisiana. These scientists, he added, "tore the veil of hype" from the program. "Washington must periodically be reminded that political rhetoric, even if employed by the most skillful of communicators, has no dominion over the laws of physics."

One feature that distinguished the boycott from other protests, says Ann Krumboltz of the Union of Concerned Scientists, was that it developed as a "totally spontaneous grassroots movement, not sponsored or organized by arms control groups. That was part of its strength. It was started by a handful of scientists at a few universities, and it spread like wildfire."

"What we are witnessing is the third major uprising of the nation's scientists against an element of U.S. weapons policy," said California Representative George Brown. The other precedents he cited were scientists' opposition to atmospheric nuclear tests in the late 1950s, which led to the Limited Test Ban Treaty, and opposition to antiballistic missiles ten years later, which led to the ABM treaty of 1972.

Perhaps an even closer parallel occurred in postwar West Germany in 1957, when 18 of that nation's most prominent scientists signed a public declaration refusing to participate in the government proposed atomic bomb project. The protest completely killed the program. . . .

Did the Boycott Work?

What happened to the Star Wars boycott? More than two years after its inception, what effect, if any, has it had on the SDI program? Has it impeded SDI research? Has it mobilized protest against space-based warfare?

"There has been absolutely no impact," a spokesman from the SDI office claimed on October 29, 1987. "We have a large and capable group of people working on SDI, so we just haven't felt any impact." When asked whether the fact that so many of the nation's top scientists refuse to participate in the program has forced the SDI Organization to rely on other, perhaps less capable researchers, he said, "Now we're getting into the realm of hypothetics. The bottom line is that there's been absolutely no impact."

Available evidence, however, contradicts this assertion. "Support for SDI in Congress is now very thin, and there is no support for Reagan's Star Wars budget," claimed a congressional aide involved in SDI issues on Capitol Hill. To what degree the boycott alone was responsible for this shift, he could not determine, "but it all adds up," he said. "One after the other, there has been an unrelenting stream of scientific groups raising serious questions about the Star Wars program. That influences both Congress and the public."

"SDI is in real trouble," said former Undersecretary of Defense Richard Perle. Not only did Congress try to cut $2 billion from Reagan's 1988 Star Wars budget, it is also pushing for restrictions on Star Wars testing. If this continues, Perle added, "they will have effectively killed the program." . . .

The Bigger Picture

Recently, organizers have begun to move the debate to a broader examination of military research. "How many times can you say Star Wars is bad?" asks Rich Cowan of MIT's Science Action Coordinating Committee (SACC), which distributed the SDI pledge among MIT students. "Once you've distributed 3,000 leaflets on how bad Star Wars is, you face the law of diminishing returns."

At MIT, two committees are now investigating the question of military research on campus. SACC wants MIT to give students the freedom to reject projects that are not ethically acceptable to them. "We want MIT to guarantee that no student will be denied funding because he or she refuses to work on military-related research," said Cowan.

United Campuses to Prevent Nuclear War shares these goals. In addition to its arms control efforts, this national organization helps establish student internship programs with peace groups. "We want students to know there are alternatives to working in the military," said their executive director, April Moore. In terms of weapons research on campus, Moore said, "we feel students have a right to know where the money is coming from, and we encourage them to find out."

A student group at Cornell is doing just that—preparing a report on university research funding. "That's something I'd like to see a lot of universities do," says Chris Moore, one of the group's founders. They're sponsoring a panel discussion by Cornell faculty who refuse to take military funding. Another symposium will look at military and industrial collaboration on campus to see whether it poses a threat to academic freedom.

"We're trying to widen the debate that started with the Star Wars boycott and move on up to more basic issues, questioning the partnership between scientists and the military," Chris Moore explained. "The boycott set a precedent, but it was a boycott of very specific kinds of research. Regardless of what you do with Star Wars money, even if your research is harmless, by taking the money you're endorsing Star Wars. That argument extends to DOD money in general. It shouldn't surprise scientists that the defense budget is skyrocketing under Reagan. By taking money, they're endorsing it."

As a follow-up to the Star Wars boycott, Chris Moore suggests circulating a less specific pledge about military funding in general. "Who knows," he said, "you might get a surprising number of people to sign."

University of California–Berkeley physicist Charles Schwartz thinks boycotts and petitions are a fine place to start, "but signing a petition is relatively easy. For most people, it doesn't cause too much discomfort, and it doesn't solve the basic problem." To avoid training potential weapons makers, Schwartz has decided not to teach physics to engineering or physics majors. He has called on other physicists to do the same, generating a worldwide strike that would involve a "collective and gradual withdrawal of our services in all ways that contribute to the arms race."

Herbert Bernstein, a theoretical physicist teaching at Hampshire College, is taking a different tack. Rather than merely challenging the applications of science—whether for Star Wars or other military projects—he is examining the nature of science itself. "Instead of refusing to apply your science, I'm asking if you can change what science is so that it is possible to be both smart and good," said Bernstein. "In other words, can you reconstruct science so that it combines disciplinary excellence with social good?"

MIT mechanical engineering professor Donald Probstein would rather use science and engineering to advance social wellbeing. Probstein, a missile expert, was reluctant to turn down Star Wars funding, because of the scarcity of other funding sources. But he did refuse the SDI money. "There are many important problems I can contribute to, especially in areas of environment and energy," he said, "problems I think require solving for the benefit of mankind. I'd like to spend my lifetime working on those problems."

EDITORS' NOTES

1. See Chapter 2, "Disrupting the 'AAA\$.'"
2. See Chapter 9, "Science for the People and the World"; and Kelly Moore, *Disrupting Science: Social Movements, American Science, and the Politics of the Military 1945–1975* (Princeton, NJ: Princeton University Press, 2008), 180–81.
3. Sarah Bridger, *Scientists at War: The Ethics of Cold War Weapons Research* (Cambridge, MA: Harvard University Press, 2015), 238 and, for more on the March 4 Movement, see 155, 163–71; also see Moore, *Disrupting Science*, 137–46. For more on the 1972 Anti-Ballistic Missile Treaty, see William Burr, "The Secret History of the ABM Treaty," National Security Archive website, November 8, 2001, http://nsarchive.gwu.edu/NSAEBB/NSAEBB60/#2 (accessed January 4, 2017). President George W. Bush withdrew the United States from Anti-Ballistic Missile Treaty in 2002, claiming that the treaty prevented the nation from developing defenses against terrorist and "rogue state" missile attacks.
4. Moore, *Disrupting Science*, 146, 161.
5. The gathering took place in Berkeley. See Martin Brown, ed., *The Social Responsibility of the Scientist* (New York: Free Press, 1971), 18, which also quotes this pledge.
6. For more on SftP and the Jason Group, see Bridger, *Scientists at War*, 149–54; and Moore, *Disrupting Science*, 169–77.
7. Madison SftP, "The Struggle Against Army Math," *Science for the People* 6, no. 1 (January 1974): 26. For more on the Sterling Hall bombing and its influence upon U.S. politics, see Daniel S. Chard, *Nixon's War on Terrorism: The FBI, Leftist Guerrillas, and the Origins of Watergate* (Chapel Hill, NC: University of North Carolina Press, forthcoming); and Tom Bates, *RADs: The 1970 Bombing of the Army Math Research Center and Its Aftermath* (New York: Harper Collins, 1992).
8. *Science for the People* 13, no. 4, "Militarism and Science" (August 1981).
9. For more on this movement, see Bridger, *Scientists at War*, 245–69.
10. This changed after the terrorist attacks of September 11, 2001, which the administration of President George W. Bush used as a pretext for invasions of Afghanistan and Iraq.
11. The *Pentagon Papers* was a classified Department of Defense monograph on the history of U.S. political and military involvement in Vietnam from 1945 to 1967. Among other things, the report demonstrated that American Presidents from Harry S. Truman to Lyndon B. Johnson had lied to the public and Congress about U.S. military operations, and that the scale of the war was far larger than what had been reported in the mainstream media. Daniel Ellsberg, a former Defense Department aide and policy analyst for the RAND Corporation, leaked the *Pentagon Papers* to the *New York Times* in 1971. The *Pentagon Papers* provided the first public documentation of the Jason Group's involvement in the development of U.S. weapons for use in Vietnam, and was a critical source informing the Berkeley SESPA collective's research for this booklet.
12. STAG stands for the U.S. Army Strategy and Tactics Analysis Group.

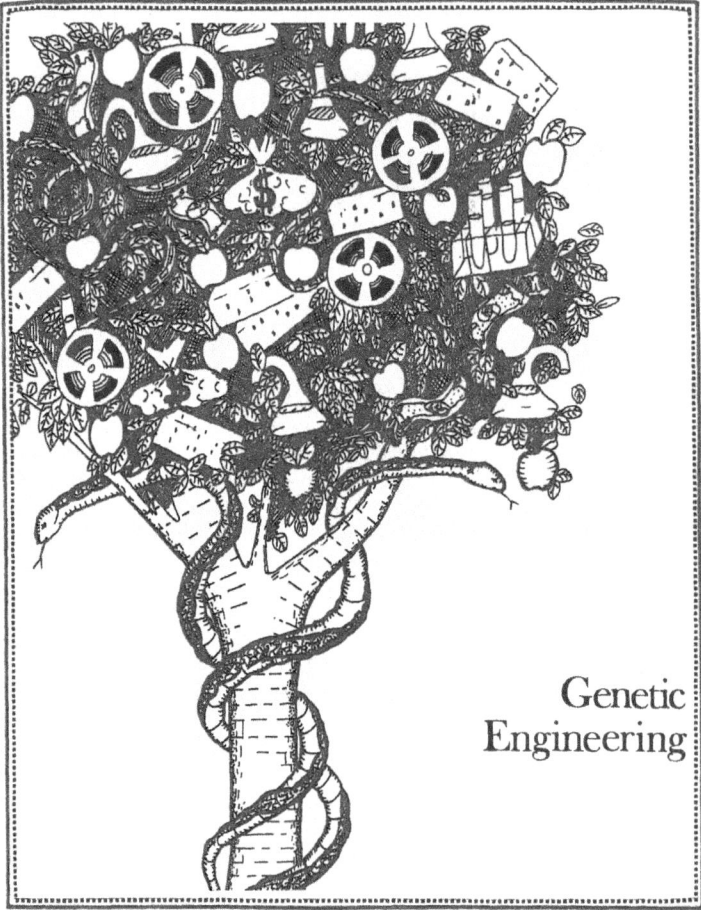

Genetic
Engineering

SCIENCE AND SOCIETY SERIES
NO 3

FIGURE 4. Cover of SftP booklet *Genetic Engineering*. Illustration by Mettie Whipple, a periodic contributor of art to SftP publications.

CHAPTER 4

Biology and Medicine

Alyssa Botelho

Science for the People firmly believed that biology and medicine should be seen as sites for correcting societal ills, not as realms of politically "neutral" investigation. SftP members engaged directly with workers to interpret and critique scientific information on health risks from asbestos, industrial chemicals, and other workplace hazards.[1] More broadly, the group used community organizing and educational campaigns to help the public understand the social and political contexts that shaped biomedical research. In these efforts, SftP engaged mass media and institutional allies, and succeeded in spreading their message beyond existing radical circles to mainstream audiences. SftP's Boston chapter, which included a large share of the group's biologists and health workers, receives special attention here.

From its founding, SftP promoted an alternative, socially conscious model of biology education. In the early 1970s, the Boston Science Teaching Group produced and distributed a series of pamphlets around the northeastern United States on topics ranging from genetics to ecology. Boston SftP members, many of them professional educators, also volunteered as biology teachers in the city's underserved schools. Boston members Rita Arditti and Tom Strunk worked especially hard to reform college biology curricula. In "Objecting to Objectivity: A Course in Biology" (Document 4.1), the pair chronicled their experience teaching a socially conscious first-year biology course together at Boston University in 1971.

SftP also held a longstanding commitment to strengthening community health infrastructure.[2] The group worked in solidarity with the Young

85

Lords Organization and the Black Panther Party to bring health care to people of color who so often could not access the medical system as patients or practitioners.[3] SftP also carried out projects with other New Left health organizations that fought for just and equitable health care, including the Medical Committee for Human Rights and the Health Policy Advisory Center (Health/PAC).[4,5] In addition, SftP's feminist members wrote extensively on women's health and reproductive rights from the organization's early days (see Chapter 5, "Race and Gender").[6]

In keeping with their broader economic analysis, SftP also illuminated how capitalist interests influenced the U.S. biomedical research agenda.[7] The 1971 National Cancer Act, signed by President Richard Nixon, was a special point of concern for the group.[8] In his 1980 article "The Politics of Cancer Research" (Document 4.5), Wayne State University medical researcher and SftP member John Valentine argued that the National Cancer Act neglected to fund studies that investigated the broad "causes" of cancer, such as poor preventive health care and exposure to environmental and occupational carcinogens, in favor of supporting research on molecular pathways of disease. Valentine also questioned the use of public funds to develop novel chemotherapies. Some of that money, he suggested, could be better spent studying how workplace exposures and consumer products might increase the risk for contracting cancers in the first place.

Nineteen seventy-five was a formative year for SftP's biologists. The publication of Harvard biologist E. O. Wilson's *Sociobiology: The New Synthesis* sparked one of SftP's fiercest and most renowned rebuttals of genetic determinism.[9] In *Sociobiology,* Wilson proposed that social behaviors are in part inherited, and shaped by natural selection across generations. Though the majority of the volume focused on lower species, Wilson extrapolated in his concluding chapter that human behaviors such as warfare, sexual exploitation, and xenophobia could be rooted in our genetic makeup. In an oft-cited *New York of Review of Books* piece (Document 4.3), biologists in Boston SftP's Sociobiology Study Group and allied colleagues banded together to raise their concerns about Wilson's claims, arguing that such science could propagate faulty and unjust rationalizations of difference among genders, races, and other social categories on the basis of DNA. The Sociobiology Study Group, however, was not a fully united front: many women members felt that sociobiological explanations of gender difference were not challenged strongly enough, and some feminists left the group amidst this strife (see Chapter 5, "Race and Gender").

In the wake of *Sociobiology,* SftP extended its fight against biological deter-minism to a number of other issues that unfolded in the 1970s. One was SftP's campaign to discredit research on XYY syndrome, a now debunked medical theory that boys born with a second male "Y" chromosome were "super-males" prone to deviant and criminal tendencies.[10] SftP members pointed out that early investigations of the XYY condition in the United Kingdom and the United States studied only men committed to prisons and institutions for the mentally ill. Without studying the broader population, they argued, such research exhibited severe selection bias for mental disability or criminal behavior in XYY males. SftP's attack on the theory, led by Harvard biolo-gist Jonathan Beckwith and MIT biologist Jonathan King, escalated when Harvard Medical School psychiatrist Stanley Walzer spearheaded a XYY screening program for newborn boys at Boston Lying-In Hospital.[11] In 1974, Beckwith and his colleagues filed a complaint about the study's legitimacy and methods with Harvard Medical School's standing committee on medical research. Though the committee ruled in the study's favor (199–35), Walzer eventually discontinued the newborn screening portion of his study due to continued pressure from SftP and allied groups, including the Children's Defense Fund. The 1975 article "Actions on XYY Research" (Document 4.2) recounts this episode. During these years, SftP also questioned the extent to which sex roles are biologically determined, and scrutinized the use of IQ testing as a metric for intelligence.[12] Many SftP members and affiliated thinkers, including Anne Fausto-Sterling, Ruth Hubbard, Stephen Jay Gould, Steven Rose, Leon Kamin, Richard Lewontin, and Richard Levins, went on to write extensively on biological determinism, building a foundation for science and technology studies scholars who would scrutinize the entangle-ment of biology and politics in later years.[13]

SftP's fight against recombinant DNA technology, launched in 1976, built on the organization's previous activism in important ways.[14] Developed in 1973, the technology allowed scientists to swap genes of interest from one organism to another—within and across species—for the first time in his-tory.[15] Recombinant DNA opponents raised the specter of genetic engineering in humans, and voiced concerns that genetic engineering would lead to new forms of biological warfare that could contaminate people and the land.[16] SftP critics also predicted, accurately, that the technology would commercialize biomedical research.[17] In the 1980s, recombinant techniques paved the way for the mass production of insulin, interferon, and other drugs now at the foundation of our modern pharmaceutical industry. Many scientists across the nation, including SftP's biologists, opposed moving ahead with recombinant DNA research before its environmental and public health hazards were rigorously tested. This story is laid out in Bob Park and Scott Thacher's 1977 "Dealing with Experts: The Recombinant DNA Debate" (Document 4.4). As they did in other causes, SftP sought to reframe discussion of recombinant DNA technology to focus on critical questions of democracy and equity, urging scientists and the public to reflect on who decides what research gets done, and whom such research serves.

Document 4.1

Rita Arditti and Tom Strunk, "Objecting to Objectivity: A Course in Biology," *Science for the People* 4, no. 5 (September 1972): 16–20.

Rita Arditti and Tom Strunk's piece is one of several that the September 1972 magazine devoted to issues in science education. The authors discussed their experience creating a first-year biology course with a social issues component at Boston University during the 1971–72 school year. Their syllabus covered myriad topics: genetic engineering and its social implications; human reproduction and its control via contraception, sterilization, and abortion; the ethics of human experimentation; the biological basis of human behavior; and methods of science communication.

During the second semester of the academic year 1971–1972, an opportunity to create a course dealing with the connections between biology and society arose at Boston University. We had been teaching general biology for a semester to freshmen students in the Division of General Education, a two-year program for first and second year students, where an interdisciplinary approach is supposed to be stressed. The program covers natural sciences (biology and physics), the humanities and the social sciences. As is the case in most academic institutions, the science courses have had difficulty in developing and maintaining student interest or even simply assuring their presence at lectures or smaller class meetings.

No wonder. Teachers in general expect students to memorize facts and names while connections are not made between scientific knowledge and real life, and scientific work is made to appear as though happening in a vacuum, beyond and above the social and political conditions of the times. When the courses end, the ritual of exams cleanses the wounds and everyone goes home, relieved. The facts and names are quickly forgotten to make room for the next layer of "knowledge."

At the end of the first semester a proposal was made by a group of teachers: instead of giving another semester of general biology to the freshman class, why not offer areas or study which differed in content, so that students would have some choice in their scientific curriculum, and we could thereby pursue our own interests as well. Students manifesting their discontent with the straight biology course helped to create a receptive atmosphere. Nevertheless, when the proposal was accepted we were surprised.

The two other full-time teachers gave courses on human genetics and behavior and ecology. We chose to present a program which we called biology and social issues. Students reacted strongly in favor of the second semester reform and very quickly we found ourselves overwhelmed with applications for our course. Here is the outline of the course we presented:

I. Introduction to Human Embryology and Genetics

    A. Genetic Engineering

        1. Cloning

        2. Somatic cell alteration

        3. Virus therapy

        4. Control of sex

    B. Physical and social limitations and implications

        1. Human gene maps

        2. Polygenic inheritance

        3. Problems of prenatal diagnosis

II. Reproduction

    A. Mechanism of hormone action

    B. Human reproduction

        1. Role of the female sex hormones

        2. Role of the male sex hormones

        3. Pregnancy

    C. Birth control, sterilization, and abortion

        1. History of contraception, abortion, and infanticide

        2. Theories of how the oral and intrauterine contraceptives work

        3. Current research

        4. Public policies and organizations

    D. Population growth

        1. Growth curves

        2. Theories of Malthus and Marx

    E. Social disease, a case study of venereal disease

III. Human Beings as Experimental Animals

    A. Similarities with other laboratory animals

    B. Differences

C. Ethics and responsibilities
    1. The drug industry
    2. Role of the FDA
    3. Genetic or ethnic weapons

IV. Biological Basis of Some Human Behavior

  A. Biological theories of territoriality and aggression
  B. The effect of certain drugs on behavior
  C. Current theories of controlling behavior by chemical means

V. The Scientific Community

  A. Methods of scientific communication
  B. The politics of pure versus applied research
  C. Who are scientists?
  D. The future of science

. . . Each week we lectured on one of the topics that we had announced and handed out articles that covered other aspects of the subject. We had recommended as background reading *The Biological Time Bomb* by Gordon Rattray Taylor and the New England Free Press pamphlet, *Women and Their Bodies.*

We deliberately chose articles that either had appeared in magazines for the general public or were written in a language that did not require special effort to understand. Also some of our articles expressed strong emotions and opinions like population (Dick Gregory's *My Answer to Genocide*) or birth control (*Off the Pill* by Judith Coburn). We found them incredibly effective in exposing the social implications of biological knowledge.

We would like now to illustrate the way we presented the course by describing how we dealt with several different topics.

I. *Control of sex.* We began by giving an idea of the ways in which it can be eventually achieved in humans and a description of the present status of the research. That naturally led into the question of what side effects this knowledge will have if spread freely in our society. We had to question the value or reasons for this kind of research, the need or lack of need for it, the idea of a society which regulates the number of people of a certain sex and the sex imbalances that would result, affecting the whole structure of society.

II. *Current advances in prenatal diagnosis.* We described the primary technique, amniocentesis (taking a sample of amniotic fluid). We then spoke about the cases in which parents might want to abort a fetus after getting information of a genetic disease affecting it or the cases in which social pressures might play a role in trying to affect or obtain a certain type of decision. We looked at genetic counseling and talked about the delicacy and importance of such activity.

III. *Cloning.* Watson's article *The Future of Asexual Reproduction* was an instance where people best grasped the implications of the new biology for the future of mankind, and the absolute necessity for everybody to be informed about what is happening in science today. Just how close are we today to making replicas of humans and test-tube babies? Who is going to decide who will be replicated and how many copies would be made?

   As the feelings of helplessness and frustration built up in the fact of the implications of a technology out of control, a way to deal with many of the questions, within the system, was introduced through a discussion of Senate Resolution 75. This is a proposal to form a commission to hold public hearings on questions of biomedical advances and ethical guidelines. We talked about the people and organizations who opposed the resolution, as well as those who favored it. Students offered many excellent revisions, most of which were designed to expand the responsibility of the commission and its availability to the public.

IV. *Reproduction.* On the subject of reproduction and birth control, one of us (R.A.) got, quite frankly, carried away. We discussed the basic biology involved and then got into the ideology of birth control research (almost exclusively devoted to control of the female reproductive system), a clear example of how the values in society influence the direction in which research develops. We carefully discussed the pill and examined the role of the FDA, AMA and drug lobby in suppressing information about known side effects. Virtually every facet of abortion was also exposed. How does a human fetus develop? When is abortion safe, what methods are used and when? How does the system work in New York? Whose rights are involved and how? And many more questions.

V. *Population growth and control.* We approached this historically by reviewing the arguments of Malthus and Marx. An interesting parallel was offered when we examined today's controversy between Ehrlich and Commoner of population and pollution, who argue, respectively (broadly), for "zero population growth" and "zero economic growth." Technology's inability to foresee and deal with its own side effects, already in evidence from genetic engineering and contraception, was again obvious in the environmental crisis and forced us to ask if we really trusted the technology that brought us to this point to extricate us from it.

VI. *Behavior and aggression.* We discussed Lorentz's views on human aggression, Erich Fromm's theory and we presented the AFSC slide show on the electronic battlefield in VietNam, a superb example of how corporations and war profit [from] ideology [that] exploit[s] the potential for destruction in the human species.

   In dealing with behavior, we asked what determines our own behavior, from TV to institutions, the role of obedience in maintaining social structure

(Stanley Milgram's experiments on obedience), drugs for children (see article *The Case of Ritalin*) and the revival of psychosurgery. At the same time, other events were developing that would expand our learning environment greatly. After a two-year moratorium Marine Corps recruiters were invited on campus and a peaceful protest was turned into a violent confrontation as the Boston Tactical Police Force was called in by the BU administration to smash the demonstration. They did exactly that, with clubs and attack dogs, and arrested 33 students. By the time we were dealing with human aggression in class, anti-war activities and political retaliation were in full swing. Law and order, and political and domestic violence were seen in context with the immediate events as we moved into war, genocide and VietNam.

For our last lecture we invited Science for the People to talk about their organization and what it tries to accomplish. They discussed the university, the kinds of curriculum that is offered in our society and whose interests scientists serve. As examples of alternative actions we spoke about the Medical Committee on Human Rights, Science for the People, the Free Health clinics and pregnancy and abortion counseling services.

[In the full article, the authors included student feedback from end-of-course evaluations about this socially conscious biology curriculum. They also included a teaching bibliography of readings they used in their course.—eds.]

Document 4.2

The Genetic Engineering Group, "Actions on XYY Research," *Science for the People* 7, no. 1 (January 1975): 4.

During the 1960s, a series of scientific studies performed in the United States and Britain began linking men born "XYY"—having inherited two "Y" male sex chromosomes instead of one—with mental disability, aggressive tendencies, and criminal behavior. The research was one of many instances, Science for the People argued, in which scientists wrongly claimed that "deviant" behavior was genetically determined and clinically identifiable. When psychiatrists at Boston's Lying-in Hospital undertook an XYY genetic screening program of newborn boys, Boston SftP's Genetic Engineering Group immediately mobilized in protest. This 1975 piece, "Actions on XYY Research," described their public fight. There remains no evidence today for a causal relationship between an XYY genotype and antisocial behavior.

The September issue of *Science for the People* carried an article describing a genetic screening project in progress at a Boston Hospital, in which newborn infants are tested for the presence of an extra Y chromosome.

The psychological and behavioral development of those with the extra Y chromosome (1 in 1000) is followed by a group of psychiatrists, to see if the children develop "antisocial" behavior. The study came to the attention of the Genetic Engineering Group (GEG) of Science for the People. We were opposed to this kind of study for numerous reasons:

1. There is little or no evidence for a causal relationship between the XYY chromosome constitution and so-called antisocial behavior.

2. The intervention of the investigators is more likely to damage than to aid those in the project (the great majority of XYY males are normal individuals), because the investigator's intervention is liable to be a self-fulfilling prophecy.

3. Many parents of these children are drawn into the study by subtle deceit, not by truly informed consent.

4. Such studies represent one facet of a larger movement to attribute social unrest to intrinsic genetic factors, rather than to oppression and unjust social conditions.

In addition to bringing such studies to public view, the GEG decided to also proceed through hospital channels. Critiques were prepared and presented to the Harvard Medical School, with the request that the continuation of the study be reviewed. This led to a hearing on October 4 before a special committee on inquiry of the Medical School.

Though most of us are scientists, none of us are professionals in the precise area of the research. Thus our actions were surprising and upsetting to the Medical School Faculty, who are steeped in their own elite professionalism. In particular, the Faculty Professionals tend to view any criticism of their action as a threat to "academic freedoms" even if these actions involve harming human subjects.

We presented our critique, and also offered witnesses, such as an admitting aide at the hospital. The other side presented their defense, much of which served in fact to point up the questionable propriety of such research. Up to a point, our criticism was effective. Most members of the committee recognized that truly informed consent was not being obtained. However, our criticism struck more deeply in questioning the propriety for much clinical investigation. The committee was clearly worried that if one study was stopped, the same could happen to other investigations with human subjects. The power of research precedent was also raised in the opposite context; the researchers implied that the existing screening programs (e.g. for the metabolic defect phenylketonuria—PKU) justified their chromosomal screening studies. This made the importance of preventing even this small study clearer to us, since it will obviously be used to justify larger intrusions into the lives of people. Among the revelations that emerged during the proceedings was the fact that the research is supported by the Crime and Delinquency Division of the National Institute of Mental Health.

Aspects of our case against the study have been reported in the *New York Times* (November 15, 1974), the *Boston Globe* (November 16, 1974), and on local Boston television. Media coverage is one way of informing the public of research programs which endanger their subjects and benefit no one (except perhaps the investigators in their career pursuits).

At the time of this writing the committee is deliberating the issue and is scheduled to report out their findings about Christmas time. If the committee decides to permit the study to continue, the GEG will continue the fight and try more energetically to bring the issue to public attention via newspaper coverage, magazine articles, etc. We have recently published a more extensive analysis in *New Scientist,* Nov. 14, 1974.

—The Genetic Engineering Group

Document 4.3

Elizabeth Allen et al., "Against 'Sociobiology,'" *New York Review of Books,* November 13, 1975, http://www.nybooks.com/articles/archives/1975/nov/13/ against-sociobiology/, accessed November 1, 2014.

One of Science for the People's most extensive campaigns was its fight against Harvard University biologist E. O. Wilson's *Sociobiology: The New Synthesis,* which laid out the theory that social behaviors are shaped and inherited over generations through the force of natural selection. SftP biologists were especially concerned about Wilson's extrapolation that violent human behaviors could be hardwired in human genetics. The theory, SftP members argued, "allow[ed] Wilson to confirm selectively certain contemporary behavior as adaptive and 'natural' and thereby justify the present social order." In this oft-cited *New York Review of Books* piece, several SftP members and affiliates, including Barbara and Jonathan Beckwith, Steven Chorover, David Culver, Stephen Jay Gould, Ruth Hubbard, Richard Lewontin, and Herb Schreier, critiqued elements of Wilson's theory that provided genetic justifications for the status quo and the inequities that remained entrenched within it.

In response to:
Mindless Societies from the August 7, 1975 issue
    The following letter was prepared by a group of university faculty and scientists, high school teachers, doctors, and students who work in the Boston area.

To the Editors:

    Beginning with Darwin's theories of natural selection 125 years ago, new biological and genetic information has played a significant role in the development of social and political policy. From Herbert Spencer, who coined the phrase "survival of the fittest," to Konrad Lorenz, Robert Ardrey, and now E. O. Wilson, we have seen proclaimed the primacy of natural selection in determining most important characteristics of human behavior. These theories have resulted in a deterministic view of human societies and human action. Another form of this "biological determinism" appears in the claim that genetic theory and data can explain the origin of certain social problems, e.g., the suggestion by eugenicists such as Davenport in the early twentieth century that a host of examples of "deviant" behavior—criminality, alcoholism, etc.— are genetically based; or the more recent claims for a genetic basis of racial differences in intelligence by Arthur Jensen, William Shockley and others.

Each time these ideas have resurfaced the claim has been made that they were based on new scientific information. Yet each time, even though strong scientific arguments have been presented to show the absurdity of these theories, they have not died. The reason for the survival of these recurrent determinist theories is that they consistently tend to provide a genetic justification of the status quo and of existing privileges for certain groups according to class, race or sex. Historically, powerful countries or ruling groups within them have drawn support for the maintenance or extension of their power from these products of the scientific community. For example, John D. Rockefeller, Sr. said, "The growth of a large business is merely a survival of the fittest. . . . It is merely the working out of a law of nature and a law of God." These theories provided an important basis for the enactment of sterilization laws and restrictive immigration laws by the United States between 1910 and 1930 and also for the eugenics policies which led to the establishment of gas chambers in Nazi Germany.

The latest attempt to reinvigorate these tired theories comes with the alleged creation of a new discipline, sociobiology. This past summer we have been treated to a wave of publicity and laudatory reviews of E. O. Wilson's book, *Sociobiology: The New Synthesis,* including that of C. H. Waddington [*NYR,* August 7]. The praise included a front page *New York Times* article which contained the following statement:

Sociobiology carries with it the revolutionary implication that much of man's behavior toward his fellows . . . may be as much a product of evolution as is the structure of the hand or the size of the brain. (*New York Times,* May 28)

Such publicity lends credence to the assertion that "we are on the verge of breakthroughs in the effort to understand our place in the scheme of things" (*New York Times Book Review,* June 27). Like others before him, Wilson's "breakthrough" is an attempt to introduce rigor and scope into the scientific study of society. However, Wilson dissociates himself from earlier biological determinists by accusing them of employing an "advocacy method" (deliberately selecting facts to support preconceived notions) generating unfalsifiable hypotheses. He purports to take a more solidly scientific approach using a wealth of new information. We think that this information has little relevance to human behavior, and the supposedly objective, scientific approach in reality conceals political assumptions. Thus, we are presented with yet another defense of the status quo as an inevitable consequence of "human nature."

In his attempt to graft speculation about human behavior onto a biological core, Wilson uses a number of strategies and sleights of hand which dispel any claim for logical or factual continuity. Of the twenty-seven chapters of *Sociobiology,* the middle twenty-five deal largely with animals, especially insects, while only the first and last chapters focus on humans. Thus, Wilson places 500 pages of double column biology between his first chapter on "The Morality of the Gene" and the last chapter, "From Sociobiology to Sociology." But Wilson's claim for objectivity rests entirely upon the extent to which his last chapter follows logically and inevitably from the fact and theory that come before. Many readers of *Sociobiology,* we fear, will be persuaded that this is the case. However, Wilson's claim to continuity fails for the following reasons:

1. Wilson sees "behavior and social structure as 'organs,'—extensions of the genes that exist because of their superior adaptive value." In speaking of indoctrinability, for example, he asserts that "humans are absurdly easy to indoctrinate" and therefore "conformer genes" must exist. Likewise, Wilson speaks of the "genes favoring spite" and asserts that spite occurs because humans are intelligent and can fathom its selective advantages. Similar arguments apply to "homosexuality genes" and genes for "creativity, entrepreneurship, drive and mental stamina." But there is no evidence for the existence of such genes. Thus, for Wilson, what exists is adaptive, what is adaptive is good, therefore what exists is good. However, when Wilson is forced to deal with phenomena such as social unrest, his explanatory framework becomes amazingly elastic. Such behavior is capriciously dismissed with the explanation that it is maladaptive, and therefore has simply failed to evolve. Hence, social unrest may be due to the obsolescence of our moral codes, for as Wilson sees it we still operate with a "formalized code" as simple as that of "members of hunter-gatherer societies." Xenophobia represents a corresponding failure to keep pace with social evolution, our "intergroup responses . . . still crude and primitive."

      This approach allows Wilson to confirm selectively certain contemporary behavior as adaptive and "natural" and thereby justify the present social order. The only basis for Wilson's definition of adaptive and mal-adaptive, however, is his own preferences. While he rejects the "advocacy approach" and claims scientific objectivity, Wilson reinforces his own speculations about a "human nature," i.e., that a great variety of human behavior is genetically determined, a position which does not follow from his evidence.

2. Another of Wilson's strategies involves a leap of faith from what might be to "what is." For example, as Wilson attempts to shift his arguments smoothly from the nonhuman to human behavior, he encounters a factor which differentiates the two: cultural transmission. Of course, Wilson is not unaware of the problem. He presents (p. 550) Dobzhansky's "extreme orthodox view of environmentalism": Culture is not inherited through genes; it is acquired by learning from other human beings. . . . In a sense human genes have surrendered their primacy in human evolution to an entirely new nonbiological or superorganic agent, culture.

But he ends the paragraph saying "the very opposite could be true." And suddenly, in the next sentence, the opposite does become true as Wilson calls for "the necessity of anthropological genetics." In other words, we must study the process by which culture is inherited through genes. Thus, it is Wilson's own preference for genetic explanations which is used to persuade the reader to make this jump.

3. Does Wilson's analysis of studies in nonhuman behavior provide him with a basis for understanding human behavior? An appeal to the "continuity of nature" based on evolutionary theory will not suffice. While evolutionary analysis provides a model for interpreting animal behavior, it does not establish any logical connection between behavior patterns in animal and human societies. But Wilson requires such a connection in order to use the vast amounts of animal evidence he has collected. One subtle way in which Wilson attempts to link animals and humans is to use metaphors from human societies to describe characteristics of animal societies.

For instance, in insect populations, Wilson applies the traditional metaphors of "slavery" and "caste," "specialists" and "generalists" in order to establish a descriptive framework. Thus, he promotes the analogy between human and animal societies and leads one to believe that behavior patterns in the two have the same basis. Also, institutions such as slavery are made to seem natural in human societies because of their "universal" existence in the biological kingdom. But metaphor and presumed analogy cannot be allowed to mask the absence of evidence. . . .

What we are left with then is a particular theory about human nature, which has no scientific support, and which upholds the concept of a world with social arrangements remarkably similar to the world which E. O. Wilson inhabits. We are not denying that there are genetic components to human behavior. But we suspect that human biological universals are to be discovered more in the generalities of eating, excreting and sleeping than in such specific and highly variable habits as warfare, sexual exploitation of women and the use of money as a medium of exchange. What Wilson's book illustrates to us is the enormous difficulty in separating out not only the effects of environment (e.g., cultural transmission) but also the personal and social class prejudice of the researcher. Wilson joins the long parade of biological determinists whose work has served to buttress the institutions of their society by exonerating them from responsibility for social problems.

From what we have seen of the social and political impact of such theories in the past, we feel strongly that we should speak out against them. We must take "Sociobiology" seriously, then, not because we feel that it provides a scientific basis for its discussion of human behavior, but because it appears to signal a new wave of biological determinist theories.

> Elizabeth Allen, premedical student, Brandeis University; Barbara Beckwith, teacher, Watertown Public High School; Jon Beckwith, professor, Harvard Medical School; Steven Chorover, professor of psychology, MIT; David Culver, visiting professor of biology, Harvard School of Public Health, professor of biology, Northwestern; Margaret Duncan, research assistant, Harvard Medical School; Steven [sic—eds.] Gould, professor in the Museum of Comparative Zoology at Harvard University; Ruth Hubbard, professor of biology, Harvard University; Hiroshi Inouye, resident fellow, Harvard Medical School; Anthony Leeds, professor of anthropology, Boston University; Richard Lewontin, professor of biology, Harvard University; Chuck Madansky, graduate student in microbiology, Harvard Medical School; Larry Miller, student, Harvard Medical School; Reed Pyeritz, doctor, Peter Bent Brigham Hospital, Boston; Miriam Rosenthal, research associate, Harvard School of Public Health; Herb Schreier, psychiatrist, Massachusetts General Hospital. (Affiliations for identification only.)

Editors' Note: We regret that C. H. Waddington, who would have been asked to reply to this letter, died on September 26.

Document 4.4

Bob Park and Scott Thacher, "Dealing with Experts: The Recombinant DNA Debate," *Science for the People* 9, no. 5 (September–October 1977): 28–35.

This selection outlined the history of the recombinant DNA debate as it flared in research centers around the country during the 1970s. Bob Park and Scott Thacher described the reasoning voiced by both the technology's supporters and its opponents, with special focus on the Boston Science for the People chapter's Genetic Engineering Group, a key faction of anti-recombinant DNA biologists. The group, which included Richard Lewontin, Ruth Hubbard, Jonathan King, and Jonathan Beckwith, fought fiercely against the construction of a high-containment lab for recombinant DNA work at Harvard University. Some members testified publicly against their academic colleagues in a series of hearings before the Cambridge mayor and City Council in the summer of 1976. Heeding their testimony, the city council placed a moratorium on recombinant DNA research in Cambridge for almost seven months. Only after a committee of nine lay citizens (one of whom was SftP member Sheldon Krimsky) analyzed the research hazards did Cambridge allow recombinant DNA work to resume with new restrictions. The partnership between SftP's biologists and the lay committee, Park and Thacher argued, was a striking experiment in charging non-experts with evaluating and regulating scientific risk.

Open Debate on Usually Closed Issues

Debate on recombinant DNA research, both in and out of science, reveals that a Pandora's box has been pried open; social control of science is a live issue. Specific questions arise in three areas—the ostensible benefits, probable uses, and unintentional hazards. But we can go further and ask what underlies the disagreement among experts themselves and then ask how government policy in science could become the province of the people?

One benefit promised from recombinant DNA technology is a breakthrough in world food production using new, specially engineered species of plants, which it is claimed would significantly reduce world hunger. This invites examination of the past effects of the Green Revolution—increased yields from selected hybrid varieties of rice, corn, and wheat. The results have not been to feed the hungry.[1] Predictions of new drug sources and super therapies for intractable disease demand looking at the economic and social origins of most disease and health problems, questioning medical research priorities in general, and exposing what the high technology, "technical fix" approach to health care means.

While conceivably new therapies will be able to correct some of the noncontroversial genetic defects known, there are many other conditions—virtually any characteristic with a claimed genetic predisposition—where the "correction" would amount to a form of genetic repression of individuals by society. Who decides when human variability becomes a genetic "defect"?[2] We need to spell out the implications—present and future—of emphasizing genetic fixes over giving society the treatment: they include declining social services, increasing channeling of individuals (IQ in education, occupational hazard vulnerability in employment), and ultimately suppression of deviance, dissent, unrest, and other "maladaptive" behavior. . . .

The Cambridge Experimentation Review Board

Just as final NIH Guidelines were about to be issued in June, 1976, Harvard University's plans to build a P3* facility came to light. Aware of Harvard's intentions, an interested City Councillor, Barbara Ackermann, attended a low-key "public" meeting called by Harvard's Committee on Research Policy to discuss the P3 plans. Simultaneously, the facility was announced in the lead article of a local alternative newspaper and immediately hazardous research in Cambridge became a burning issue, fanned by some local politicians running hard to catch up. They included Mayor Al Vellucci who gained national attention for his efforts.** Thus recombinant DNA research became the focus of lengthy City Council meetings at which numerous opposing presentations were given and to which hundreds of people came, not all of them academically affiliated. An unprecedented 6-month moratorium on P3 and P4 recombinant research resulted, an act heard 'round the world, and equally startling, a citizens' review committee made up of non-experts was created to advise on the research hazard.

The experience of the Cambridge Experimentation Review Board (CERB) warrants close inspection as an example of public participation in making science policy. CERB, at the City Council's direction, was selected by the City Manager and consisted of people with neither personal interest in recombinant DNA research nor related professional interests, as with research scientists. Board members—all Cambridge residents, with an equal number of men and women—included a nurse, a social worker, two physicians, a businessman, a saleswoman, a university faculty member, a homemaker and an engineer. Taking its narrow assignment of dealing only with the immediate public health-safety issues, CERB met in both open and closed sessions biweekly for over 4 months and heard 75 hours of testimony ranging from NIH dignitaries and renowned advocates of the research to lab technicians and members of Science for the People. The board's final position allowed the research to proceed but with significantly stricter requirements than NIH. These included strengthening institutional biohazards committees, monitoring escape of vectors,[†] conducting local epidemiological studies, and setting up a city-wide biohazards committee. In addition, CERB recommended that the federal government extend the NIH Guidelines to cover industry, maintain a registry of workers in recombinant DNA labs, and fund health monitoring. CERB rejected assurances from Harvard and NIH scientists that the voluntary NIH Guidelines were a more-than-adequate protection against exceedingly improbable or inconceivable events. The CERB deliberations led to a city ordinance incorporating their recommendations and were in part responsible for the near-passing of another law banning P3 and P4 research indefinitely (defeated 6:5). CERB's most important contribution was to show that non-experts could judge experts and make creditable public policy judgments. . . .

There were deficiencies in the CERB conclusions, but first let's examine how CERB was able to do what it did. CERB avoided becoming beholden to Harvard, MIT, or the science establishment in part because of the selection process that formed the board, but also because the development of an authority structure or hierarchy was minimized. For example, the original chairperson, who was also Acting Commissioner of Health and Hospitals in Cambridge, removed himself as a voting member on grounds of possible conflict of interest. In addition, all members were encouraged to take part in defining unresolved issues.[5] Finally, at least some members of the committee had a clear perception of political power and the people's interests, as well as an active commitment to working for those interests. . . .

The shortcomings of the CERB report reflect conditions which no citizens' committee could have easily overcome. It is unlikely that any representative committee (feeling the immense weight of world attention on its actions) could have strayed very far from the middle of the road in the absence of a visible migration of popular opinion on the issues. While there is considerable consciousness of the hazards possible in recombinant DNA research, very little organization or examination of the issues in political terms has developed on a mass scale. . . .

There are therefore two main lessons from CERB: 1) With some essential but rarely achievable prerequisites, a citizens' committee can acquire substantial critical expertise free of direct control by nearby institutions and can to some extent reject dominant and respected views. 2) Without a developed progressive movement concretely involved in similar or related issues locally, there are severe limitations to what even a well-selected citizen committee can do in forging an advanced position. This of course confirms the basic strategy of relying on "mass work"—going to, and being part of, the general populace rather than concentrating on influencing law makers, policy-level scientists, or other persons in high places. . . .

Conclusion

Whether or not strong, meaningful laws are passed, requiring the slow, careful development of recombinant DNA technology—and whether they are enforced—depends on the critical consciousness of the people. The task of progressive science workers is to facilitate this process. Furthermore this objective makes sense only if it is broadened to include all interrelated areas, e.g., medical research priorities, occupational and environmental health, and genetic engineering uses. So too, the value of citizens' committees depends on informed popular opinion and agitation. Conceivably, legitimate citizens' committees could be arranged by coalitions of organizations in communities, independent of government, to help clarify technical disputes.

Evaluating experts is a political process. However, there is obviously no guarantee that politically progressive and responsible experts will necessarily have more reliable technical opinions and interpretations of fact. Ideally then, experts should be experienced in collectively defining positions and principles—participating with other, non-expert, working people. In this way the technical discipline and political sensitivities of experts will grow in good directions, along with everyone else's. Organizations are therefore needed in which both experts and non-experts can collaborate in non-elitist and anti-sexist practice toward progressive goals.

When working people begin to routinely and systematically evaluate the credibility of experts, the face of technology will change: governments and business will be less free to design our future against our interest.

Bob Park and Scott Thacher are members of the Recombinant DNA Group of the Boston chapter of SftP. Bob has worked in clinical trials research in the drug industry and is planning to attend public health school. Scott is a graduate student in biophysics at Harvard, studying membrane biology.

References

1. H. M. Cleaver, "The Contradictions of the Green Revolution," *Monthly Review*, June 1972; Nicholas Wade, "Green Revolution (1): A Just Technology, Often Unjust in Use," *Science,* 186, 1093, 1974.
2. Jon Beckwith, "Recombinant DNA: Does the Fault Lie Within Our Genes?," *Science for the People,* May–June 1977, p. 14.
* P3: the second highest level of laboratory "containment," ranging P1–P4, for keeping experimental organisms isolated and preventing their escape into the real world, from which they could never be recalled.
** The response of the politicians reflects more than just awareness within their constituencies of recombinant DNA issues. Cambridge has long been dominated by the imperial giants of Harvard and MIT, usually with cooperation from most city politicians, with effects which have included the removal of most of Cambridge's industrial employment and the constant encroachment on traditional working class neighborhoods by university expansion and housing for students, faculty, and the technological elite. In the 60's and early 70's, extensive industrial properties were bought up by the MIT-government-aerospace team to be transformed into an electronics, computers and weapons research center. (Technology Square, for example, is a former site of numerous manufacturing plants.) The details of this process are contained in *Harvard, Urban Imperialist,* 1969, published by the Anti-expansion, Anti-ROTC committee at Harvard. The rent control law, finally passed in the late 60's with little help from most politicians, was a significant victory reflecting the widespread anger of the people against institutions like Harvard and MIT. The recombinant DNA issue was for the people of Cambridge but another example of imperial decision-making, and many politicians could not afford to let it pass.
† Vectors: organisms containing, in this case, hybrid DNA.
5. "The Cambridge Experimentation Review Board," (report of), *Bulletin of the Atomic Scientists,* May 1977, p. 22.

Document 4.5

John Valentine, "The Politics of Cancer Research," *Science for the People* **12, no. 3 (May–June 1980): 22–28.**

The foreword of Science for the People's 1980 "Cancer" issue lauded John Valentine for "lay[ing] bare a complex web in which government, public, and private institutions interlock to insure [*sic*—eds.] that only profitable 'cures' for cancer are likely to be discovered." Valentine, a medical researcher at Wayne State University in Detroit, recent graduate of the cell and molecular biology program at the University of Michigan, and SftP's Midwest coordinator, examined how research in cancer therapeutics had become a burgeoning biomedical industry while work in cancer prevention, especially with regard to occupational health, languished. His article highlighted lopsided allocation of government funds for cancer research as well as socioeconomic disparities in cancer incidence and prognosis.

> *The doctors said as they took their fees / There is no cure for this disease*
> —*Traditional folk song*

Detroit's new Radiation Oncology Center is a $5 million project within the new Detroit Medical Center, a single massive institution designed to cover most of that region's health needs. The center will have its own $4 million neutron therapy center for treating cancer, complete with a miniature cyclotron. Such a strategy is reminiscent of curing war with hydrogen bombs. The alternative to dealing with cancer after it has begun is the series of regular warnings from the government to avoid certain cancer-causing chemicals that are around everyone. Only sporadically are some of those chemicals removed from the industrial or retail market. This reinforces the popular emphasis on preventing cancer by controlling diet and "lifestyle."

The possible courses of action to deal with cancer often conflict. We can exert government control over diet and environment, but these regulations are met with protests about lost jobs, compromised freedom, or impossible enforcement—or with risk assessments stating that the problems are balanced by the benefit to society. Throughout this debate, the results of a huge amount of research seem to have very little certitude. It is almost never heard that "X causes cancer of the Y. So that's that. Take it off the market." We almost never hear, either, that "a simple cure is around the corner so don't worry."

Why is the question of cancer causation answered by little more than subterfuge and trends? Why is the research so uncertain? Why does prevention seem to be completely a matter of individual choice yet often impossible in spite of individual acts of will? For example, how is it that only recently has asbestos been publicly linked to lung cancer, when the association between asbestos and cancer was so obvious medically by 1918 that insurance companies stopped selling policies to asbestos workers in the U.S. and Canada?[1]

Cancer research in this country has become a bureaucracy and an industry, and certain avenues of research languish because of this. Cancer prevention and its research are not in the interests of the medical establishment, and cause contradictions in our economic system. This article will examine the broad issue of cancer research: it includes analogies to past improvements in public health, a description of research fund distribution, some political analysis, and some discussion of action.

Theories about Cancer

Two theories describe the origin of cancer (carcinogenesis). A viral theory argues that an infectious agent or native ubiquitous viruses trigger cell growth abnormalities. An environmental theory says that cancer is the result of chemical or other alteration (mutation) of the genetic material, DNA. Functioning as a physiological regulator, DNA is constantly active. If several regulatory genes are mutated and no longer contain the information they once did, loss of control over cell growth can occur, says the environmental theory. These are not mutually exclusive theories; variations often include parts of both. It is important to note that though the two theories may be only different approaches to the same process of carcinogenesis, they imply very different courses of action, and research is clearly split between the different approaches.

The Viral Emphasis

The viral theory allows us to view cancer as a communicable disease that attacks the population indiscriminately. It is popular with the medical research establishment. The study of a viral mechanism is amenable to investigation by existing techniques in molecular biology and implies the possibility of a universal vaccine to prevent cancer. However, viruses seem to be implicated in only a few cancers, and even then external environmental triggers seem to have a role in viral carcinogenesis. Also, the cancers (i.e., presumptive viruses) spread in a familial pattern rather than across populations, unlike common infectious diseases. . . .

The Environmental Emphasis

The environmental theory or emphasis on cancer engenders public health solutions to cancer. The analogy of cancer prevention to previous reductions of health problems illuminates contradictions in cancer research.

It has been estimated that most of our improved health in the last century is due to improved sanitation and nutrition—public health measures. According to one study, 69 percent of decreased mortality over this period is due to reduction of eleven infectious diseases.[3] Diseases treated with specific medical measures (such as polio) account for 3 percent of the reduction in mortality. About 97 percent of the reduction is attributed to "standard of living" improvements. The exponential rise in medical costs and treatment began only after 90 percent of the decline in mortality had occurred.

A more specific parallel between cancer and past health improvements is that with antibiotics. The size, shape, cost and limited accessibility of cancer treatment ("cure") can already be seen by analogy to the administration of antibiotics. The future of cancer treatment would seem to be refinement of techniques, development of drugs and therapeutic compounds, and increasing dependence on a particular industrialized technology, if the chemotherapeutic-surgical approach to treatment and research is further pursued. There is no question that antibiotics are an invaluable tool, but their use is misunderstood. It is unlikely that cancer would be cured in a single simple step by a new "miracle cure," just as treatment is almost never simple with antibiotics, the old "miracle cure." . . .

It should also be added that an understanding of primary causation (who gets cancer and where) rather than mechanisms of action of environmental agents, has historical precedent. Social study of disease preceded biochemical understanding. For example, good nutrition has an accepted role in good health, even though the functions of many necessary nutrients are still unclear.

Historical precedent and technical arguments make a strong case for a focus by research institutions on environmental studies and the ecology of carcinogens and people, rather than on the viral and molecular process of carcinogenesis. Why has this not occurred? Is it a matter of inertia? A conflict of interests? Economic stakes? A reflection of a particular social and economic system? . . .

Political Conflict

Clearly, at all levels of funding and control by federal and private institutions, there is an aversion to studies of environmental causes of cancer. When such studies are done, little action is taken. It would be difficult to defend this inaction by saying "the data aren't all in," because we balk about even collecting data about our environment. It is easy to say that doctors occupy positions throughout these institutions, so they decide matters in a self-interested way. It is more insightful to look deeper into the social and economic fabric of the system that supports our medical system and its cancer research. . . .

The affluent class in this society benefits most from a treatment oriented attack on cancer, since cancer rates are highest among the poorer groups such as workers and Blacks. To treat rather than prevent cancers would make most sense to the lowest incidence group. Treatment would make the most sense to those who could count on the best treatment. Thus, there is a contradiction between ignoring our present political and economic system and endeavoring to prevent cancer.

Research and Action

Much emphasis has been placed on dietary and lifestyle changes as the most important preventative measures against cancer and ill health. "There is a growing realization that lifestyle plays an important role in the ecology of disease. If there is a health crisis in America today, it is largely a crisis of lifestyle in which destructive habits such as alcohol use, drug addiction, lack of exercise, malnutrition, overeating, cigarette smoking, careless driving, and sexual promiscuity create health problems."[23] Put more bluntly, "cancer occurs because of something we do—we eat certain foods, we drink, we smoke, we choose a certain way to live."[24] In this admonition, the victim is blamed for cancer resulting from her or his "lifestyle." (Imagine telling the tubercular child laborers in Chicago, in Upton Sinclair's "The Jungle," that their problem was diet and then giving them six points of "wise nutrition"!) . . .

There are truths about dietary prevention of cancer that are derived from research efforts. Rather than ignore them, it is useful to consider the nature of our food sources. Most of the food bought by the American public in supermarkets is a chemical-industrial product—refined, processed, transported, and marketed so as to yield higher profits. This attitude toward food (and toward our environment and much of the hardware that surrounds us) allows "lifestyle" to be lumped more easily under the broader category of industrialchemical environmental "insults," which must be more extensively included in our research programs if cancer is to be effectively battled. In other words, our food and objects around us should be considered just more environmental chemicals.

Testing for Carcinogens

There is a great deal of confusion surrounding the testing of chemicals (occupational insults, food, petrochemicals, etc.) for carcinogenicity. Part of the problem has already been discussed; only 1 percent of the NCI budget goes into testing, and the documentation registry program is neglected. Much of the controversy and ambiguity could be eliminated by testing and epidemiological follow-up.

There are some 70,000 chemicals currently in industrial use and about 700 new ones are added each year, it is widely acknowledged. Even if only a few of these are carcinogenic, a serious health hazard is present. Thus far, assays have correlated well with epidemiological studies to the extent that all of the chemicals showing carcinogenicity in animal tests show some correlation with human epidemiological studies when such human data are available.[26]

In addition to testing, it might be decided that certain chemicals are not needed after their cost to society is considered. . . . For those chemicals deemed necessary, testing should be easy. Testing would be exhaustive if even 1 percent of the $100 billion cost of cancer to society[28] were not externalized (excluded) from corporate profit calculations. The cost of testing each of the 700 new chemicals each year is $200,000. The total, $140 million, is .4 percent of the gross profits of the chemical industry in 1976.[29] The costs are trivial. If the expected rise of cancer incidence in the early 1980s occurs, "trivial" will barely describe the cost ratio between testing carcinogens and the cost to society of cancer. . . .

[R]ather than the data not all being in yet, we are not researching the fundamental ecology between people and the chemical environment. When we do act, great impediments arise from non-scientific and economic forces such as business interests, the medical industrial lobby, and the ideology of a non-representative capitalist ruling class. The major solution to cancer—social planning—has little to do with present cancer research.

The entire social environment should be considered so that the very need for the existence of certain industries and chemicals could be an overall consideration in cancer research.[33] It might be shown empirically that good health is inconsistent with a system that allows private companies to externalize from their responsibilities the effects of their processes and products on society. "A framework for clinical investigation that links disease directly to the structure of capitalism is likely to face indifference or active discouragement from the state," so an approach to researching cancer goes far beyond simple debate of technical points within the medical-academic arena.[34] The research must be politicized at the laboratory and institutional levels and must include social and economic considerations. To politicize cancer research will surely challenge the institutions and ideology of capitalist health care practice.

References

1. Armelagos, G., and Katz, P., "Technology, Health, and Disease in America," in *Ecologist,* 7(7), p. 35, 1978.
3. McKinley, S., and McKinley, J., "The Questionable Effects of Medical Measures on the Decline of Mortality in the United States in the 20th Century," monograph, 1978.
23. Armelagos, p. 33.
24. Gonzales, N., "Preventing," in *Today's Health,* May 1976, p. 30.
26. *National Cancer Program, Hearings Before the Subcommittee on Health and Scientific Research of the Committee on Labor and Human Resources, United States Senate* (U.S. Government Printing Office, 1979), pp. 195–97.
28. *NCP Hearings,* p. 469.
29. Ibid.
33. Conrad, F., "Society May Be Dangerous to Your Health," in *Science for the People* 11(2), pp. 14–19, 1979.
34. Waitzkin, H., "A Marxist View of Medical Care," in *Science for the People* 10(6), pp. 31–42, 1978.

EDITORS' NOTES

1. Frank Mirer, "Occupational Health: Time for Us to Get to Work," *Science for the People,* 4, no. 6 (November 1972): 4–7; *Science for the People* 7, no. 5, "Occupational Health and Safety" (September 1975).

2. *Science for the People* 10, no. 6, "Special Issue on Health Care" (November–December 1978).

3. For more information on the Black Panther Party's free medical clinics and contributions to public health, see Alondra Nelson, *Body and Soul: The Black Panther Party and the Fight against Medical Discrimination* (Minneapolis: University of Minnesota Press, 2011).

4. Science for the People reprinted Health/PAC educational materials in *Science for the People* on multiple occasions, including "The Structure of American Health Care," *Science for the People* 3, no. 2 (March 1976): 17–20; "Free Clinics," *Science for the People* 4, no. 1 (January 1972): 22–26.

5. See Kelly Moore, *Disrupting Science: Social Movements, American Scientists, and the Politics of the Military, 1945–1975* (Princeton, NJ: Princeton University Press, 2008); 160; John Dittmer, *The Good Doctors: The Medical Committee for Human Rights and the Struggle for Social Justice in Health Care* (New York: Bloomsbury Press, 2009); Merlin Chowkwanyun, "The New Left and Public Health: The Health Policy Advisory Center, Community Organizing, and the Big Business of Health, 1967–1975," *American Journal of Public Health* 101, no. 2 (February 2011): 238–49.

6. Rita Arditti, Claire Huga, and Cynthia Kneen, "Birth Control in Amerika," *Science for the People* 2, no. 4 (December 1970): 28–31; Rita Arditti, "Women's Biology in a Man's World," *Science for the People* 5, no. 4 (July 1973): 39–42; Ruth Hubbard, "Human Embryo and Gene Manipulation," *Science for the People* 15, no. 3 (May–June 1983): 24–27; Barbara Beckwith, "Women's Health Book Collective: Women Empowering Women," *Science for the People* 13, no. 5 (September–October 1981): 19–22; *Science for the People* 16, no. 2 "Special Babies Issue" (March–April 1984).

7. John Feltheimer, "The U.S. Ethical Drug Industry," *Science for the People* 4, no. 4 (July 1972): 12–14, 28–32.

8. Joel Swartz, "Cancer: A Social & Political Problem," *Science for the People* 4, no. 4 (July 1972): 26–28; Allen Silverstone, "Priorities in Cancer Research: Occupational and Environmental Carcinogenesis," *Science for the People* 8, no. 3 (May 1976): 19–20; Samuel S. Epstein, "Epidemic! Cancer-Producing Society," *Science for the People* 8, no. 4 (July 1976): 4–11; *Science for the People* 12, no. 3, "Cancer," (May–June 1980).

9. E. O. Wilson, *Sociobiology: The New Synthesis* (Cambridge, MA: Harvard University Press, 1975).

10. For more information on SftP's involvement in the XYY controversy, see Nathaniel Comfort, *The Science of Human Perfection: How Genes Became the Heart of American Medicine* (New Haven: Yale University Press, 2012), 223–25.

11. Jon Beckwith and Jonathan King, "The XYY syndrome: A Dangerous Myth," *New Scientist,* November 14, 1974, 474–76; Jane E. Brody, "Scientists' Group Terms Boston Study of Children with Extra Sex Chromosome Unethical and Harmful," *New York Times,* November 15, 1974, 16.

12. Freda Salzman, "Are Sex Roles Biologically Determined," *Science for the People* 9, no. 4 (July–August 1977): 27–32; *Science for the People* 6, no. 2, "IQ" (March 1974).

13. Anne Fausto-Sterling, *Myths of Gender: Biological Theories about Women and Men* (New York: Basic Books, 1992); Ruth Hubbard, *The Politics of Women's Biology* (New Brunswick, NJ: Rutgers University Press, 1990); Stephen Jay Gould, *The Mismeasure of Man* (New York: W.W. Norton, 1981); Richard Lewontin, Steven Rose, and Leon J. Kamin, *Not in Our Genes: Biology, Ideology, and Human Nature* (New York: Pantheon Books, 1984); Richard Levins and Richard Lewontin, *The Dialectical Biologist* (Cambridge, MA: Harvard University Press, 1985).

14. For a detailed account of the recombinant DNA controversy, see Sheldon Krimsky, *Genetic Alchemy: The Social History of the Recombinant DNA Controversy* (Cambridge, MA: MIT Press, 1984).

15. Stanley Cohen et al., "Construction of Biologically Functional Bacterial Plasmids in Vitro," *Proceedings of the National Academy of Sciences USA* 70, no. 11 (1973): 3240–44.

16. "Gene Implantation: Hazards of Genetic Engineering," *Science for the People* 8, no. 2 (March 1976): 10–12; *Science for the People* 17, no. 3, "Decoding Biotechnology" (May–June 1985).

17. Kathy Yih, "Biotechnology Becomes Big Business," *Science for the People* 12, no. 5 (September–October 1980): 5–7.

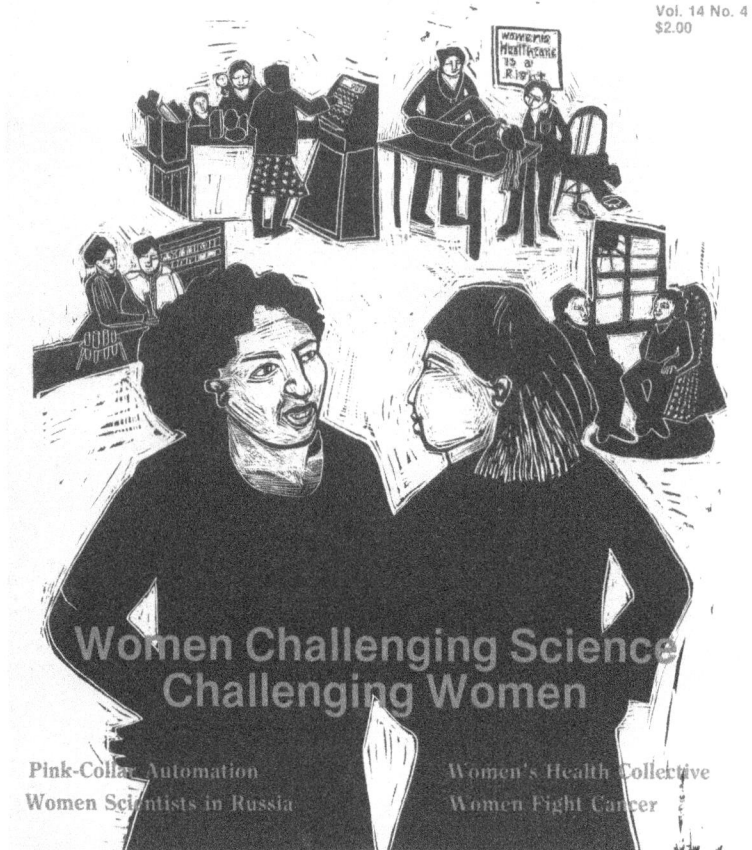

FIGURE 5. Cover of *Science for the People* 14, no. 4 (July–August 1982). The image highlights SftP's fight against sexism in everyday scientific practice and in scientific ideologies. This magazine issue, which was produced by a special editorial collective of seven women SftP members, explored feminist issues in science. Reprinted here with permission from Bonnie Acker.

CHAPTER 5

Race and Gender

Alyssa Botelho

From its early days, Science for the People advocated extensively on behalf of women and people of color, challenging sexist and racist practices in both the laboratory and the clinic. The organization debunked biologically deter-minist theories that reinforced notions of inherent difference between races and genders (also see Chapter 4, "Biology and Medicine"). Members also promoted policies to combat the second-class status of women and people of color in society, including equal pay, gender parity, and affirmative action in the scientific and medical workforce.

SftP's history is infused with the spirit of the 1970s feminist movement, which addressed issues surrounding sexuality, reproductive rights, family structure, domestic violence, and workplace inequality. The organization included several prominent feminist members, such as Rita Arditti, Barbara Beckwith, Ruth Hubbard, Freda Salzman, and Anne Fausto-Sterling. These women—many of whom trained in the sciences—were prolific writers and activists, and their work was integral in the development of feminist science studies.[1] All served for extended periods on *Science for the People* magazine's editorial board, and from as early as its second issue (Document 5.1), the publication reflected their commitment to tackling the challenges women face in pursuing careers in science. However, these feminist members faced intra-organizational hurdles. Though they worked hard to make race and gender fundamental axes of analysis in all realms of SftP's activism, many of these women felt that their male colleagues' lack of engagement prevented the organization from achieving a sustained feminist critique of science in the same way that the group developed anti-capitalist and anti-militaristic critiques. In Kelly Moore's *Disrupting Science,* Rita Arditti remembers that focusing on feminism in SftP "was a constant struggle. . . . To bring a feminist perspective was a risky thing to do . . . and one had to be on the defensive . . . to keep pounding [in] that it was meaningful."[2] Though she never faced overt opposition, Arditti felt that her colleagues might have participated in feminist causes because they felt obligated, not because they genuinely shared her concerns.

Still, this small but active core of women and male allies in SftP wrote about feminist issues and science in powerful and novel ways. They wrote extensively, for example, about gender dynamics in the laboratory and the broader academic community. They also fought for equal pay and gender parity in university admissions and faculty hiring. "The sociology of the laboratory life is structured by class, sex, and race, as is the rest of society," Hubbard wrote in one *Science for the People* magazine issue, stressing that activists had to investigate how labor was negotiated and divided among lab members in order to truly understand how scientific knowledge is made.[3] Some SftP members explored the ways in which the language of biology and medicine was inherently "male," and thus primed to communicate male interests.[4] Others sought to empower women to make their own health decisions and create a medical system that would be able to fully meet women's needs.[5] The group paid special attention to new reproductive technologies such as hormonal birth control, fetal genetic screening, and *in vitro* fertilization.[6] SftP members were wary that such technologies could be used to disproportionately remove the control of pregnancy and childbirth from certain groups of women, particularly working-class women and women of color.

SftP's efforts toward racial equality ran in parallel, and often intertwined, with feminist commitments. Though SftP was a predominantly white organization, several SftP members held ties to the Black Panther Party and were allies to their cause. In an early magazine issue, the group published communications from Black Panthers who urged scientists to develop a "free science" program for black people to further their scientific education and bring their knowledge back to their communities.[7] SftP also focused on uncovering and ameliorating occupational health hazards that black workers and other ethnic minorities faced in the United States and abroad.[8] Finally, the group stood in solidarity with students across the country who were targeted in attacks on affirmative action.[9] In 1976, SftP's Boston chapter wrote a reflection (Document 5.2) on one such highly publicized attack at Harvard Medical School. Some issues of *Science for the People* magazine featured pieces by black physicians, researchers, and advocates.[10]

The publication of biologist E. O. Wilson's *Sociobiology: The New Synthesis* in 1975 galvanized SftP to think deeply about the ways in which biology legitimized social inequality between races and sexes (also see Chapter 4, "Biology and Medicine").[11] Boston SftP members formed the Sociobiology Study Group to challenge Wilson's framework, fearing that evolutionary explanations for social behaviors would reinforce a cultural status quo that worked against historically disenfranchised groups. SftP feminists scrutinized claims of inherent difference between men and women, arguing that such sociobiological theories kept women from advancing in society from a young age.[12] However, many women members felt that the Sociobiology Study Group did not challenge sociobiological explanations of gender difference strongly enough (especially with regard to women's abilities to succeed in science). Feminist members Ruth Hubbard and Freda Salzman eventually left the study group due to this internal conflict.[13] SftP also tied their critique of *Sociobiology*, which sought to identify evolutionary origins for homosexuality, to their support of the gay rights movement. In a valuable 1980 piece (Document 5.3), SftP member Doug Futuyma argued that while a sociobiological explanation for homosexuality might initially sound appealing, the search for such a theory implied that homosexuality was an "individual" problem, and distracted from the larger challenge of addressing oppression of gay people.

Harvard University biologist Richard Lewontin, who contributed to a 1982 special issue "Racism in Science," was especially committed to disproving a scientific basis for the concept of race. In that article (Document 5.4) and other works, he argued that while geographical and physical categorizations of human populations into "races" might have social significance, genetics research shows that such racial groupings are in fact *not* genetically distinct.[14] The stakes were high for Lewontin and other SftP biologists who sought alternative explanations for the stark disparities in women and racial minorities' social experience. As Ruth Hubbard once put it: "Biologists have the authority to tell us what is natural and what is human. They sort nature from culture, and what is more political than that?"[15]

Document 5.1

"Equality for Women in Science," *Science for the People* **2, no. 2 (August 1970): 10–11.**

In this early piece, the *Science for the People* editorial board argued that the scientific community could not increase public understanding of their research and fully promote human welfare "while women in science are relegated to second-class status." The article described the many ways in which women are culturally and economically oppressed, and paid particular attention to the challenges female scientists face in the workplace. The authors then proposed a number of strategies to remedy such discrimination. Among other things, the authors called for the establishment of adequate public school counseling for women interested in entering the science, technology, engineering, and math fields; gender parity among graduate students and departmental faculty; equal pay; and adequate health care and childcare support for female scientists. The article closed by urging the leaders of the American Association for the Advancement of Science to commit to these initiatives and pressure their members to fight for the advancement of women in their workplaces.

The stated goals of the AAAS are:

to further the work of scientists,

to facilitate cooperation among them,

to improve the effectiveness of science in the promotion of human welfare, and

to increase public understanding and appreciation of the importance and promise of the methods of science in human progress.

None of these objectives can be realized while women in science are relegated to second-class status. Female scientists do not escape the oppression faced by all women in our society. They are oppressed economically and culturally-trained for inferior roles and exploited as sex objects and consumers.

Such sexual discrimination is no accident. It serves, in a variety of ways, the interests of those who dominate the economy of this country. It provides them with a source of ideologically justified cheap labor, and as a consequence drives all wages down. It establishes 'wives' as unpaid household workers and child raisers, as well as a body of willing consumers. At the same time, the limitations on the creative development of women deprive society of the full contributions of over one half its members.

It is important to note that sexual oppression is both pervasive and institutionalized; within the scientific community it takes many forms. Educational tracking by sex from elementary school on channels women into subordinate roles and stereotypes. While men are trained to develop 'logical' patterns of thought, women are encouraged to be 'intuitive.' Math and science are seen as male prerogatives. Vocational counseling in high schools and colleges pressures women into family roles, clerical work and, if professions are considered, into the service fields: teaching, social work, nursing, etc. Those few women who manage to transcend such socialization and choose scientific careers, encounter a vicious circle of exploitation. Quotas are placed on graduate school admissions and justified by the self-fulfilling prophecies that most women will be unable to finish because they will marry, have children, and lack the emotional stability and drive to meet the arduous initiation rites of the profession. The still fewer who complete their training continue to find themselves faced with male chauvinist ideology. They are forced to choose between family and profession, while men never make that choice.

As scientists, they are limited by being placed in subordinate positions, rarely being given their own labs or first authorship on papers, and, the most glaring inequity, being paid less than their male colleagues for equal work. They are automatically and illegally barred from certain jobs, particularly in industry[,] and cut off from tenured and supervisory positions.

Moreover, the psychological harassment is constant and debasing. Casual remarks continually define the female scientists simply in relation to her sex, from compliments on her looks to 'you think like a man.' She is placed in the schizophrenic position of being treated as either a dehumanized worker or a feminine toy.

Universities hold a strategic position with regard to all manifestations of this problem, since they help create and transmit the ideology of male supremacy.

Moreover, the practices of sexual discrimination which permeate all institutions where AAAS members work and study are contradictory to the declared goals of the AAAS. Clearly we cannot 'further the work of scientists' while denigrating in so many ways the contributions and potential of women in the profession. Sexual discrimination makes 'cooperation among scientists' an ironic platitude. The 'effectiveness of science in the promotion of human welfare' is hardly furthered by denying half of humanity the opportunity to pursue scientific careers, or by wasting this tremendous reservoir of talent.

We therefore propose the following resolutions be adopted at the general Council meeting of the AAAS, and be fought for by AAAS members where they work.

That universities and other institutions where AAAS members work be immediately required to comply with the law of the land and pay equal wages for equal work to men and women.

That graduate school departments and medical schools admit 1/2 women and 1/2 men, regardless of the proportion of applicants, and that they take whatever steps are necessary to recruit sufficient women to comply with this demand.

That vocational counseling in high schools and colleges be totally reoriented so as not to channel women into low status, low-potential occupations.

That the universities and other institutions give priority to the hiring and promotion of women, increasing the proportion of women to 50% at all levels.

That birth control and abortion counseling be provided by university and company health services to all women.

That the curriculum of courses in psychology, sociology, anthropology, etc. be thoroughly revamped by women, to end the perpetuation and creation of male supremacist myths. Further, that sex inequality be added as a topic to all courses and texts which cover social inequalities, and that new courses be created by women in their history and oppression.

That the universities and government sponsor programs to investigate and change the subordinate status of women in our society.

That it be recognized that the actual practices of hiring, promotion and tenure discriminate against women, and that institutions have not accepted their responsibility for such inequalities.

As a first step in the right direction institutions should provide:

a) parenthood leave and family sick leave for all employees, both female and male;
b) half-time appointments for mothers and fathers who want them must be considered (Since child rearing is a social responsibility, it is preferable for both parents' work to be slowed down than for the mother's to be stopped entirely.);
c) free child care centers should be open to the communities where the institutions are located, controlled by the parents, staffed equally by male and female teachers, open 24 hours a day, 7 days a week for infants to school age children and after school for older children.

While we realize that the ultimate liberation of both women and men in our society will only come with a total social and economic revolution, we feel that it is important for us to make steps now toward destroying false notions of superiority which do not serve science, scientists, or humanity.

Document 5.2

Larry Miller, Herb Schreier, and Jon Beckwith, "Racist Outbreak at Harvard Medical School," *Science for the People* 8, no. 4 (July 1976): 20–35.

In this selection, three members of Science for the People's Genetics Group and Sociobiology Study Group recounted a recent racist incident at Harvard Medical School. In a May 1976 issue of the prestigious *New England Journal of Medicine*, Harvard physician and geneticist Bernard Davis wrote an inflammatory op-ed piece insinuating that the medical school's affirmative action policy was diminishing the academic performance of the student body and endangering future patients. The piece sparked outrage across the country, and Davis's comments were widely condemned. In the aftermath of the scandal, these SftP members expressed their support for Harvard's medical students of color, and pointed out how much more work needed to be done in Boston and across the country to correct the disparity of physicians from historically marginalized ethnic, gender, and socioeconomic groups in the United States.

> *"Professor contends medical schools' standards have dropped because of rise in minority students."*—NY Times, *May 13, 1976*
>
> *"Professor assails Blacks' performance."*—Harvard Crimson, *May 14, 1976*

In the middle of May, as students at Harvard Medical School were preparing for their exams, as many medical schools around the country were completing their admissions decisions, as President Ford spoke of "alternatives to busing," Bernard D. Davis, a Professor at Harvard Medical School, stirred up a storm the impact of which is far from over. On May 13, 1976, Davis published an article on the opinion pages of the *New England Journal of Medicine* which was a thinly veiled attack on minority admissions programs at medical schools. The article was picked up immediately by the *New York Times* and then much of the media; Davis appeared on several Boston TV stations. Davis was quoted in the *Times* as warning against the "temptation to award medical diplomas on a charitable basis" and suggesting that some medical diplomas might be awarded to "a person who might leave a swath of unnecessary deaths behind him." The clear-cut insinuation was that an increase in minority doctors could cost patients' lives.

There have been immediate and tragic effects of this publicity. First, several incidents have occurred in Boston area hospitals in which white patients have refused to be seen by black doctors—a direct result of Davis's statements. Secondly, Medical School admissions offices around the country have since contacted Harvard Medical School to learn of the "failure" of its minority admissions programs. Such programs, which were under attack already (minority admissions to medical schools declined for the first time in 1975) may have been dealt a severe blow. This is not to speak of the contribution of this slander to heating up the racist situation in Boston over the busing issue; nor of the contribution to strengthening attempts to reverse affirmative action programs.[1,2]

What did Davis base his statements on? *There were no data of any sort in his article.* There was a reference to a single student who had been unable to pass his Medical Boards, part I, in five tries, but still received a medical degree. Among the numerous responses . . . to Davis's claims were some strongly worded statements from Robert Ebert, Dean of Harvard Medical School, which totally refuted Davis's innuendos. [The authors then included a letter written by Robert Ebert to the Deans of all medical schools in the United States, denouncing Davis's statement.—eds.]

Davis and Biological Determinism

Since Davis obviously had no evidence to back up his allegations, where did they come from? The views he has put forth in this incident are quite consistent with his writings and talks given in the past few years which reflect a biological determinist perspective. This perspective has led him to publicly support such areas of research as genetics and intelligence studies, genetic engineering,[3] XYY research,[4] and, most recently, sociobiology.[5]

A thread that runs throughout his recent statements is that most members of disadvantaged groups are disadvantaged because they were born that way. Thus, we can only go so far in correcting discrimination, since the basis for discrimination is the inherent lack of ability in certain groups. While he equivocates, the following excerpts from a speech [he] presented at the Cambridge Forum on April 10, 1976, illustrated this perspective:

> . . . [S]cience tells us that we sow confusion, if we will fail to distinguish social equality, which is a normative matter, from biological equality, which is an empirical matter, for we can manipulate our social structure, but we cannot manipulate our genes. *Science also tells us that environmental measures can compensate to some degree for various genetic defects, but only within limits.* Hence social justice must be built around the reality of our genetic diversity.

> . . . *What Davis has assumed here is that those groups which are now under-represented in such high status jobs are less well-endowed overall in the qualities that lead to those jobs.* In other words, those groups which are excluded now are excluded due to lack of the requisite innate abilities. Perhaps a few group members can achieve "high status jobs" but most are simply genetically unable. The crucial step in Davis's argument is simply left out—he never even considers the possibility that the disadvantaged groups may be genetically equal or even superior to the current dominant groups. Further, he simply assumes that the abilities required to attain "high status jobs" are genetic. Both assumptions can only come from Davis's own beliefs about the source of differences between groups, and both are obviously consistent with racist proclamations of genetic inferiority. Thus, even if we accept Davis's premise concerning genetic diversity, his conclusions are groundless.

While he makes no evidence or logical basis, Davis makes these irrational claims under the guise of objective science ("Science tells us . . ."). This misuse of his status as a scientist to promote his own opinions as scientific fact is inexcusable. It is bad enough that he claims a scientific basis for illogical theories which are immediately useful to those promoting racism; but he now has extended this unfounded perspective into the sphere of social policy by his attack on minority programs at Harvard Medical School. . . .

For years, we in Science for the People and others have been exposing the dangers and the fallacies of contemporary biological determinist theories.[8, 9] These theories usually begin with racist, sexist or class-based assumptions, are marked by shoddy or fraudulent research and logic, and serve to provide ideological support for the continued functioning of oppressive social institutions. In fact, the questions upon which most of this research is based are only of interest to those promoting the *status quo. This is not neutral research which is being misused.* David's extension of his own brand of biological determinism into directly harmful public statements and the rapidity with which they are picked up and publicized illustrates the seriousness with which these ideas should be taken and the need to confront them. This case also illustrates how prestigious scientific journals (*Science* and the *New England Journal of Medicine*) are quite open to promoting reactionary social policy in the name *of* science and health care.

Medical Schools and Health Care

The major issue raised in this controversy is equal opportunity for medical education for blacks, Chicanos, Boricuas, Native Americans, and other minorities, and also those from lower socioeconomic classes. These groups form a definite minority of physicians. But the issue of equal opportunity in turn has important implications for health, in terms of the distribution of physicians and influences on a community's health. The maldistribution of physicians and other health care workers by geographical area and income has been widely demonstrated; central urban areas, some rural areas, and many working-class areas have an inadequate supply of physicians, and even then many residents cannot afford high-priced health care. The past several decades have demonstrated that, for both financial and personal reasons, medical students recruited from the white middle and upper classes do not practice in these areas, where physicians are most needed.

While recruiting efforts have *slowly* begun to address the inadequate supply of black and women physicians, the percentage from working-class backgrounds has not changed in 50 years.[10] The result of the selection of white male middle class students to attend medical schools is not only unequal access to health care for a large part of the population, but also that physicians have little experience in their own backgrounds with the health needs of a large part of the population.

This class domination of medicine is certainly a contributing factor to the crisis in medical care that exists in this country. Infant mortality rates, which are twice as high for non-whites as for whites in some areas, reach the levels of some underdeveloped countries.[11] Longevity statistics are the worst in the industrialized world.[12] Five thousand communities are without a single primary care physician, yet more surgeons than needed are produced (which may account for the thousands of needless operations performed each year[13]), while a meager 1.4% of current interns and residents are training in general practice programs.[14] . . .

The establishment of the large university medical center as the new leader of American medicine has been welcomed by some as "perhaps the most profound and promising development in the evolution of medical care."[16] The centers became important forces in advancing the treatment of specific diseases, but they have, in effect, retarded the development of an equitable, effective and efficient system of health care for most people. Competition for prestige and funds, a desire to do "important" work, and a willingness to carry out certain research because there was money available to do so, caused human priorities to suffer. Things have changed little for the majority of Americans. Despite remarkable technological advances, a 1971 Citizens Board of Inquiry into Health Services for Americans reported that:

> The United States has failed to provide adequate health services to the vast majority of its citizens. The system is in disarray. . . . Consumers have few meaningful options in health care today. . . .[17]

Because of the relative autonomy these centers enjoy in determining the selection of future physicians and the direction of medical education, they have contributed to what has been called the "obsolescence of the American physician . . . his inappropriate orientation to disease and to people, the economic (fee for service) and societal (one to one) framework of the physician-patient relationship, the traditional notion of a patient-centered rather than a community-centered responsibility. . . ."[18] Students are chosen mainly by criteria that select for those with scientific research interests and those who will go into specialties. The criteria work against people who, for example, would find satisfaction giving primary care in a small community.[19] . . .

Conclusion

Davis's foray into the public arena with his attack on minority admissions programs raises several issues.

First, this incident shows the direct links between the resurgent "academic" biological determinist theories and racist, sexist, and anti-poor and working-class social policy. While Davis has limited himself mainly to attacks on minority programs, others have used essentially the same arguments against women and lower socioeconomic classes.[23] These arguments are used to support admissions policies which contribute to the continuation of a costly, class-biased, archaic medical system and the consequent neglect of the health needs of most people in our society. In addition, the domination of medicine and medical research by white middle and upper class men further distorts research objectives and practices. For instance, it is male medical researchers who have favored directing contraceptive development towards the female reproductive physiology, thus leaving the burden of contraception on women, and the dangers of contraceptive testing on mainly Third World women.[24]

The education of more minority, women and working class students to be physicians is a highly desirable goal, and some inequities and oppressive features of medicine may be ameliorated. Some of the doctors from these groups may even help to begin the process whereby communities can gain control over their own health care. However, it is unlikely by itself to produce meaningful and lasting change in medical care in this country. As long as medical school admissions and training are oriented towards producing academicians, researchers and high-priced specialists, there will still be only a small proportion of doctors committed to improving community health.

But further, what has to be recognized here is that providing health care is not the same as promoting health. Amidst all the concern about health care providers, it must be recalled that the major influences on a community's health are income, job situation[,] housing, environment, community self-reliance, etc.—factors generally determined outside the community by those who control the sources of capital, such as corporations and landlords.[25] And it is the same group of large corporations who dominate the health care industry. Thus, in both generating and helping to maintain a community's health, control comes from without. Only by organized community involvement in and control of health care and living conditions can true health be achieved.

Larry Miller, Herb Schreier, and Jon Beckwith are all active in both the Genetics Group and the Sociobiology Group of Science for the People. Larry is a medical student at Harvard. Jon teaches in the Microbiology Department at Harvard Medical School and was instrumental in getting the minority student program established there in 1968. Herb is a child psychiatrist at Mass General Hospital and at the East Boston Health Clinic.

References

1. See, for example, editorials in *Science* magazine— Oct. 17, 1975, Dec. 19, 1975, and Feb. 13, 1976.
2. N. Glazer. *Affirmative Discrimination.* Basic Books, 1976.
3. B. D. Davis. Editorial in *Science,* Oct. 25, 1974.
4. B. D. Davis. Editorial in *Science,* Sept. 26, 1975.
5. B. D. Davis. *New England Journal of Medicine.* 293, 1375, 1976.
8. See articles on IQ, XYY and Sociobiology in *IQ: Scientific or Social Controversy.* edited

by Genetics and Social Policy Group of Science for the People. Available from SESPA, 16 Union Square, Somerville, MA 02143 for $1.25.

9. N. Block and G. Dworkin. *The IQ Controversy.* Pantheon paperback, 1976. (An excellent collection of articles.)

10. V. Navarro. *Int. J. Health Services* 5, 74 (1975).

11. H. A. Schreier. *Pharos.* vol. 38 no. 3, July 1975.

12. B. and J. Ehrenreich. *Social Policy* May/June, 1974.

13. *N.Y. Times,* January 27, 1976, p. 1.

14. R. H. Ebert. *Scientific American* 229, no. 3, Sept. 1973. 15. *Report of the Committee on the Costs of Medical Care for American People.* Chicago, Univ. of Chicago, 1932.

16. J. Knowles. *Scient. Amer.* 229, 128, 1973.

17. *Heal Yourself.* Report of the Citizens Board of Inquiry into Health Services for Americans. Washington D.C., 1971.

18. M. Michaelson. *N.Y. Rev.* 32, July 1, 1971.

19. E.L. Kelly. *J. Med. Educ. Supplement,* 32, 185, 1957.

23. R. Herrnstein, "I.Q." *The Atlantic Monthly,* Sept. 1971; E.O. Wilson, *N.Y. Times Sunday Magazine,* Oct. 12, 1975. p. 38.

24. R. Arditti, this issue, and *Science for the People* 6, no. 5, Sept. 1974, p. 8.

25. J. Kosa *et al. Poverty and Health.* Harvard University Press, 1975.

Document 5.3

Doug Futuyma, "Is There a Gay Gene? Does It Matter?," *Science for the People* 12, no. 1 (January–February 1980): 10–15.

In this selection, State University of New York–Stony Brook ecologist Doug Futuyma analyzed E. O. Wilson's recent theorizing about the biological origins of homosexuality. Futuyma, a gay man, applauded Wilson's efforts to push back against the notion that homosexuality is pathological or "unnatural." But Futuyma also warned that a deterministic understanding of homosexuality was scientifically unsatisfying and dangerous in its own right. He highlighted the many ways in which seeking a biological justification for homosexuality could distract, and even hinder, activists from tackling the larger challenges in seeking rights for gay people. Echoing the view of Science for the People more broadly, Futuyma concluded that using evolutionary theory to inform ethics can only lead us astray from efforts to drive social progress.

As most readers of *Science for the People* are aware, speculations about the evolutionary and genetic bases of human behavior have stirred controversy since the publication of E. O. Wilson's *Sociobiology: The New Synthesis* in 1975.[1] In the early stages of the debate, Wilson[2] claimed innocence of any concern with the political and social implications of sociobiological theory: but in *On Human Nature*,[3] he acknowledges these implications by explicit discussion of social issues. Much sociobiological speculation . . . seems ready made for the forces of oppression: apparently little more than Social Darwinism clad in new jargon, it seems to rationalize sexism, xenophobia (including racism), and capitalism, whether its authors intend such rationalizations or not. Indeed, Wilson denies any such intention in *On Human Nature,* and goes further: he clearly is proud to present sociobiological hypotheses that purport to affirm human rights and egalitarianism. . . .

Wilson suggests there is "a strong possibility that homosexuality is normal in a biological sense, that it is a distinctive, beneficent behavior that evolved as an important element of early human social organization. Homosexuals may be the genetic carriers of some of mankind's rare altruistic impulses." Thus "the traditional Judeo-Christian view of homosexual behavior is inadequate and probably wrong," and "it would be tragic to continue to discriminate against homosexuals on the basis of religious dogma supported by the unlikely assumption that they are biologically unnatural."[6]

As a gay person, I can only applaud Wilson's humanitarian concern: I agree that discrimination against gays is tragic. I consider the traditional Judeo-Christian view of homosexuality to be barbaric, and I consider the oppression of gays, in Christian and non-Christian societies alike, an evil that demands moral outrage. However, I find Wilson's argument scientifically unsatisfying and politically dangerous: and precisely because this is one of the rare sociobiological arguments that arrives at an appealing libertarian conclusion, I would like to analyze it with the confidence that I will not be accused of fearing the awful truths that sociobiology threatens to reveal. . . .

The Sociobiological Theory of Homosexuality

By assuming that homosexual behavior is an evolved trait, which therefore must have some genetic basis, Wilson must confront the problem: How could homosexuality evolve if homosexuals, by not reproducing as much as heterosexuals (presumably), tend not to propagate the very genes that predispose them to homosexual behavior? The answer that emerges from sociobiological theory is very simple. Genes predisposing an individual to homosexuality may be carried, even if not expressed, by the relatives of homosexuals (because related individuals, of course, inherit many of the same genes from their common ancestors). Thus if homosexuals, freed from preoccupation with their own children, helped to raise their nieces or nephews, the genes for homosexuality carried by these relatives would survive and be propagated. Such genes could actually be advantageous, in the sense that they would improve the chances for survival of related individuals who carry copies of those same genes. This is one of many applications of the theory of "kin selection," which can explain the evolution of many traits, such as altruistic behavior, that seem socially beneficial, yet detrimental to the individual that displays the trait. In fact, Wilson ventures that homosexuals' solicitude for relatives might be extended into a genetically programmed tendency to be exceptionally altruistic in general.

By this argument from "kin selection," one could predict either that (1) homosexuals and heterosexuals carry different genes, on average, predisposing them to their respective sexual orientations; or (2) heterosexuals and homosexuals might all have the same genotype, but a genotype that specifically programs one to develop into the heterosexual or the homosexual mode depending on which would be the most adaptive—just as a tree may develop thin flexible leaves in the shade, but thick, drought-resistant leaves if it develops in a drier, more exposed site. The first thesis, favored by Wilson,[14] may be called the hypothesis of genetic polymorphism (polymorphism is the existence of two or more genotypes within a population). The second, entertained by Weinrich,[15] may be called the developmental switch hypothesis. It resembles the idea of Kinsey that we develop sexual orientation in response to our early environment except that the developmental switch postulates that homosexuality and heterosexuality are specific, adaptive responses to certain environmental or social conditions.

The Genetic Polymorphism Hypothesis

Are humans genetically polymorphic for sexual orientation? Do gay people have different genes from straights? There is a large early literature that supposed so, some of which is almost laughably naive. For example, T. Lang believed that male homosexuals might really be genetic females (with two X chromosomes rather than an X and a Y) in male bodies, and claimed that the sex ratio among the siblings of German male homosexuals was shifted toward a preponderance of males, as if some of the genetic females in these families had been transformed into apparently male homosexuals.[16] (This study isn't quite as amusing when one reads that Lang obtained his list of homosexuals from secret police lists in the 1930s.)

There is a confused, contradictory literature on whether or not homosexuals differ hormonally from heterosexuals. Whether they do or not, a hormonal difference would not imply a genetic difference in any case, since hormone levels are affected by a multitude of physiological and environmental factors. The *only* acceptable evidence that differences in sexual orientation might be genetically based would have to come from the study of relatives—from evidence of transmission within families. But in humans, relatives (e.g., siblings) share not only genes, but a panoply of common environmental factors: parental attitudes, learning experiences, playmates (including each other), and so forth. That is, children inherit not only their parents' genes, but their attitudes, values, religious beliefs, and so on. To demonstrate a genetic basis for behavior, it is necessary to separate the potential genetic component of this inheritance from the non-genetic component. This is why the studies of separately reared twins and of adopted children have been the only source of data that are even momentarily worth considering in the controversy over the inheritance of IQ.[17] . . . In the case of sexual orientation, no such data exist.

The Developmental Switch Hypothesis

The other possible version of the kin-selection argument is that gay people, rather than having special genes for homosexuality, have the same genes as heterosexuals but genes which specifically program either homosexuality or heterosexuality, depending on which would be adaptive for the individual. For example, Weinrich has suggested that it might be appropriate to become homosexual if one's physical condition precluded the likelihood of becoming a successful parent.[24] This idea is quite similar to the "learning" theory of Kinsey et al., which holds that sexual orientation, like our tendency to become extroverted or introverted, peaceful or belligerent, analytical or fanciful, arises through a long succession of conscious or unconscious responses to innumerable experiences or stimuli. The difference is that the evolutionary notion of an adaptive "developmental switch" is a biological determinist view—we are genetically programmed for specific responses to specific situations—whereas the "learning" theory is as free of determinism as a psychological theory of personality development can be.

The subtle distinction between these theories can be illustrated by a rather absurd analogy. Why do some people speak with New England accents and others with Georgian accents? A "learning" theory would hold that as children we develop our particular speech patterns by responding to a succession of stimuli the sounds we hear and imitate. A "biological determinist" theory might suppose that our environment triggers a physiological change, perhaps in the vocal cords, so that we develop either broad a's or a slow drawl, depending on whether our childhood winters were cold or warm. The one theory emphasizes the action of environmental events on an initially "clean slate"; the other invokes specific genetically controlled alterations in the developing person, that then affect the responses to environmental events. . . .

If Wilson cannot offer a way of telling whether our genotype programs or simply permits various paths of development, his determinist theory is untestable, and so is bad science—or isn't scientific at all, some philosophers would say.[25] The only tests of the theory that Wilson offers are actually very weak. Biological determinists are fond of pointing out similarities between human behavior and that of other mammals as evidence of the evolutionary, hence biological, foundations of human behavior. And Wilson indeed notes that homosexual behavior has been observed in many species, especially of primates. But every evolutionary biologist is aware that the similarities between very different species may not be homologous, with the same genetic foundation, but analogous, like the fish-like form of fishes and porpoises. . . . Wilson's other line of defense is to argue that if homosexuality is genetically programmed because of its kin-selected advantage, we would expect homosexuals to play special, people-oriented, social roles. I'm not quite sure of how he logically arrives at this conclusion, but in any case he cites as evidence cases of homosexual or transvestite men playing the role of shaman or berdache in some pre-industrial cultures, and the supposed tendency of homosexuals to enter upwardly mobile, white collar professions in western industrial societies. The evidence that either of these claims is true is far from compelling (because, for example, homosexuals may simply "come out" more often if they are in these professions); and I fear that by citing this "evidence" Wilson may contribute to the propagation of stereotyped myths about how different gay people are from heterosexuals. But there is strong reason to believe that if gays tend to enter special professions in our society, they do so in response to social pressures that make some professions safer than others. In other words, these roles are imposed, not prompted by a biological imperative. And it is certainly possible that social imposition was as important in pre-industrial cultures as in our own. The evidence that homosexuality is a genetically programmed adaptive developmental pathway is absurdly weak.

Does it Matter?

Wilson's argument that homosexuality is biologically "natural" and the more general argument that it is "genetic" or "inborn" appeals to a great many gay people . . . for at least two reasons: the answer it provides to heterosexual bigots who claim that homosexuality is an "unnatural" "crime against nature"; and the secret satisfaction it gives to inwardly guilty homosexuals that their sexual orientation isn't their fault, for it was programmed into them by a biological imperative which absolves them from responsibility.

Insofar as any deterministic theory of the origin of homosexuality panders to "gay guilt," it is, I feel, psychologically and politically counterproductive. Above all else, gay people need to cultivate self-acceptance, and to cleanse themselves of the notion that they need to blame their orientation on anyone or anything—for this implies that their orientation is a fault.

Indeed, the entire focus on the causes of homosexuality is scientifically questionable and politically repressive. To concentrate on discerning the causes of homosexuality is, first, implicitly to judge it a personal or social problem, and to divert attention from the more pressing, liberating questions: What cure is there for society's homophobic, oppressive attitudes? And how can we help people whose judgment of their own worth has been warped by repressive societal values?

Moreover, the focus on the causes of homosexuality is flawed at its very base. The behavioral traits for which biological bases have been sought are most often the characteristics that are perceived as politically or socially threatening. There hasn't been very much debate over the possible genetic basis of the ability to whistle, or of people's variable appreciation of Beethoven, or, in the realm of sexual orientation, of the degree to which we are sexually and emotionally attracted to people on the basis of their hair color, intellectual depth, or other physical or personal characteristics. Attraction to people on the basis of their sex is singled out for analysis as a special, separate characteristic—it is reified—because it is viewed as a social problem, not because it is scientifically interesting to any unusual degree, or because it is a separable, independent part of the personality. Indeed, the greatest insult to gay people, and the greatest scientific error, may be to divorce "sexual orientation" from the emotional context of feelings and responses that an individual has toward other people—a complex of responses in which the sex of other people enters as only one of many interdependent variables. We do not have simple knee-jerk responses to the single stimulus "male" or "female"—we have complex emotional, affectional, and erotic responses to the multitude of stimuli another individual presents; and it is folly to suppose that the response to the person's sex is genetically or psychologically separable from the rest of us.

Insofar as the sociobiological theory of homosexuality serves as an argument for gay rights and social acceptance, it is unfortunately a flawed and indeed dangerous argument. It is dangerous because it is certainly within the realm of possibility that tomorrow's research could disprove the hypothesis that homosexuality has any biological foundation whatever—and where then lies the argument for gay rights? It is a flawed argument because it accepts and rests on the same profoundly nonsensical assumption that supports heterosexual bigotry: that "what is biologically natural is good; what is not, is bad"—the notion that our morals, ethics, and laws should be shaped to fit our biological urges, as we conceive them to be. To give Wilson credit, he remarks that "it would be . . . illogical, and unfortunate, to make past genetic adaptedness a necessary criterion for current acceptance"; but in the same breath he says that "it would be tragic to discriminate against homosexuals on the basis of religious dogma supported by the unlikely assumption that they are biologically unnatural"—implying, as he does so often in his book, that biology should indeed inform ethics.

. . . Women, racial minorities, and gay people are entitled to freedom from discrimination not because of their biology, but because of our idealistic conception of the dignity of the individual. Whatever our biological evolution has been, our ethics are part of our cultural evolution, in which we have come to strive for humanitarianism and to combat oppression out of respect for human dignity.

Doug Futuyma teaches in the Department of Ecology and Evolution at the State University of New York at Stony Brook and does research on the genetics and ecology of insects. His book *Evolutionary Biology* was published recently by Sinauer Associates (Sunderland, MA). Doug and his mate, Bruce Smith, live in Stony Brook.

References

1. E. O. Wilson, *Sociobiology: The New Synthesis* (Harvard University Press, 1978). For early critiques see, e.g., Sociobiology Study Group, "Sociobiology—Another Biological Determinism," in *BioScience* 26, 1978, pp. 182–86 and Sociobiology Study Group, "Sociobiology—A New Biological Determinism," in Ann Arbor Science for the People (eds.), *Biology as a Social Weapon* (Burgess, 1977), pp. 133–49.
2. E. O. Wilson, "Academic Vigilantism and the Political Significance of Sociobiology," in *BioScience* 26, 1976, pp. 183–90.

3. E. O. Wilson, *On Human Nature* (Harvard University Press, 1978).

6. Wilson, 1978.

14. Wilson, 1978.

15. J. D. Weinrich, *Human Reproductive Strategy: The Importance of Income Unpredicability, and the Evolution of Non-reproduction,* Ph. D. dissertation (Harvard University, 1976); and J. D. Weinrich, quoted in D. Stein, "Why Gays are Smarter than Straights: Homosexuality and Sociobiology," in *Christopher Street* 3:1, 1978, pp. 9–14.

16. T. Lang, "Studies on the Genetic Determination of Homosexuality," in *Journal of Nervous and Mental Disease* 92, 1940, pp. 55–64.

17. R. C. Lewontin, "Genetic Aspects of Intelligence," in *Annual Review of Genetics* 9, 1975, pp. 387–405.

24. Weinrich, 1976 and 1978.

25. K. Popper, *The Logic of Scientific Discovery* (Harper and Row, 1968).

Document 5.4

Richard Lewontin, "Are the Races Different?," *Science for the People* 14, no. 2 (March–April 1982): 10–14.

In *Science for the People* magazine's special issue "Racism in Science," Harvard University evolutionary biologist Richard Lewontin argued that "race" is neither scientifically founded nor a useful descriptive category. Citing a series of recent population genetics studies, Lewontin explained that the majority of genetic variation in the human species exists within a given human "race" rather than between any two "races." Ultimately, Lewontin demonstrated that while some physical traits such as complexion, hair, and facial features vary across ethnic and other geographic groups, "racial" differences end there. Lewontin is professor emeritus at Harvard University. Before his tenure at Harvard, he was a population geneticist at the University of Chicago and a founding member of the Chicago chapter of Science for the People.

Racism claims there are major inherited differences in temperament, mental abilities, energy, and so on between human groups even though no evidence exists for such inherited differences. Racism draws credibility from what seem to be obvious differences in some physical traits like color, hair form, or facial features. "After all," it is argued, "races differ so markedly in such inherited physical traits, so isn't it reasonable that they would differ in mental ones as well?" To understand the real situation we need to look at what is really known about genetic differences between people and to examine the very concept of "race" itself.

Race Is Only Skin Deep

In the nineteenth century and before, "race" was a fuzzy concept that included many kinds of relationships. Sometimes it meant the whole species as "the human race"; sometimes a nation or tribe as "the race of Englishmen"; and sometimes merely a family as "He is the last of his race." All that held these notions together was that members of a "race" were somehow related by ties of kinship and that their shared characteristics were somehow passed from generation to generation.

Beginning in the middle of the nineteenth century, with the popularity of Darwin's theory of evolution, biologists began to use the concept of "race" in a different way. It simply came to mean "kind," an identifiably different form of organism within a species. So there were light-bellied and dark-bellied "races" of mice or banded or unbanded shell "races" of snails. But defining "races" simply as observable kinds produced two curious situations. First, members of different "races" often existed side by side within a population. There might be 25 different "races" of beetles, all members of the same species, living side by side in the same local population. Second, brothers and sisters might be members of two different races, since the characters that differentiated races were sometimes influenced by alternative forms of a single gene. So, a female mouse of the light-bellied "races" could produce offspring of both light-bellied and dark-bellied races, depending on her mate. Obviously there was no limit to the number of "races" that could be described within a species, depending on the whim of the observer.

Around 1940 biologists, under the influence of discoveries in population genetics, made a major change in their understanding of race. Experiments on the genetics of organisms taken from natural populations made it clear that there was a great deal of genetic variation between individuals even in the same family, not to speak of the same population. It was discovered that many of the "races" of animals previously described and named were simply alternative hereditary forms that could appear within a family. Different local geographic populations did not differ from each other absolutely, but only in the relative frequency of different characters. For example, in human blood groups, some individuals were type A, some type B, some AB, and some O. No population was exclusively of one blood type. The difference between African, Asian, and European populations was only in the proportion of the four kinds.

These findings led to the concept of "geographical race," as a population of varying individuals, freely mating among each other, but different in average proportions of various genes from other populations. Any local random breeding population that was even slightly different in proportion of different gene forms from other populations was a geographical race. This new view of race had two powerful effects. First, no individual could be regarded as a "typical" member of a race. Older textbooks of anthropology would often show photographs of "typical" Australian aborigines, tropical Africans, and Japanese, listing as many as 50 or 100 "races," each with its typical example. Once it was recognized that every population was highly variable and differed largely in average proportions of different forms from other populations, the concept of the type specimen became meaningless.

The second consequence of the new view of race was that since every population differs slightly from every other one on the average, all local interbreeding populations are "races," so race really loses its significance as a concept. The Kikuyu of East Africa differ from the Japanese in gene frequencies, but they also differ from their neighbors, the Masai, and although the extent of the differences might be less in one case than in the other, it is only a matter of degree. This means that the social and historical definitions of race that put the two East African tribes in the same "race," but put the Japanese in a different "race," were purely arbitrary. How much difference in the frequencies of A, B, AB, and O blood groups does one require before deciding it is large enough to declare two local populations are in separate "races"?

All People Look Alike

In ordinary parlance we still speak of Africans as one race, Europeans as another, Asians as another. And this distinction corresponds to our everyday sensory impressions. No one would mistake a Masai for a Japanese or either for a Finn. Despite variation from individual to individual within these groups, the differences between groups in skin color, hair form, and some facial features makes them clearly different. Racism takes these evident differences and claims that they demonstrate major genetic separation between "races." Is there any truth in this assertion?

We must remember that we are conditioned to observe precisely those features and that our ability to distinguish individuals as opposed to types is an artifact of our upbringing. We have no difficulty at all in telling apart individuals in our own group, but "they" all look alike. Once, in upper Egypt, my wife was approached by an Egyptian who began a lively conversation with her under the impression that he knew her. After she repeatedly protested that he was mistaken, he apologized, saying, in effect, "I'm sorry but all you European women look alike."

Superiority Is in the Eyes of the Beholder

If we could look at a random sample of different genes, not biased by our socialization, how much difference would there be between major geographical groups, say between Africans and Australian aborigines, as opposed to the differences between individuals within these groups? It is, in fact, possible to answer that question.

During the last 40 years, using the techniques of immunology and of protein chemistry, it has been possible to identify a large number of human genes that code for specific enzymes and other proteins. Very large numbers of individuals from all over the world have been tested to determine their genetic constitution with respect to such proteins, since only a small sample of blood is needed to make these determinations. About 150 different genetically coded proteins have been examined and the results are very illuminating for our understanding of human genetic variation.

It turns out that 75 percent of the different kinds of proteins are identical in all individuals tested from whatever population, with the exception of an occasional rare mutation. These so-called monomorphic proteins are common to all human beings of all races, and the species is essentially uniform with respect to the genes that code them. The other 25 percent are polymorphic proteins. That is, there exist two or more alternative forms of the protein, coded by alternative forms of a gene, that are reasonably common in our species. We can use these polymorphic genes to ask how much difference there is between populations, as compared with the difference between individuals within populations.

An example of a highly polymorphic gene is the one that determines the ABO blood type. There are three alternative forms of the gene which we will symbolize by A, B, and O, and every population in the world is characterized by some particular mixture of the three. For example, Belgians have about 26 percent A, 6 percent B, and the remaining 68 percent is O. Among Pygmies of the Congo, the proportions are 23 percent A, 22 percent B, and 55 percent O. . . .

A major finding from the study of such polymorphic genes is that none of these genes perfectly discriminates one "racial" group from another. That is, there is no gene known that is 100 percent of one form in one race and 100 percent of a different form in some other race. Reciprocally, some genes that are very variable from individual to individual show no average difference at all between major races.

. . . Of all human genetic variation known for enzymes and other proteins, and where it has been possible to actually count up the frequencies of different forms of the genes and so get an objective estimate of genetic variation, 85 percent turns out to be between individuals within the same local population, tribe, or nation. A further 8 percent is between tribes or nations within a major "race," and the remaining 7 percent is between major "races." That means that the genetic variation between one Spaniard and another, or between one Masai and another, is 85 percent of all human genetic variation, while only 15 percent is accounted for by breaking people up into groups. If everyone on earth became extinct except for the Kikuyu of East Africa, about 85 percent of all human variability would still be present in the reconstituted species. A few gene forms would be lost like the FY^b allele of the Duffy blood group that is known only in American Indians, but little else would be changed.

Who's Who?

. . . In practice, "racial" categories are established that correspond to major skin color groups, and all of the borderline cases are distributed among these or made into new races according to the whim of the scientist. But it turns out not to matter much how the groups are assigned because the differences between major "racial" categories, no matter how defined, turn out to be small.

The result of the study of genetic variation is in sharp contrast with the everyday impression that major "races" are well differentiated. Clearly, those superficial differences in hair form, skin color, and facial features that are used to distinguish "races" from each other are not typical of human genes in general. Human "racial" differentiation is, indeed, only skin deep. Any use of racial categories must take its justification from some source other than biology. The remarkable feature of human evolution and history has been the very small degree of divergence between geographical populations as compared with the genetic variation among individuals.

Richard Lewontin is a population geneticist at the Comparative Museum of Natural History at Harvard University. He is a longtime member of Science for the People.

EDITORS' NOTES

1. For further work by these feminist members and related scholars, see Rita Arditti, Pat Brennan, and Steve Cavrak, eds., *Science and Liberation* (Montreal: Black Rose Books, 1980); Anne Fausto-Sterling, *Myths of Gender: Biological Theories about Women and Men* (New York: Basic Books, 1985); Donna Haraway, *Primate Visions: Gender, Race, and Nature in the World of Modern Science* (New York: Routledge, 1989); Sandra Harding, *The Science Question in Feminism* (Ithaca, NY: Cornell University Press, 1986); Ruth Hubbard, *The Politics of Women's Biology* (New Brunswick, NJ: Rutgers University Press, 1990); Evelyn Fox Keller, *Reflections on Gender in Science* (New Haven, CT: Yale University Press, 1985).

2. Kelly Moore, *Disrupting Science: Social Movements, American Scientists, and the Politics of the Military, 1945–1975* (Princeton, NJ: Princeton University Press, 2008), 184.

3. Ruth Hubbard, "Facts and Feminism," *Science for the People* 18, no. 2 (March–April 1986): 16–20, 26.

4. Rita Arditti, "Women as Objects: Science and Sexual Politics," *Science for the People* 6, no. 5 (September 1974): 8–11, 29–30; Evelyn Fox Keller, *Reflections on Gender in Science* (New Haven, CT: Yale University Press, 1985).

5. Barbara Beckwith, "Women's Health Book Collective: Women Empowering Women," *Science for the People* 13, no. 5 (September–October 1981): 19–22; *Science for the People* 14, no. 4, "Women Challenging Science Challenging Women" (July–August 1982).

6. Rita Arditti, Claire Huga, and Cynthia Kneen, "Birth Control in Amerika," *Science for the People* 2, no. 4 (December 1970): 28–31; Rita Arditti, "Women's Biology in a Man's World," *Science for the People* 5, no. 4 (July 1973): 39–42; Ruth Hubbard, "Human Embryo and Gene Manipulation," *Science for the People* 15, no. 3 (May–June 1983): 24–27; *Science for the People* 16, no. 2, "Special Babies Issue" (March–April 1984).

7. Herb Fox, "Panthers Suggest a 'Free Science Program' to SESPA-Science for the People," *Science for the People* 2, no. 4 (December 1970): 26.

8. Morris Davis, "Black Workers and Occupational Hazards," *Science for the People* 12, no. 2 (March–April 1980): 29–31; Tomás Morales-Cardona and Gilberto Concepción Suárez, "Industrial Safety & Health in Puerto Rico," *Science for the People* 7, no. 5 (September 1975): 36–37.

9. Affirmative Action Workshop, "Defend Affirmative Action," *Science for the People* 11, no. 4 (July–August 1979): 19.

10. Connie Phillips, "A Black Psychiatrist Examines Racism: An Interview with Dr. Alvin F. Poussaint," *Science for the People* 14, no. 2 (March–April 1982): 21–24; Rod Toneye,

"Institutionalized Racism in the Medical Profession," *Science for the People* 14, no. 6 (November–December 1982): 21–24.

11. E. O. Wilson, *Sociobiology: The New Synthesis* (Cambridge, MA: Harvard University Press, 1975).

12. *Science for the People* 9, no. 4, "Are Sex Roles Biologically Determined?" (July–August 1977); *Science for the People* 13, no. 5, "Science and the Attack on Women" (September–October 1981).

13. Jonathan Beckwith, email message to Sigrid Schmalzer, December 31, 2016.

14. Richard Lewontin, "The Apportionment of Human Diversity," *Evolutionary Biology* 6 (1972): 381–98.

15. Ruth Hubbard, *The Politics of Women's Biology* (New Brunswick, NJ: Rutgers University Press, 1990), 209.

FIGURE 6. Cover of *Science for the People* 11, no. 3 (May–June 1979). The image, a collage of two photographs by Ellen Shub, demonstrates the emphasis SftP placed on issues of industrialization and exploitive labor practices in agriculture under capitalism. Photo © Ellen Shub. Reprinted here with permission from Ellen Shub.

CHAPTER 6

Agriculture, Ecology, and Food

Sigrid Schmalzer

Agriculture was an important focus for Science for the People; it was one of the areas in which the organization's members collaborated most effectively with other groups; and it has produced some of SftP's strongest legacies, as former members have continued to work within organizations like the New World Agriculture and Ecology Group, the Pesticide Action Network, and the Consumers Union. The production of food is of obvious and inevitable relevance to anyone concerned with social inequities, and the environmental consequences arising from different agricultural approaches offers further reason for popular concern. Beyond these widely recognized issues, agriculture presents fertile ground for Marxist analysis. In such "applied" fields, the integration of theory and practice is of obvious importance. Moreover, agriculture not only involves complex biological systems, and is thus ripe for Marxist arguments against reductionism—it is also inescapably linked to social and political factors and therefore presents an almost incontrovertible case for considering science within its social and political contexts. SftP members tackled agricultural issues on a number of fronts: they critiqued the theories underlying agricultural policy, analyzed the political economy of food production and distribution, produced educational materials for use in middle and high schools, collaborated with farm labor organizers, and engaged in solidarity efforts in Latin America.

Environmental issues were of central concern to SftP members who worked on agriculture, but here as elsewhere SftP's analysis differed profoundly from mainstream liberal environmentalism. In his 1977 essay "Ecological

Determinism" (Document 6.1), professor of ecology and evolutionary biology John Vandermeer offered a systematic deconstruction of widely accepted
understandings of the threats posed by overpopulation. Debunking the "myth
of overpopulation" was an essential starting point for SftP's analysis of agricultural issues, since much U.S. domestic and foreign agricultural policy rested
on claims about population pressures. In "Ecological Determinism," Vandermeer critiqued the reductionist scientific logic at play in assumptions about
overpopulation (whether held by "reactionaries" or "liberals"), in which every
ecological problem was imagined to boil down to the single factor of population. More specifically, the essay advanced the Marxist position that an understanding of population—as with any other issue—must account for social and
political factors, especially for the workings of institutional power structures.

SftP shared more ground with liberal environmentalists on questions
related to industrial agriculture, particularly regarding the increasing reliance on agro-chemicals. To some extent, SftP's opposition to the reductionist
tendencies of agricultural research (and biological research more generally)
also overlapped with the perspectives of environmentalists hostile to mod-
ernism. However, in place of Romantic holism and nostalgic appeals to a
pre-industrial form of "natural" living, SftP members typically embraced
a self-consciously pragmatic, rational, and critical approach to identifying
agricultural solutions. As SftP member and Harvard biologist Richard
Levins later said, "Instead of having to decide between large-scale industrial
style production and a 'small is beautiful' approach *a priori*," the scale of
agricultural work should be recognized as "dependent on natural and social
conditions" and should be "adjusted to the watershed, climatic zones and
topography, population density, distribution of available resources, and the
mobility of pests and their enemies."[1] Here again, SftP's Marxist analysis
provided the essential difference: capitalism, rather than industrialism per
se, posed the critical problem, and so SftP focused squarely on the inequities
and exploitations generated by the capitalist political economy. Evolutionary biologist Richard Lewontin's 1982 article "Agricultural Research and
the Penetration of Capital" (Document 6.2) perfectly captures the core of
the SftP critique. Lewontin clearly articulated the difference between farming and agriculture: "Farming is growing peanuts. Agriculture is turning
petroleum into peanut butter." He further advanced the central argument
"that capital has completely penetrated agricultural production . . . and that
technological change has played the same role in that penetration as it has
in all other productive sectors." This article has been widely engaged by STS
scholars who focus on the history of agriculture.[2]

While Lewontin's article was published in *Science for the People* magazine, and so reached mainly habitual readers of political criticism, SftP was committed to engaging with a wider public. The *Feed, Need, Greed* curriculum constitutes one of the most innovative such efforts for SftP on any issue. This high school curriculum was originally published in 1974 as *Feed, Need, Greed: Where Will It Lead?* but the portion excerpted here (Document 6.3) came from the expanded 1980 version, *Feed, Need, Greed: Food, Resources & Population*. The volume's authors, Connie Phillips and Sue Tafler, remember printing "a few hundred" copies, which they sold from tables at National Science Teachers Association conferences and AAAS meetings; anecdotal reports suggested that the curriculum was adopted in biology and "science and society" courses.[3] Notably, the volume began with a unit on "Population and Resources" devoted to debunking claims about overpopulation and thus the need for capital-intensive agriculture. The selection included here offers a window onto SftP's analysis of the relationships among capitalism, racism, and imperialism. It underscores SftP's deep commitment to representing the experiences of workers and Third World people, and to incorporating their voices into SftP publications.[4]

These themes appear also in the fourth selection, a 1983 magazine article by Uriel Kitron and Brian Schultz, "Alternatives in Agriculture: A Report from the New World Agriculture Group" (Document 6.4). NWAG, later renamed New World Agriculture and Ecology Group (NWAEG), was formed in 1977 by concerned scientists, many of whom were already SftP members in the Ann Arbor chapter.[5] The article offers a concrete example of how members of SftP engaged in agricultural solidarity work with Third World countries, in this case with Nicaragua. This was by no means SftP's first such effort. As will be explored further in Chapter 9, "Science for the People and the World," in 1973 and 1978, Science for the People sent delegations to the People's Republic of China; the first of these had reported very favorably on agricultural science in a socialist-revolutionary society, and the second had taken food and agriculture as its specific focus.[6] Later, SftP members—most notably Richard Levins—would forge deep connections to Cuban agricultural science. But in the 1980s Nicaragua presented the most exciting opportunity for SftP (and especially NWAG) to develop Third World solidarity in revolutionary agricultural science.

"Alternatives in Agriculture" further testifies to the ability of SftP members to make meaningful alliances with labor organizations, in particular the Farm Labor Organizing Committee (FLOC). FLOC was founded in 1967 by migrant farmworker Baldemar Velásquez, who modeled the organization after Cesar Chavez's California-based United Farm Workers. In the late 1970s

FLOC gained national attention and improved labor conditions for migrant farmworkers in the Ohio tomato industry by organizing a strike and boycott against canned food manufacturers Campbell's and Libby's.[7] In 1977, the Ann Arbor chapter of SftP formed a "FLOC Support Group" to coordinate solidarity efforts.[8] "Alternatives in Agriculture" showcases some of the roles that members of SftP and NWAG sought to play in this struggle. One way SftP and NWAG activists contributed to the FLOC struggle was by promoting the technology of intercropping—that is, planting multiple crops in a single plot, for example by alternating rows. SftP's 1978 delegation to China had returned especially excited by the ecological benefits achieved through intercropping there,[9] and in the U.S. context of the tomato workers' struggles and the threat mechanized harvesting posed to labor, it took on an additional social dimension. Finally, this article shows SftP members plugging into the labor movement by researching the consequences of pesticide use for farmworkers, a project that finds a clear echo in the work that former SftP member Margaret Reeves now pursues with Pesticide Action Network.

Document 6.1

John Vandermeer, "Ecological Determinism," in Ann Arbor Science for the People Editorial Collective, ed., *Biology as a Social Weapon* (Minneapolis: Burgess Publishing Co., 1977), 108–22.

The volume in which this essay appeared emerged from a conference organized by the Ann Arbor chapter of Science for the People; other essays critiqued the purported link between race and IQ, biological theories of sexual difference, and research that supposedly demonstrated increased aggression in individuals with XYY chromosomal irregularities. In his contribution, John Vandermeer moved the discussion from the more familiar SftP terrain of genetic determinism to the realm of ecology in order to challenge widely accepted beliefs about the deterministic role supposedly played by population in the environmental crises of the day. Only a small portion of the essay is reproduced here, but it is well worth reading in full, especially for its step-by-step explication of both "fascist" and "liberal" renderings of the "population bomb." John Vandermeer, then as now a professor at the University of Michigan and an active member of SftP, was also a founding member of the New World Agriculture Group.

The environmental crisis has matured somewhat since the sixties. This process seems to have changed crisis into paradox. In case after case, crises can more appropriately be called ecological paradoxes . . .

Air pollution in many major cities reaches dangerous levels, but the auto industry lobbies to defer legislation on emission controls. People starve in Latin America, but the secretary of agriculture notes that food is part of our "negotiating package."[3] Every ecological "problem" seems to carry with it something structural that renders the problem insoluble, at least in the near future. It is certainly an ironic situation that freedom for the average woman and man seems to be freedom to choose between ecological ruin or economic ruin, death by poison or death by starvation. People will insist on an understanding of the cause of a contradiction that affects their lives so directly.

But, by the time the paradoxical nature of the environmental crisis became obvious to the public, an apparent cause of that fundamental contradiction had been firmly entrenched in the public's consciousness. The basic problem was seen as too many people. If there were not so many people in Latin America, Latin Americans would have enough food to go around. If there were not so many people in the United States, the staggering number of automobiles would no longer exist. Virtually every ecological and environmental problem could be, and was, plausibly tied to the specter of too many people.

As the "population problem" became central to the ecological movement, a host of important factors were swept under the rug. Many of these factors are beginning to reemerge, but, in the minds of many people, the so-called population problem still remains an important causal factor in the generation of the sort of ecological paradoxes described above. . . .

[In the body of the paper, Vandermeer outlines and critiques what he terms "reactionary" and "liberal" versions of the myth of overpopulation.—eds.]

If the ecological problems that exist are, in fact, severe enough to threaten our very lives and if there are always structural reasons why these problems cannot be solved, it would seem to follow that the structure itself must be changed. In fact, in the early sixties, it seemed as though we were on the brink of a mass awakening to this consciousness. The repeated disclosures of environmental rape began awakening people to the realities of ecology. A growing awareness of the fundamentally political nature of the environmental crisis might soon have followed. But science saved the day again! Nothing is structurally wrong—there are just too many people. Latin Americans starve not because our coffee and bananas grow on their farmland but because there are too many Latin Americans. The putrid air in Gary, Indiana, does not result from the steel corporation profits but from too many people demanding steel. Every ecological problem can be tied to an overabundance of people. . . .

Scientists and technicians, in their sadly naive attempts at remaining "objective" in pursuing their "value-free" science, have frequently been made into unwilling conscripts, who unwittingly serve the very cause of the problems they wish to solve. Ecologists, I think, are the most obvious example of such service. In a truly passionate desire to save the world from ecological disaster, they have sometimes sacrificed a complete analysis of cause and effect for the pragmatic "what can we do here and now." If we cannot hope to control the monster United Brands, maybe we can talk Latin Americans into having fewer babies. If we do see the need for regional planning, let the global corporations do it, since no one else will in the near future.

This kind of copout, obviously, will not help to solve the problem; indeed, it will only exacerbate it. What we need to do is to attack the problem at its core. We must eliminate the fundamental system that holds profit above ecology, that continues to enslave both humanity and nature.

. . . Yes, we are in a crisis situation. Fascist solutions are both humanistically and ecologically unsound. Liberal solutions cannot be achieved within our present socioeconomic system. Clearly, the solution to environmental problems requires a radically different kind of politics.

References

3. Lerza, C. 1975. The world food conference: A summary. In *Food for the people, not for profit*, eds. C. Lerza and M. Jacobson. New York: Ballantine Books, p. 279.

Document 6.2

Richard Lewontin, "Agricultural Research and the Penetration of Capital," *Science for the People* 14, no. 1 (January–February, 1982): 12–17.

In this oft-cited essay, Richard Lewontin laid out the essential elements necessary for a Marxist analysis of agricultural science and technology. With this approach, he treated scientific research as just one aspect of agriculture within the larger context of the capitalist political economy. When SftP began, Lewontin was a population geneticist at the University of Chicago and a founding member of the Chicago chapter; by 1982 he had taken a position at Harvard University, where he is now professor emeritus.

Agricultural production in the United States seems to present a difficulty to political economic theory. On the face of it, it seems that an important sphere of production has resisted the usual advance of capitalist penetration. Although ships and shoes are produced by a relatively small number of corporations of very large size and huge capital investment, the production of cabbages has remained firmly in the hands of 2.5 million petty producers. Why is it that the technological change and concentration of capital that we see in the manufacturing, transportation, extractive industries, etc. has not taken over agricultural production as well? An answer sometimes given is that agriculture has simply lagged behind and that monopoly capitalism is finally catching up with it. Thus, the number of farms is decreasing (from 5.7 million in 1900 to 2.7 million in 1975), the average size of farms is increasing (146 acres in 1900 to 404 acres in 1975), and big enterprises are taking over huge acreages (the proportion of all farms that are over 1000 acres has risen from 0.8% to 5.5% in the same period). This answer does not really meet the facts, however. Of the three million farm operators who disappeared between 1900 and the present, 2 million were tenancies. The proportion of all farms run by managers rather than family units has not changed (less than 1% of farms), and big corporations have actually divested themselves of farm land in recent years. There is simply no rush to make farms into immense General Motors corporations.

Farming vs. Agriculture

The basic problem in confronting the analysis of capitalist development in agriculture is the confusion between farming and agriculture. Farming is the process of turning seed, fertilizer, pesticide and water into cattle, potatoes, corn and cotton by using land, machinery and human labor on the farm. Agriculture includes farming, but it also includes all those productive processes that go into making, transporting and selling the seed, machinery and chemicals that the farmer uses, and all of the transportation, food processing and selling that go on from the moment a potato leaves the farm until the moment it enters the consumer's mouth as a potato chip. Farming is growing peanuts. Agriculture is turning petroleum into peanut butter. It is the claim of this article that capital has completely penetrated agricultural production when viewed as a complete process in the U.S. and that technological change has played the same role in that penetration as it has in all other productive sectors. That is, the owners of large amounts of capital are the ones who control and profit from agriculture. It is a corollary of this claim that agricultural research, although directly responsive to the demands of farmers, is, in fact, carried out on terms set by capital concentration.

Historical Development: Inputs

The most striking change in the nature of agricultural production in the U.S. since the turn of the century is the change in the composition of inputs into farm production. These inputs are the seed, fertilizer, energy, water, land and labor that the farmer uses in production. The total value of these inputs in any year can be calculated by weighting the physical amount of each by its price (adjusted for inflation). This value can then be compared from year to year by establishing some year as an arbitrary base with the index value 100 and expressing all other years relative to it.

The total amount of inputs into farming rose from an index value of 84 in 1910 to about 100 in 1975, not a very great increase. But the nature of these inputs changed drastically. Inputs produced on the farm itself went from an index value of 175 down to 90 between 1910 and 1975, while the index value of inputs the farmer purchased from outside the farm rose from 38 to 105. That is, farmers used to grow their own seed, raise their own horses and mules, raise the hay the livestock ate, and spread manure from these animals on the land. Now farmers buy their seed from Pioneer Hybrid Seed Co., their "mules" from the Ford Motor Company, the "hay" to feed these "mules" from Exxon, and the "manure" from Union Carbide. Thus, farming has changed from a productive process that originated most of its own inputs and converted them into outputs, to a process that passes materials and energy through from an external supplier to an external buyer.

The consequence of this change can be seen in the sources of the market value of consumer products. At each stage of a productive process, as a raw material is converted to a partly finished form then to a finished product, and then into an item for the consumer some value is added to the material by the labor expended. Iron and coal are cheaper than the steel that is made from them; the steel is cheaper than the girder made from it; and the girders are cheaper than the bridge built from them. At each stage the transformation of form by the labor expended on it adds value, and the total value added is the difference in price between the original raw materials and the final product consumed.

At present, only 10% of the value added in agriculture is actually added on the farm. About 40% of the value is added in creating the inputs (fertilizer, machinery, seeds, hired labor, fuel, pesticides, etc.), and 50% is added in processing, transportation and exchange after the farm commodities leave the farm gate. Another facet of this structure of production is that, although the percent of the labor force engaged in farming has dropped from 40% to 4% since 1900 (a loss of about 4.3 million family workers and about 4 million farm laborers), there has been a growth in those who supply, service, transport, transform and produce farm inputs and farm outputs so that there are now about 6 persons engaged in off-farm agricultural work for every person working on the farm. To sum up, farm production is now only a small fraction of agricultural production.

Productivity

The second major historical fact concerns the detailed nature of the production process on the farm and of farm productivity. Total farm productivity, measured as the ratio of farm outputs to farm inputs, went from an index value of 53 in 1910 to 113 in 1975. That is, for each dollar spent by the farmer on farm inputs, the value of what the farmer produced more than doubled. It is extremely difficult to estimate total inputs in the 19th century, but labor productivity increased, depending on the crop, by a factor of 2–3. The increase in farm productivity took place in stages corresponding to important technological innovations. The first period, beginning in about 1840 to about the turn of the century, was marked by a tremendous increase in labor productivity because of the introduction of farm machinery. The steel plow, the harvester, the combine and stationary steam engine increased labor productivity in grain production, for example, by up to 8 times in dry regions where full combines could be used. This development in machinery, however, came to a stagnant period around the end of the 19th century because of the lack of traction power. Only small multiple plows could be pulled by horse teams. Stationary steam engines for threshing had to be fed with grain by horse and wagon; rudimentary steam tractors had poor maneuverability. Then, after the first World War, the automotive industry developed flexible, powerful, mobile traction. Internal combustion engines, diesel engines, the differential that allows rear wheels to move independently, and inflatable tires made farm tractors that could pull heavy loads and maneuver in tight places. The final spurt of machinery adoption was between 1937 and 1950.

Chemical Inputs

The third major change was after World War II with the immense growth in chemical inputs into agriculture. This was a consequence of two factors. First, chemical plants had been built at government expense during the war so that chemical companies found themselves with immense unused plant capacity. The price of fertilizer fell dramatically compared with other inputs. Second, export markets increased dramatically because of European demand, so production had to be increased quickly, and fertilizers were the fastest, cheapest way. Chemical inputs to farming increased by a factor of 7 times between 1946 and 1976.

There are three features to note about these technological changes:

1) They were not the product of agricultural research, but of entrepreneurial capitalism. McCormick and Hussey, who invented reaping machines in the 1830's, were typical inventor entrepreneurs of early industrial capitalism; and the flourishing of the first phase of mechanization was a consequence of industrial capitalism. McCormick was a Virginia farm boy who invented a successful reaping machine in 1831, patented an improved model in 1834, and by 1841 established a large factory for its production in Chicago. The changes in traction power were a direct spinoff of the development of the automobile as the leading American industry, and the fertilizer and pesticide "revolution" was a consequence of the economic structure of the chemical industries and strong export demand.

2) At all times, but especially for mechanization, it is the labor process which is at the heart of the change. Farmers, like other producers, are under a constant pressure to reduce labor costs. The spread of the reaper came 20 years before the famous Civil War labor shortage. But, in addition, farmers are under an unusually strong pressure to control the labor process, not simply to reduce the payroll. A strike by harvest workers results in total loss of the product, not simply postponement of production. Carelessness causes crop loss or damage.

But it is very hard to supervise farm labor and to regulate its speed. Therefore, piece work is common in harvesting. But piece work puts a premium on total speed without quality control. Mechanization provides control over speed and quality, as well as guaranteeing production. No strikes, no shortages. In this connection, it is interesting that the early vegetable farming "machines" were simply large horizontal platforms, pulled by a tractor, on which workers lay to tend or harvest the plants. The farmer or foreman drove the tractor. This reverse assembly line in which workers are moved across the work not only reduced the labor force, but also controlled the speed of work and allowed close supervision of the process. It was made possible by Henry Ford.

3) The effect of the technology is to reduce the value added on the farm and increase the value of purchased inputs. That is, the chief consequence of technological innovation to increase on-farm productivity has been to make on-farm productivity less and less important in determining agricultural value. Major changes in all aspects of farming technology are in the same direction. Thus, hybrid seed is a purchased input replacing the older self-generated seed, mechanized irrigation replaces labor-intensive ditching, etc. It is important to note that all changes in value added on the farm are not the consequence of technological change in agriculture. Changes in factor prices in inputs and processing as a result of technological changes or political changes (oil prices) also change the proportion of value added on the farm.

Agricultural Research

Where does agricultural research fit in? The research carried out by suppliers—seed companies, machinery companies, chemical companies—is clearly designed to maximize the use of purchased inputs. But the same happens in socialized research. Our field studies of agricultural research scientists in state agricultural experiment stations give a consistent picture. Research workers usually come from farm backgrounds or at least small town agricultural service communities. Their ideology is to serve the farmer by making farming more profitable, more risk-free and easier as a way of life. They also say that benefits to the farmer will trickle down to the consumer. In actual practice, most agricultural research is directly responsive to the demands of farmers (what agricultural research scientists call "progressive" farmers, i.e. larger and richer farmers) in the state. But the critical point is that the demands of the farmers are determined by the system of production and marketing in which they are trapped. Thus, the farmer becomes the agent by which the providers of inputs and purchasers of outputs use the socialized establishment of research. Agricultural research serves the *needs* of capital by responding to the demands of farmers, because of the total control by capital of the chain of agricultural production and marketing.

On the production side the influence is obvious. Farmers buy huge amounts of herbicide to replace cultivation. Weed science departments in schools of agriculture spend their time testing and evaluating herbicide treatment combinations, leaching rates and toxicity. Agricultural engineering departments design machines for application of herbicides and redesign other machines for weed-free fields. Plant breeders breed varieties for earliness to take advantage of herbicide treatments. In plant breeding the hybrid seed method has become omnipresent because it makes the purchase of seed from a seed company necessary. But, more than that, the objective of the breeding program is to provide varieties that make maximal use of heavy fertilizer application (short, stiff stalks to prevent lodging, proper root development, etc.). All phases of research are directed by the nature of purchased inputs.

On the marketing side the same dependence is evident. Just as the procession of farm inputs—seed, fertilizer, pesticides and machinery—is highly monopolized, so purchase of farm outputs is in the hands of monopoly buyers (monopsonists). Cargill buys grain, Hunt buys tomatoes, and Anderson-Clayton buys cotton. Cargill pays for soybeans based on the regional average protein content. But there is a negative correlation between yield and protein, so it will not pay a farmer to use a higher protein variety with less yield. Therefore, plant breeders go for yield, not protein. Canneries make contracts with farmers which govern all the inputs and require delivery of a particular type of tomato at a particular time. Again, breeders comply with the "demands of the farmers" for just the right tomato.

In summary, because farmers are a small (although essential) part of the production of foods, the conditions of their part of production are set by the monopolistic providers and buyers of farm inputs and outputs. Therefore, the agricultural research establishment, by serving the proximate demands of farmers, is, in fact, a research establishment captured by capital. The farmers are only the messengers. The messages are written in the corporate headquarters. . . .

Document 6.3

"Harvest of Shame," in Science for the People, ed., *Feed, Need, Greed: Food, Resources & Population* (Boston: Science for the People, 1980), 50–54.

Feed, Need, Greed was a high-school curriculum originally developed in 1974, and then revised and expanded in 1980, by the Food and Nutrition Group of Science for the People's Boston chapter. Unit I sought to "explode the population myth." Unit II offered a social and political analysis of the twin problems of hunger and obesity. Unit III (from which this selection is drawn) critiqued the capitalist and imperialist underpinnings of the "Nutritional-Industrial Complex" and included discussion of another of SftP's signature efforts, the defense of breastfeeding (especially in the Third World) against infant formula manufacturers. Unit IV, optimistically entitled "Building a New World," presented an array of suggestions for organizing.

Cutting Cane in Florida

Roberto left his family in Jamaica to come to Florida to harvest sugar cane on a small farm. Like 25% of Jamaicans he was jobless. Lacking access to welfare or social security programs, he had little choice but to become a migrant worker. Every morning at 6:00 Roberto climbs into the truck to go to the field. The truck is overcrowded with standing men and the cane cutting knives are out in the open. Roberto tries to stay away from those knives since he knows sometimes that the heavy truck goes off the side of the road and workers get hurt. Roberto arrives in the field to wait for the crew leader to assign him a quarter of a mile long row of cane that is his average daily "task." Roberto hurries up knowing that if he doesn't harvest at least a ton each hour he will be sent home to Jamaica. It is 6:45 in the morning, the crew leader finishes assigning rows, opens his notebook and puts in front of Roberto's name: "starting time, 6:45." The cane is 12 to 14 feet high and very thick. Roberto uses a sharp knife to cut stalks. To protect himself he wears awkward metal guards for his feet, shins and hands like medieval armor, and long sleeves and a hat to protect himself from sticky cane fibers. He sees a dangerous snake and wants to strike at it with his knife; fortunately he stops, remembering that the grower prohibits killing snakes because they eat rats.

Roberto has problems breathing. Ashes are surrounding him because the field is first burned to remove leaves before the workers harvest it. It is 12:00, lunch time. To be able to earn more Roberto eats in a hurry. The crew leader marks half an hour lunch in front of Roberto's name. The sun is high now and Roberto is hotter and hotter in his heavy clothes. He tries to work fast but carefully. He knows that he won't get hospitalized if he cuts off one of his toes or fingers even though 3% of his wages are given to a "medical insurance." His hourly wage is $3.23. An American worker would demand $5 an hour for this kind of job.

It is almost 8:30 at night and it is becoming dark as Roberto finishes his row. He is dead tired. He goes back to his quarters, a tiny room for ten workers. They lie down in bed and talk. They are deciding whether to go on strike for better working conditions. Some of the men are scared to be sent home.

This is the contract under which they are working:

— the contract is signed between the Jamaican government and Florida sugar growers. There is no contract between worker and grower.
— any act of misconduct or disobedience and the worker is deported to Jamaica at his own expense
— Federal minimum wage laws cover only the largest farms (and these laws usually are not enforced)
— workers should not be forced to work more than 8 hours a day, six days a week
— housing should be free
— the price of meals is deducted from the worker's wages
— the grower should supply the same medical care and compensation for work-related injuries and diseases that are required for American workers by state law.

Role play: Some students will play the part of Jamaican migrant workers and some students will play the part of the Florida growers as they confront each other the next morning. One student will play the part of the local judge who is a brother-in-law of the main sugar grower.

Canned Imperialism

The Bajio Valley is one of Mexico's richest agricultural valleys. Del Monte became interested in the region because the labor is so much cheaper than in the United States. When Del Monte first sent its technicians to Bajio in 1959, they found a fertile land with corn and bean production predominating and serving as the basis for the local diet. Some of the land was owned by Mexican campesinos each caring for 10 to 20 acres. Some of the land was held in ejidos (large State-owned farms) subdivided into small plots, worked by ejidatarios (tenant farmers). Mexican law prohibited the sale of these lands and restricted ownership by foreign corporations.

Nevertheless, Del Monte found a way to change the valley's agriculture. Because agricultural credit is very limited in Mexico, Del Monte introduced contract farming. Contract farming means that in order to have credit the farmer agrees to plant a set number of acres of a particular crop. The company provides seeds, machines and fertilizer. The costs of these are deducted from the farmer's income when he delivers the crop to the company's cannery. In the early 1960's Del Monte came to dominate the valley. Del Monte preferred to deal with large owners while the ejidatarios were increasingly marginalized and often forced out of production. Many have been forced to leave their villages in search of work and many migrate illegally to the United States. The large grower who already had money or land could enter new areas of production by using contract farming to increase his wealth. However they were *all* dependent on Del Monte. If a machine arrived late and the farmer lost his crop, he wouldn't receive any money and would even go into debt.

Instead of the traditional corn and beans, now peas and asparagus are extensively grown and canned in Bajio Valley for export. These are not part of the diet of the Mexican people. Canned peas are purchased only by middle and upper class Mexicans. 90% of the asparagus is shipped to industrialized countries. No longer do the people grow food for their own consumption. Their wages are too low to buy enough food. Without the complementary protein provided by meals like tortilla and frijoles (beans), malnutrition is increasing in Mexico. The Mexicans are becoming even poorer.

Discussion questions:

1. Del Monte was able to get what they wanted produced in Mexico because they could provide credit. Why do farmers need credit? When do farmers need credit most? For what?

2. Investment by American firms is usually seen as beneficial because money is provided to buy new technology which helps increase production. Let's look at this case of investment by examining the following:

   (a) what kind of food production was *increased* by Del Monte's investment?
   (b) what kind of food production was *decreased* by their investment?
   (c) name the technologies that were made available because of Del Monte's investment.
   (d) what happened to the *large* land owners as a result of the investment?
   (e) what happened to the *small* land owners as a result of the investment?
   (f) what happened to the *workers* as a result?
   (g) summarize the effects of this investment on production and on people.

Document 6.4

Uriel Kitron and Brian Schultz, "Alternatives in Agriculture: A Report from the New World Agriculture Group," *Science for the People* 15, no. 1 (January–February 1983): 25–30.

The authors of this 1983 *Science for the People* magazine article were both active members of the Ann Arbor chapter of Science for the People, the New World Agriculture Group (NWAG), and the Farm Labor Organizing Committee (FLOC) Support Group. At the time, Uriel Kitron was an Israeli ecologist and public health worker living in Ann Arbor; today he is a professor of environmental studies at Emory College. Brian Schultz was then working with John Vandermeer as a graduate student in ecology and served on the first NWAG delegation to Nicaragua; he is now a professor of ecology and entomology at Hampshire College. The full article provides more details on the Nicaragua project. The excerpt that follows focuses on NWAG's work with FLOC and includes two boxes from the original article highlighting NWAG's statement of purpose for collaboration with the Nicaraguan government and a FLOC resolution on pesticides.

For fifteen years *Science for the People* has asserted that a science truly for the people must also be done with and by the people. Progressive scientists must form close alliances with working class organizations such as progressive unions in order to find out what their interests are, rather than attempt to impose our conceptions from a distance. We must help facilitate radical organizing and learning that challenge exploitive power relations. Progressive scientists support democratic, socialist countries in their struggle against imperialism, by seeking to develop technologies that reduce their dependence on hostile, developed nations, and by helping them to avoid some of the ecological mistakes made during recent capitalist developments.

This support work includes exposing the class-based nature of current technologies, but further, it includes researching, developing, and publicizing alternative, "transitional" technologies that do not represent the interests of the ruling class, but aid in the struggle for liberation by oppressed classes. Such technologies will serve as a tool for workers to achieve lasting gains, and must not substitute for or hinder progressive social change. The so-called appropriate or alternative technologies are often appropriate only in a technical sense, and often ignore the social, political, and economic changes.[1]

In 1977 a group of progressive North American scientists formed the New World Agriculture Group (NWAG) to develop transitional technologies and encourage progressive agricultural initiatives. NWAG (pronounced "new-ag") has chapters in Ann Arbor, Berkeley, Boston, Ithaca, and Montreal, as well as active individuals in other cities. Most of us are ecologists, social scientists, or public health practitioners associated with universities, and many of us are members of Science for the People. NWAG attempts to find and develop alternative methods of agricultural production that are ecologically rational, in the sense of protecting the environment and preserving long term productive capacity, and that help bring an end to the exploitation of workers and the unequal distribution of wealth. We reject the myth that science and technology are neutral or apolitical. Throughout history, technology has often been developed to strengthen the position of a small elite, at the expense of oppressed people. Mechanization as a weapon to control labor is perhaps the most familiar example, in agriculture as well as industry.[2]

In this article we present two examples of current attempts by NWAG to put some of these ideas into practice. NWAG has begun a program of collaboration and technical assistance with the people of Nicaragua. Decades of mismanagement under the Somoza dynasty, damage from the war, and finally, the flight of capital following the revolution which overthrew Somoza in 1979, have all crippled production and left Nicaragua with huge debts.[3] NWAG hopes to aid the Nicaraguans to rebuild their agriculture by increasing food production for all the people and by minimizing dependence upon expensive, imported chemical inputs, such as pesticides and inorganic fertilizers.

Since 1977 members of NWAG and Science for the People have been actively supporting the Farm Labor Organizing Committee (FLOC)[4] by writing articles, fundraising, teaching, campus organizing, and more direct action (for example, locating tomato fields for picketing; helping on picket lines; talking to other labor unions). Building upon this foundation of political work, we have directed our research toward studying methods of agricultural production that may be useful in FLOC's struggle by, for example, opposing the spread of agricultural mechanization as a means of breaking labor unions. We also recently began to work with FLOC in the Farm Labor Research Project (FLRP), collecting and evaluating information about pesticides and farmworker health and safety in the midwestern United States. . . .

Cooperation with the Farm Labor Organizing Committee

After working with FLOC for several years, NWAG members decided to choose areas of research in ecological agriculture that might be helpful in FLOC's struggle against tomato mechanization and related technologies used in the tomato fields. While FLOC members do not oppose in principle mechanization as a way of reducing the amount of tedious work needed to grow food, they realize that agricultural mechanization has often been used to break labor unions.[8] One common effect of mechanization has been to displace migrant workers who, by becoming organized, present a threat to current labor practices. FLOC insists that farmworkers as well as growers should benefit from mechanization (through shorter hours, less child labor, retraining and placement in new jobs, and other methods) rather than simply being cast aside when their services seem expendable. Finding feasible alternatives using hand labor could slow the spread of job-displacing mechanization.

Intercropping has the potential to be one such method. Researchers in NWAG have found that intercropping is usually more productive and more labor intensive than monoculture cropping. Although it has been associated with the tropics, intercropping was also well known in the midwestern U.S. until the advent of mechanization in the 1940s made large monocultures more profitable to large investors.[9] At present most intercrops cannot be harvested mechanically. Existing harvesting equipment (except in the People's Republic of China[10]) has been developed with one crop in mind. Intercropping thus seems to offer a way of maintaining jobs for farmworkers as well as producing higher yields than mechanized monocultures. Even if mechanical harvesting methods for intercrops can be developed, the delay in developing such techniques would at least give FLOC more time to grow and organize. Failures to incorporate successful intercropping techniques can be publicized to illustrate the true goal of processors—breaking labor unions. Thus we have attempted to use intercropping as a useful, transitional technology serving the cause of farm labor.

Starting with the 1980 growing season at the University of Michigan in Ann Arbor, we decided to experiment with the intercropping of tomatoes with other crops commonly grown in the Midwest, first cucumbers, later soybeans. Cucumbers, like tomatoes, are a high-risk, high-return crop usually grown second in priority to grain crops in the Midwest as a chance for extra profits. Intercropping has sometimes been found to reduce risk beyond that obtained simply by growing more than one monoculture.[11] Furthermore, as legumes, soybeans can serve to convert atmospheric nitrogen to a useable form for a nonlegume "companion" crop such as tomatoes. The preliminary results from three years of experience have been promising. Tomatoes and cucumbers as well as tomatoes and soybeans have yielded as much as 31% more overall when grown together in our small-scale experiments. We have, however, been too slow in publicizing at a popular level our results and the potential advantages of intercropping in general. Several of us have begun to devote more effort to writing articles for local grower magazines, attending and speaking at farmers' conferences and poster sessions, and setting up trials on commercial farms and on land rented specifically for large-scale demonstrations. Perhaps because our backgrounds are in the basic sciences, we have tended to become overly mesmerized by scientific minutiae, at the expense of paying sufficient attention to popularization. We do hope that if intercropping proves feasible in production, farmers will find it to their advantage to join in a just solution to the conflict between farmworkers and processors, rather than switch crops or attempt to mechanize the problem away.

The Farm Labor Research Project

More recently, NWAG began to work with the Farm Labor Research Project (FLRP). Initiated by FLOC in 1982, FLRP (pronounced "flerp") is a research and public education effort focused on the problems of migrant farmworkers in Ohio,

Indiana and Michigan. Working in cooperation with FLOC, the project coordinates research on migrant living and working conditions, wages, and the impact of mechanization on jobs. FLRP, NWAG, and SftP jointly established a "pesticide task force," and NWAG and FLOC support group members have started working on specific issues affecting farmworker safety. We study methods to monitor the use of pesticides, exposure of workers to pesticides, the impact of pesticides on agricultural pests, and the development of alternative technologies such as intercropping and biological pest control. FLOC uses this information for outreach and community organizing programs within and outside of the farm worker community.

FLOC has been interested in training organizers to quickly recognize, document, and report specific cases of pesticide-related accidents and violations for use in publicity and, possibly legal actions. The FLRP pesticide task force has collected information about the pesticides that are used on tomatoes in Ohio and Michigan. Our initial findings were presented as a reference manual and in a set of talks at a meeting of FLOC organizers in Toledo, who were preparing to go into the field to talk to workers. The manual includes a brief description of the pesticide problem, symptoms of pesticide poisonings, and health and exposure effects of the 40 or so pesticides currently in use in tomato fields in Ohio. The manual concludes with a brief discussion on the excessive use of pesticides, and potential alternative methods of pest control.

In the presentation by the task force to farm worker organizers, discussion focused on information useful in organizing. We discussed common pesticides and their poisoning symptoms, pesticide package labels and poisoning information, legal rights with respect to pesticide use, the loss of effectiveness of pesticides (due to pest resistance and the destruction of beneficial insect predator[12]), and alternative methods of pest control. We emphasized that pesticide regulations are rarely enforced, and that only organized workers can expect to obtain real improvements in working conditions. We showed how, given the existence of alternatives, exposure to pesticides need not be accepted as an unavoidable part of a farmworker's job. We ended our talk by describing how chemical and food processing companies are interested in profits, not controlling insects[13] or protecting farmworkers.

We gave a similar presentation for a conference of farmworkers in Holland, Michigan; others are being planned. We are also producing pamphlets, slide shows, and other media to spread information about pesticides, health effects, and the legal rights of farm workers in the Midwest. This aspect of FLRP is part of assisting the FLOC organizers, but we hope that the project will also generate mutual participation and enthusiasm on the part of organizers and farmworkers. . . .

In summary, NWAG attempts to use our knowledge and skills as agricultural scientists to contribute to work that promotes progressive social change, such as strengthening the position of Midwestern farm labor or Nicaraguan revolutionary independence. It is important to take our direction from meaningful collaboration with the organizations with which we ally, rather than attempt to impose our misconceptions upon them, as "experts" have too often done in the past. In this way

NWAG hopes to pursue not only science for the people, but also science with the people and by the people.

Statement of Purpose for Collaboration Between NWAG and the Nicaraguan Government

1. To aid the Nicaraguans in their efforts to develop agriculture in a manner which is in harmony with the revolution's goals, by: a. increasing yields, both in terms of food production and economic value, b. reducing the vulnerability of the agricultural system to natural disaster and economic uncertainty, c. developing a technology which protects the health of agricultural workers and the environment.

2. To help develop the scientific community in Nicaragua so as to achieve intellectual autonomy free of dependence on imperialist science, promote the integration of theoretical research with the achievement of practical goals, and encourage the kind of science which can see technical problems in their social and human context.

3. To express our own solidarity with the Sandinista revolution and defy any blockade which the U.S. government may impose.

Resolution from FLOC's 2nd Constitutional Convention

Whereas, many of the pesticides used in the Midwest are highly toxic, both in terms of acute toxicity and in terms of long range effects, such as cancer and birth defects, and

Whereas, farmworkers are continuously exposed to pesticides, and suffer from illness, disability and reduced life span, and

Whereas, farmworkers are often exposed to pesticides without their knowledge and consent, and

Whereas, cases of pesticide poisoning typically go untreated, unreported and uncompensated, and

Whereas, the use of pesticides results in environmental destruction and

Whereas, effectiveness of pesticides is often questionable, and can even make pest problems worse,

Therefore be it resolved that FLOC denounces the indiscriminate and unnecessary use of pesticides in the Midwest, and

Further be it resolved that FLOC calls for strong regulations regarding the use of pesticides, exposure of farmworkers to pesticides and compensation in the case of pesticide poisoning,

And be it further resolved that FLOC voices support for the development of alternative methods of pest control,

Furthermore be it resolved that a permanent task force be developed by the Farm Labor Research Project and FLOC to study pesticide effects, to educate our members and to take action in appropriate ways on this crucial issue.

References

1. See R. Navarro, "Is Appropriate Technology the Solution for the Third World?" *Science for the People,* vol. 13 no. 3, 1981, p. 13.
2. J. Vandermeer, "Agricultural Research and Social Conflict," *Science for the People,* vol. 13 no. 1, 1981, p. 5.
3. R. Burbach and T. Drainin, "Nicaragua's Revolution." *NACLA,* vol. 14 no. 3, 1980, pp.2–35.
4. For history of FLOC see: P. Downs, R. Rice, J. Vandermeer, and K. Yih, "Migrant Workers, Farmers, and the Mechanization of Agriculture: the Tomato Industry in Ohio." *Science for the People,* vol. 11 no. 3, 1979, p. 7. B. Schultz, "FLOC Update: The Struggle Continues." *Science for the People,* vol. 14 no. 1, 1982, p. 5.
8. Friedland *et al, Manufacturing Green Gold.*
9. R. H. Morrish, "Crop Mixture Trials in Michigan," *Michigan State College Agricultural Station Special Bulletin* 256, 1934.
10. M. K. Hansen and S. J. Risch, "Food and Agriculture in China, Part I," *Science for the People,* vol. 11 no. 3, 1979, pp. 39–45.
11. M. R. Rao and R. W. Willey, "Evaluation of Yield Stability in Intercropping: Studies on Sorghum/Pigeonpea," *Experimental Agriculture,* vol. 16 pp. 105–12.
12. R. van den Bosch, *The Pesticide Conspiracy,* Anchor Press, 1980.
13. *Ibid.*

Acknowledgements: Kathy Yih and John Vandermeer participated in writing parts of this article. This article, in part, is condensed from "The Tomato is Red" in: *The Tomato is Red,* edited by J. Silvertown and L. Birke to be published by Pluto Press.

EDITORS' NOTES

1. Richard Levins, "How Cuba is Going Ecological," *Capitalism, Nature, Socialism* 16, no. 3 (2005): 7–26, 21.
2. See, e.g., Jack Ralph Kloppenburg, *First the Seed: The Political Economy of Plant Biotechnology, 1492–2000* (Madison: University of Wisconsin Press, 2004); Deborah Fitzgerald, *The Business of Breeding: Hybrid Corn in Illinois, 1890–1940* (Ithaca, NY: Cornell University Press, 1990).
3. Connie Phillips and Sue Tafler, personal communication.
4. See also "The People Who Produce Your Food Speak," *Science for the People* 11, no. 3 (May–June, 1979): 23–34.
5. Doug Boucher and Isadore Nabi, "The New World Agriculture Group: A History," *Radical Science* 17 (1985): 88–104. (Note that Isadore Nabi was a pen name for Richard Levins.)
6. Science for the People, *China: Science Walks on Two Legs* (New York: Avon Books, 1974); Michael K. Hansen and Stephen J. Risch, "Food and Agriculture in China, Part I," *Science for the People* 11, no. 3 (May–June, 1979), 39–45; Stephen Risch and Michael Hansen, "Food and Agriculture in China, Part II," *Science for the People* 11, no. 4 (July–August, 1979): 33–38.
7. Michael Stewart Foley, *Front Porch Politics: The Forgotten Heyday of American Activism in the 1970s and 1980s* (New York: Hill and Wang, 2013), 207–10.
8. "About this Issue," *Science or the People* 11, no. 3 (May–June 1979): 4.
9. Hansen and Risch, "Food and Agriculture in China, Part I," 42.

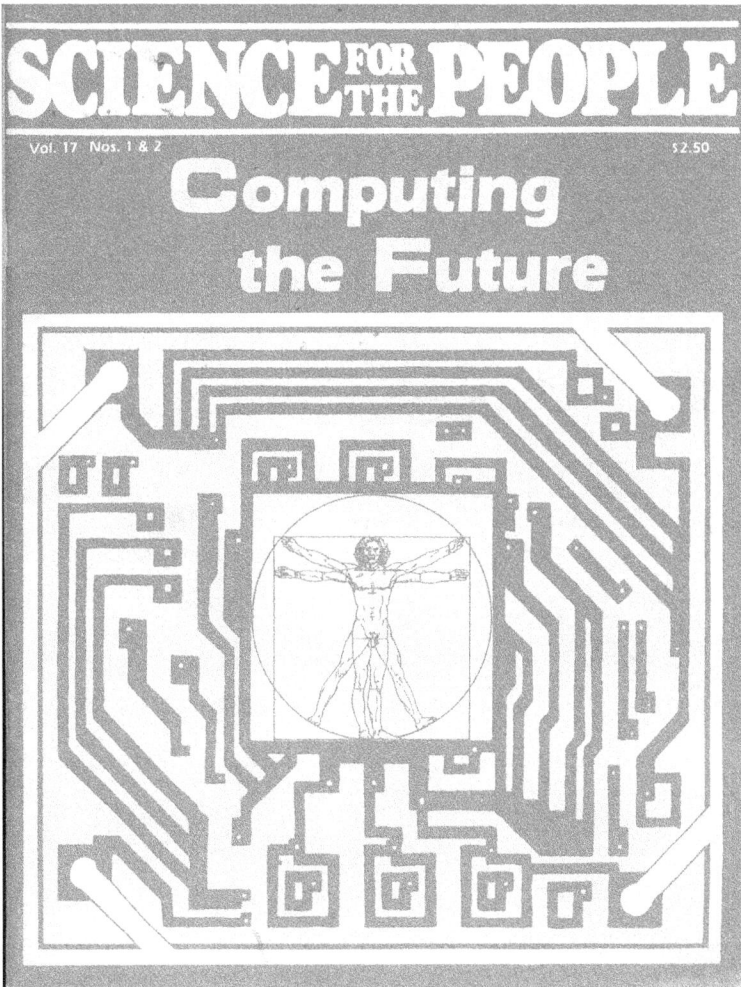

FIGURE 7. Cover of *Science for the People* 1–2 (January–February, March–April 1985). Illustration by Wen-ti Tsen, whose work periodically appeared in *Science for the People* publications. Reprinted here with permission from Wen-ti Tsen.

CHAPTER 7

Technology

Thomas Conner
and
Sigrid Schmalzer

The centrality of technology for Science for the People can be seen in the almost immediate need upon the group's founding to amend its initial name, Scientists for Social and Political Action, to Scientists and Engineers for Social and Political Action. Consistent with their Marxist predecessors, early SftP activists considered the usual privileging of science over technology (or "pure" over "applied" research) to have arisen from an elitist failure to recognize the contributions of people who work with their hands. At the same time, SftP's Marxist perspective on technology differed in fundamental ways from that of some other 1970s activists, who followed E. F. Schumacher's 1973 treatise *Small Is Beautiful* in embracing local, low-tech solutions to meet basic human needs. For most SftP members, large-scale industrial technologies were not inherently problematic, but rather problematic specifically when pursued under capitalism. Over the course of SftP's history, the organization's members contributed to popular debates over the role of technology in American society and the world, and organized local initiatives to supply fellow social justice activists with useful technology and technological assistance.

One of the first technology-related SftP projects was the Boston chapter's Technical Assistance Program (TAP). In accordance with the aims of one of the SftP's foundational documents, TAP sought to provide "technical assistance to movement organizations and oppressed people" (Document 1.1).

The TAP mini-manifesto excerpted here originally appeared as a one-page pitch in *Science for the People* magazine (Document 7.1). The document demonstrates TAP's intention to hack the anti-democratic nature of technology development by providing assistance and expertise directly to "the people"—namely, to groups organizing for social change.

Meanwhile, SftP writings highlighted a theme familiar to social critics since Marx's time: the threat technology posed to working people. David Chidakel's "The New Robots" (Document 7.2) captured a 1970s articulation of this longstanding concern. Considered from a present-day vantage point, Chidakel's article was remarkably prescient: as predicted, we are now ringing up our groceries in unstaffed self-check aisles and professionals use personal computers rather than the typing pool. Again, however, SftP members never took an anti-technology stance. The question, ultimately, came down to what technologies would most benefit humanity, particularly in an ideal socialist society.

During the 1980s, American society began to renew its faith in the fundamental goodness of technology. SftP consistently sang a different tune, however, articulating an increasingly sophisticated perspective on technology that insisted on the primacy of social and political processes. It was not alone. In this, and also in its subversion of the science/technology hierarchy, it worked in tandem with the growing academic field of science and technology studies (STS). SftP routinely stressed that technology—as not just a physical product of humanity but an element of its society—embodied social values. The point was not just that our communication is mediated increasingly by technology, or that our work is accomplished increasingly with technological assistance, or that our security depends increasingly on technological armaments and defenses. As SftP member and STS scholar Philip Bereano put it in a 1984 *Science for the People* article, "Most of us have been brought up to believe that the term 'technology' refers to physical artifacts, like a typewriter or a heating system. But that view is not sufficiently helpful in analyzing technologies in terms of their social, political, cultural and economic ramifications. I prefer to define 'technologies' as the things and the institutional (the social, political, cultural and economic) mechanisms which produce them and are affected by them."[1] The three SftP articles from the 1980s excerpted here all similarly contributed to ongoing conversations in STS about how science and technology are embedded in particular social and political contexts.[2]

In "Emerging Technologies" (Document 7.3), SftP member Seth Shulman stressed the plasticity of technology—that technology is not inert but rather always in development—and emphasized that each phase of development takes place behind the closed doors of private corporations or secretive governments. Quoting James Carroll's watershed 1971 article, "Participatory Technology," Shulman argued that this reality led to the appearance of a "technological imperative" that convinced people that opposition to harmful new technologies was futile.[3] As an alternative, Shulman offered a "blueprint" to guide communities in their struggles to gain democratic control over newly emerging technologies.

The final two documents included here further developed the themes of technology, social control, and social embeddedness. Bertram Bruce's article "Taking Control of Educational Technology" (Document 7.4)—from the 1985 *Science for the People* magazine double issue "Computing the Future," on impacts of the ongoing "computer revolution"—tackled the introduction of computers to grade-school classrooms. Bruce saw computers neither as necessarily improving education nor as necessarily undermining it; rather, he emphasized that "they are simply tools which can amplify the power people have and the social relations they engage in." He also suggested that computers could shape "social organization" in the classroom, either by placing students in a passive role with the computer as "drill master," or (in more progressive settings) by fostering mutual learning among students sharing a computer.

David Dickson's 1987 speech "Choosing Technology" (Document 7.5) reflected on the roles of science and technology in the global political order. Again, this is a special concern for Marxists, who are suspicious of technological "solutions" that fail to transform social and political relationships. Like Shulman, Dickson referred repeatedly to the role of "the public" in technological decision making. In this regard, SftP was part of a growing dialogue among academics and policy makers that became dominated by the "public understanding of science" movement in the mid-1980s.[4] However, SftP's understanding of "the public" was far more carefully differentiated than that of their liberal counterparts with respect to class, gender, and race. Their approach to the "technological imperative," too, was infused with a far greater attention to the workings of economic and military pressure. Here, as everywhere for SftP, the key analytical concept was power.

Document 7.1

Herb Fox, "Technical Assistance Program," *Science for the People* 2, no. 2 (August 1970): 7.

This is a one-page solicitation from Herb Fox, one of Science for the People's early organizers, on behalf of the Boston chapter's Technical Assistance Program (TAP), an initiative aimed at providing local community activist groups with technology, expertise, and solidarity. TAP projects included teaching basic auto repair skills, offering research helpful to community members protesting a new highway cutting through their neighborhoods, and providing electrical power to a Black Panther Party free medical clinic. The program flamed out quickly because TAP members spent more time performing unpaid work than teaching those they were assisting. Nonetheless, TAP's efforts embodied SftP's lofty goal of bringing technology and expertise to grassroots social movements.

TAP is one of the ways to put the slogan "Science for the People" into practice. In response to the expressed needs of community groups and in an attempt to give technical people a chance to counteract the frustration that comes from being misused by society, Boston-area SESPA set up TAP.

TAP's charter is to assist community political groups in situations where technical experience and knowledge can make their struggle more effective. TAP recognizes the truth of Huey Newton's famous statement, "The spirit of the people is greater than the man's technology." TAP proposes that one way that the spirit of the people is greater than the man's technology is in the capability of the "spirit" to move technically trained people to bring the "man's technology" to the side of the people's struggle.

TAP recently helped people in a working-class town in the Boston area. The people found themselves waging an uphill struggle against the "highway lobby." Another one of those obnoxious highways that destroy homes and are reducing our country to a mass of asphalt, rubber and steel was to go through the people's community. The Department of Public Works lied to the people by showing plans for a sunken highway, whereas they really started work on an elevated highway.

As usual, the community destroyers relied on the residents' ignorance and inaction, but a group of residents got together to inform their neighbors on what was in store for them and to rally opposition to the highway. Recordings of the sounds of elevated highways and of the sounds of sunken highways were provided by TAP; they set up sound equipment at public meetings. When bulldozers came the community was aroused; men, women and children put their bodies in front of the construction equipment. Construction is now held up as litigation proceeds against the Department of Public Works.

Local radical groups are now beginning to use TAP. Newsreel had a car fixed, and the Boston chapter of the Black Panther Party received information and technical assistance. A new and free community medical clinic needed electrical power because those inveterate servants of the people—the city fathers and the Edison Company—found some excuse for denying them power (ha!). TAP helped in obtaining, operating and maintaining an electrical generator. TAP has also assisted the Panthers in evaluating, purchasing and maintaining a truck and in setting up outdoor sound equipment and communications equipment.

Demystification of technology is one of TAP's objectives. In every instance technical helpers explain to the people receiving the help what they are doing and why. The aim is to pass on information and technique so that community people themselves can continue the technical work. So much so-called "specialized knowledge" is just jargon or knowing which catalogue to look in.

Organizing informal instruction groups is next on TAP's agenda. An automobile repair group is proposed where people will learn by doing. They hope to take on the repair of a vehicle to be used by a community group or the repair of vehicles needed by poor people.

Another project in the planning stage is the design and fabrication of carrier-current transmitters—an electronic device that permits broadcasting by using the electrical wiring of a building or housing project as an antenna.

Looking for a chance to use your Science for the People?

SIGN UP FOR TAP (Technical Assistance Project)

If you want to work on Sound Systems, Automobiles, Communications Equipment, Chemical Analysis, Self-Defense Mechanisms write: Science for the People . . .

Theoretically trained? We'll help you learn practical skills!

Document 7.2

David Chidakel, "The New Robots," *Science for the People* 7, no. 6
(November 1975): 6–9, 30.

In this article, engineer David Chidakel devoted special attention to the challenges that an increasingly automated workplace posed to labor. Running through the piece are two common themes in Marxist critiques of technology: first and most obvious is the practical threat that new technologies in capitalist societies pose to workers' employment; second and more subtle is the dehumanizing effect that robotic technologies have on workers, who then become even more deeply alienated from their own labor under capitalism. Though alarmist in tone, many of Chidakel's predictions about a technological takeover, including the creation of unstaffed self-check grocery checkout aisles, are now reality.

A new wave of technological change is gathering—only this time it threatens to be more than a new arrangement of control systems and conveyors. The "robot" is finally upon us and may condemn to the scrap heap people who are working not only in factories but in offices and in various service industries formerly thought immune to mechanization.

This threat is not from the robot of pulp science fiction—not from the robot that escapes its makers and builds an army of its own kind to take over the earth with clanking arms and legs and a rusty wit. This threat is from machines that lift heavy loads, do a variety of tasks with breathtaking speed and accuracy, never talk back or go on strike and seldom rest. If it is any consolation—their "intelligence" is generally not very high and it is debatable whether they are at all intelligent. What is not debatable is that they can take over tasks that humans do.

Robots are being employed as seamstresses, printers, welders, warehouse workers, armaments assemblers, clerks and machinists. At the supermarket they will soon be checking and bagging groceries; at MIT a funny little machine is said to swoosh down corridors unattended while it sweeps, mops, and waxes with a cheery lack of interest in the horrified expressions of surprised pedestrians.

None of these robots has a very human appearance. No purpose is served by adding a complete set of arms, legs, knee caps and "heads." They are really special-purpose machines that can do what automation has been heading for all along. It is just that they can act more independently, exercise more "judgment," and function in a non-mass-production situation. . . .

[M]anagement may find these sexless machines particularly seductive. Could this be their long-imagined "final solution" to the labor "problem"? What would the right to strike mean under conditions of advanced automation? Telephone workers have already found that the automatic "direct dial" equipment has diminished the leverage of a strike because a few supervisors can keep the entire operation functioning.

Can robotics increase the ability of private business to withstand public resistance? When DOW Chemical's napalm manufacture became a symbol of national disgust over the Vietnam intervention, DOW stressed that only a "handful" of workers were involved in the napalm production—a "negligible" activity they told us. As a result of advanced technology, of course, a few "reliable" workers could produce a hell of a lot of napalm! But it was their numbers, not their machinery or their production figures that was publicized by DOW . . .

Obviously this is a critical question. *Will* robotics throw people out of work? Will this mean starvation for many or can the labor movement mount a major battle as it did at the turn of the century for an eight-hour day? What *kind* of a battle could turn robotics into a benefit for workers threatened by unemployment?

It is still the case that between fifty and seventy-five percent of the US output of manufactured parts is produced in individual batches of 50 or less. This very fact seemed to make this bastion of industry (employing forty percent of the industrial labor force) immune to automation; but robotics has changed all that. Independent of assembly lines, modern robots are capable of replicating with great speed and accuracy the kind of work an individual assembler, inspector, or machinist did.[12]

Likewise in the service sector, formerly "safe" jobs are gravely threatened. Clerical and secretarial jobs may well be virtually eliminated in the next 20 years by the "paperless office" where record keeping will be all electronic. Vincent Giuliano of Arthur D Little, Inc., says that the use of paper in business should be declining within five years. Such a system would involve TV-display terminals with a keyboard at the desks of executives.[13] . . .

One by one, jobs that could be done by people with a low level of training are being encroached upon by machinery. The nervous joke that "you can be replaced by a machine" has turned into an ominous reality and there is the very real fear that we are developing an "underground of the unskilled"[17]—a growing population of people without hope (disproportionately blacks and women) who are forced to live in the twilight of a "private enterprise" technology. . . .

What are we to think about these latest developments in what some writers call "the second industrial revolution"? Under Capitalism, machinery can take away your job. That's clear. Potentially, of course, it can also provide "leisure," but such "leisure" would have to be fought for and won.

Under socialism, will robotics ultimately prove to be the key to the "workless" society? Is this a desirable concept? Would a well-planned social system be able to turn Unimates [robots produced by Unimation, Inc.] into "Serve-The-People-Mates"? Or are robots only a new form of waste?

Certainly the introduction of robotics under capitalism is an unsettling thing. As with other important technological developments, it may put another lurch in the unsmooth flow of history. Jaeger's prophesy that "these things take care of themselves" can probably have meaning only if the working class is prepared to take care of itself in the face of the peculiar logic of machine-oriented capitalism.

What will be the future of robotics? Will robots increasingly resemble their makers—walking and talking and curtsying and getting angry? None of this is impossible, but E. William Merrium of B. B. & N. doesn't think that a "truly intelligent robot" is likely before the year 2000.[19]

At the moment it is the threat from the dumb ones that must concern us.

References

12. "Computer Managed Parts Manufacture," Nathan Cook, *Scientific American,* February, 1975, p. 25.
13. "The Office of the Future," *Business Week,* June 30, 1975. p. 48.
17. Ben B. Seligman, *Most Notorious Victory,* The Free Press, New York, 1966, p. 203.
19. "Robbie the Robot—R.I.P.," David Black, *Harpers,* December 1973, p. 10.

Document 7.3

Seth Shulman, "Emerging Technologies: Toward a Blueprint for Action," *Science for the People* 17, no. 3 (May–June 1985): 16–20.

In this article, *Science for the People* magazine editorial coordinator Seth Shulman argued against the widely held belief that technology develops independently of political and economic structures. Shulman highlighted genetic engineering as a particular example of an emerging technology that posed potential unknown threats to humanity (also see Chapter 4, "Biology and Medicine"). Calling for a democratization of technology, Shulman proposed an alternative model of technological development in which the public would participate in shepherding new products into society.

Caught up as we all are in technology's "march of progress," it is easy to feel that we are merely helpless observers. Because of its seemingly unstoppable nature, some writers have called the progression of technology "autonomous," as though it proceeded somehow with a life of its own outside of our control, and in many ways this depiction seems accurate.[1] Even looking hard for historical analogies, one can find only a small handful of cases where a capability came along—a new technology emerged—and people had the good sense, after assessing its benefits and risks, to refrain from exploiting it.

Unfortunately, a review of the history of emerging technologies shows plainly that all too often we have failed to effectively guide the development and use of our own technological tools, failed to ask the right questions, or to ask them early enough. This collective inability to control our technologies is exhibited in some of the major environmental and social problems of our time such as rampant toxic waste, or vast arsenals of nuclear weapons. Jacques Ellul has stated: "There can be no human autonomy in the face of technical autonomy."[2] As we stand at the threshold of some of the most powerful technological capabilities to date, history seems certainly to have borne out Ellul's warning. To ensure our collective freedom, even our survival, we need to find ways to assert our human autonomy, our control over our own capabilities.

The emergence over the past decade of new gene-splicing techniques—genetic engineering—may well be the latest "autonomous" technological revolution. And yet, since their development, these genetic engineering techniques have already caused considerable debate. Initial questions about potential biohazards among a small coterie of scientists led to a two-year, worldwide moratorium on certain types of genetic experiments. This two-year halt allowed some time for people to assess risks and implications and was a rare and important case of people exerting direct control over the development of a new technology. The arrival of this new technology also has caused serious concern among members of the broader community, and sparked debate on the need for mechanisms to monitor and regulate its appropriate growth and development. The public concerns are as real as the technological implications are vast.

As the field of genetic engineering has quickly spawned a burgeoning biotechnology industry, so have its direct social and political implications been thrust upon a largely unwitting society. Many of these processes are well under way. Established multinational firms representing most major industries are already actively pursuing genetically engineered products including everything from less-watery tomatoes for use in ketchup to vaccines for herpes and other diseases. According to one estimate, genetically spliced drugs alone will reap an annual $15 billion for the pharmaceutical industry by the year 2000.[3] But this is just part of a bigger picture, which involves a dramatic array of products and processes on corporate agendas for agribusiness, the food and fragrance industry, chemical manufacturing, the medical establishment, and the military.

Questions of Control

Throughout the development of biotechnology the key questions have been political questions of control: who will make the decisions about how this technology is used, what mechanisms will be established to oversee it, and what provisions within this system will protect the interest of the general public against dangerous or untoward implications.

While the issue of biotechnology is unique in many respects, these questions are not. They apply when virtually any new technology comes along. The answers that we can find to these questions of regulation and control should and inevitably will draw upon previous examples of attempts to channel the direction of emerging technologies and to legislate safeguards against undesired implications.

In this context, what are our options for regulation and control? What are the possibilities for involvement by concerned individuals outside of the scientific community? And what kinds of historical analogies can we draw in this specific case? These are all questions that need attention.

Participatory Technology

In 1971, James Carroll wrote, in his article "Participatory Technology":

> To an indeterminate extent, technological processes in contemporary society have become the equivalent of a form of law—that is, an authoritative or binding expression

of social norms and values from which the individual or group may have no immediate recourse. What is at issue in the case of the computer and privacy, the supersonic transport and noise levels, highway development and the city, the antiballistic missile and national security, and the car and pollution is the authoritative allocation of social values and benefits in technological form.[4]

The issue Carroll addressed was certainly not new, but the way he couched it was. Carroll maintained that important choices were being made—essentially passed into law—often with little or no public debate of their implications, because the established systems treated them de facto as "technical" rather than social and political issues. One clear problem he identified is that, for a variety of reasons, the public has lacked adequate access to the decision-making processes involved in regulating new technologies. What Carroll was reminding us is that this needn't be the case; the public could have a significant say in such matters.

There is little doubt that the seemingly irreversible nature of technology—the "technological imperative," as some have termed it—is closely linked to the vested political and economic interests that help to propel it along. These connections have been well established in a variety of areas by many authors in the pages of *Science for the People* and elsewhere over the years.[5] One need look only at the growth of the transportation or communication networks in the United States, not to mention the military industrial complex, for clear examples. . . .

Encouraging Debate Early

The fixed nature of established technologies speaks to the vital necessity for input when it can make a difference: during the formative stages of a technology's development. While features often do become "locked in," it is important to note that technologies do not actually evolve that way. In the case of the typewriter, for example, for approximately forty years prior to the first Remington, there were dozens of prototypes of typewriter machines, each with wildly varied characteristics and keyboards. The state of affairs is not uncommon but rather is the norm as a technology emerges. As Edward Yoxen has noted in his book *The Gene Business*, new technologies

> arise through endless rounds of conjecture, experiment, persuasion, appraisal and promotion. They emerge from chains of activity, in which at many points their form and existence is in jeopardy. There is no unstoppable process that brings inventions to the market.[7]

Again, however, while the lesson is clear, its implications are fraught with difficulty. Often the public is not informed about the advent of a new technology until it is already established. In such cases, public input is forced into a reactive role, and debate is often polarized. Clearly, to have effective input during the formative stages of an emerging technology requires an informed, participatory public. In addition, however, it may also necessitate governmental or independent bodies that can monitor technical fields and raise questions of social and political implications.

Many authors have stressed the importance of viewing technologies themselves as social systems rather than simply artifacts.[8] When seen in this light, it becomes clearer what types of social arrangements a technology implies. This perspective can be important in predicting a technology's development early on, and can also help to frame the social and political questions effectively. While scientists and technical professionals often can best understand the technical aspects of a developing technology, the public invariably serves as the catalyst for open dialogue and debate of the questions raised by a new technology. In addition, even on the most technical of issues, it has been shown repeatedly that input from the public can be informed, and innovative. From a political perspective it is vital to involve as diverse a group as possible in the decision-making process, especially those most immediately at risk.[9] . . .

Encourage Debate Early: To be effective we must try to encourage debate during the formative stages of an emerging technology. Unfortunately, although there has been a good deal of debate, some of it public, on the issue of recombinant DNA technology to date, the formative stages of this technology may have already passed to a good degree. Many of the issues raised are clearly not settled, however, and people should do everything they can to inform themselves about the implications for human gene manipulation, for biological warfare, for agriculture and livestock, for pharmaceuticals, etc.

Involve Diverse Groups: A central tenet of democracy is that parties involved should have a say in decision-making. In the case of emerging technologies, it is vital to involve as diverse a group as possible in the decision-making process, especially those most immediately affected and those at risk. The Cambridge Experimental Review Board in the early debate on the safety of recombinant DNA techniques established to many the public's ability to have important, informed say on these issues. This group, made up entirely of laypeople, was effective in setting landmark policy in this area.[19]

Avoid Self Regulation: The economic demise of nuclear power exhibited in the WPPSS (Washington Public Power Supply System) loan default in Washington, or the chemical industry's fiascos such as Hooker Chemical's Love Canal or Union Carbide's Bhopal, India, have for many effectively illustrated the lesson of industry's dismal failure at self-regulation. Nonetheless, setting up regulatory bodies that can effectively serve as watchdogs is not always easy. Academic scientists are very often tied to industry concerns. Clearly public input is crucial in this area, as well, and much more needs to be learned about the establishment of appropriate mechanisms for setting national priorities. In biotechnology the time is now to establish such watchdog, regulatory bodies, and debate on this topic is well underway.

Monitor Potential Hazards: Another clear lesson from past emerging technologies is the importance of requiring the ongoing monitoring of potential health and environmental hazards. Early on in the debate on recombinant DNA, members of Science for the People called for the establishment of an independent tumor registry for workers in rDNA labs, including janitorial, and other effected [*sic*] groups. Such a registry has not been established, but historical precedent points evermore clearly to its need. The recent disclosure of Department of Energy findings of significantly higher cancer rates for workers in U.S. nuclear facilities is only the latest example of the importance of staying on top of such demographic data. In the case of biotechnology, such a registry would require minimal costs, and could help to flag potential hazards early. Requiring industry to foot the bill for such a plan seems to be an effective and reasonable way to cover the costs.

Initial Guidelines Aren't Final: Too often, we consider serious questions about a new technology settled after only the initial round of dialogue and testing. The need to establish regular, and ongoing public forums for the reexamination of initial guidelines is clear. This type of reexamination can take place at public hearings, at sessions of scientific meetings, or in independent, activist gatherings. In the current state of genetic engineering, we are witnessing a tremendous pace of technological change.

Because of this, regulations need to be continually reassessed. (As Gerry Waneck's article in this issue discusses, this is particularly true of health hazards in this area.)

Require Social and Environmental Impact Statements: When planners undertake a new project, blueprints of every system involved, and environmental impact statements are required before ground is broken. Increasingly many involved in the growth and development of new technologies are seeing the need to institute similar requirements. Indeed, the current court battle requiring an environmental impact statement from the National Institutes of Health (NIH) before field testing of recombinant DNA research is undertaken is a case in point. It is clear that we are moving in this direction, but there is much further to go. A major part of our collective blueprint for action is to call for such assessments of the implications of new, emerging technologies before they become fixed, irrevocable parts of our lives.

Seth Shulman is the Editorial Coordinator for SftP, and a freelance writer on science issues.

References

1. Langdon Winner, *Autonomous Technology,* MIT Press, 1977.
2. Jacques Ellul, *The Technological Society,* Alfred A. Knopf, 1964, p. 38.
3. *Office of Technology Assessment, Commercial Biotechnology: An International Analysis,* 1984.

4. James Carroll, "Participatory Technology," *Science,* 171, Feb. 19, 1971, pp. 648–49.

5. See for example, David Noble "Academia Incorporated," *Science for the People* 15, no. 1; Jack Manno, "The Military History of the U.S. Space Shuttle," *Science for the People* 15, no. 5; and Philip L. Bereano, ed., *Technology as a Social and Political Phenomenon,* John Wiley and Sons, 1976.

7. Edward Yoxen, *The Gene Business,* Harper and Row, 1983, p. 27.

8. See, for example, David Dickson, *The Politics of Alternative Technology,* New York, Universe Books, 1974; David Noble, *Forces of Production,* Alfred A. Knopf, 1984; Philip Bereano, "Technology and Human Freedom," *Science for the People,* Vol. 16, No. 6

9. Sheldon Krimsky, "Beyond Technocracy: New Routes for Citizen Involvement in Social Risk Assessment," in James C. Peterson, ed., *Citizen Participation in Science Policy,* The Univ. of Massachusetts Press, 1984, p. 55.

19. Cambridge Experimentation Review Board, "Guidelines for the Use of Recombinant DNA Molecule Technology in the City of Cambridge," December 21, 1976. For more on the Cambridge Experimentation Review Board, see Sheldon Krimsky, "Regulating Recombinant DNA research," in Dorothy Nelkin, *Controversy: Politics of Technical Decisions,* Sage Publications, 1979, p. 227.

Document 7.4

Bertram Bruce, "Taking Control of Educational Technology," *Science for the People* 17, no. 1–2 (March–April 1985): 37–40.

In this article, information scientist Bertram Bruce critically reflected on the emergent phenomenon of personal computer use in U.S. grade-school classrooms. Critiquing the use of school computers as a means (whether intentional or not) to promote social conformity, Bruce offered ideas on how teachers could incorporate computers into pedagogies aimed at fostering critical thinking, teamwork, communication, and human freedom.

> There is no such thing as a *neutral* educational process. Education either functions as an instrument which is used to facilitate the integration of the younger generation into the logic of the present system and bring about conformity to it, or it becomes "the practice of freedom," the means by which men and women deal critically and creatively with reality and discover how to participate in the transformation of their world.—Richard Shaull[1]

One of the central debates in education is how to prepare students to meet the needs of a technologically oriented society. A companion question concerns the ways technology should be used in teaching traditional subjects. These issues are usually discussed in terms of the efficiency of one teaching method versus another or in terms of how the limited time within the curriculum should be allocated. But prior to addressing those questions, we need to consider a more basic question about the role of computers in education: Will computers make education more of an instrument for bringing about conformity or can they assist "the practice of freedom"?

To address this question, this article takes a practical approach, by considering what computers are and how they might be used most productively in education. The examples show, among other things, that the distinction between learning about computers and learning other subjects through the use of computers is not that useful. More importantly, the examples are intended to suggest some ways to think about both progressive uses of computers in education and the creation of social and political environments in which such uses are more easily realized.

What Role Should Computers Play in Education?

Many people see computers as ideal for the present educational system, in that they can smooth some rough edges: they can protect against "cheating," they can ensure that children don't read materials they are not ready for, they can monitor student progress along pre-defined lines, limit the impact of the "teacher variable" (i.e., the power and importance of the individual teacher), and, perhaps most importantly, they can reduce costs (assuming teachers can be replaced by machines).

The alliance of these considerations with the profit motive has resulted in a tremendous push for computers in schools. Last year, for example, major computer manufacturers, led by Apple Computer, sought substantial tax breaks in return for massive installation of computers in schools. Large school districts are now purchasing computers *en masse*. Boston, for instance, recently reached an agreement with IBM to purchase 800 computers for its schools.[2] Much of this momentum has occurred with little understanding of the eventual uses and consequences of computers in schools.

Parents' legitimate concerns about jobs for their children have also fueled the current computer mania. Many parents believe that if their children learn how to program they will automatically become eligible for high-paid, high-tech jobs, not realizing that most of the employment in the high-tech field is low-paid, non-union factory work.

In contrast, others, such as the Crab-apple group, have taken decidedly negative positions about the current push for computers in schools. They argue that there are societal needs far more pressing than turning every classroom into a high-tech center. Moreover, they see the emphasis on computer programming as a misleading promise about jobs that will not be there. They also see computers as emphasizing piecemeal learning, rather than supporting more holistic, critical or creative education. . . . Finally, some feel that the use of computers in schools needs to be encouraged precisely because it does foster progressive education. . . .

The problem with all of these views is that they tend to locate the source of the computer's power to affect education in the computer itself. Thus we hear that "Computers will teach children to read," or "Computers will turn schools into assembly lines." In fact, computers *per se* do nothing; they are simply tools which can amplify the power people have and the social relations they engage in. In that sense, the positive or the negative consequences realized by computers will be caused by people making use of computers to accomplish ends for change in education.

What Kind of Tool is a Computer?

Although we often associate computers with numbers and the repetitive calculations needed by banks, insurance companies, manufacturers, and so on, the essence of the digital computer lies not in adding columns of numbers but in its function as a tool for creating, manipulating and communicating symbols, in short, as a tool for language and thinking. Many teachers have begun to see this and to use the computer as a tool for expanding children's opportunities to solve problems (using programming languages such as Logo), to develop ideas (using "microworld" simulation programs), to gain access to information (using computer networks and public databases), to explore scientific questions (using statistics programs and computers connected to measuring devices, such as thermometers), to write and to share their writing (using text editors, publishing programs, and networks). This view of computers as a symbol tool emphasizes the creation of contexts in which meaningful activities are encouraged and supported. . . .

The prevalent view of computers for the classroom, however, still seems to be one in which the computer "teaches" by controlling information and managing student efforts. Such uses limit rather than expand children's possibilities for learning. Within this restricted view, computers are seen as useful solely for teaching specific concepts or skills: punctuation, spelling, simple arithmetic calculations, state capitals, subject-verb agreement, etc., or for managing the process of instruction. If we are to go beyond this view we need to rethink some assumptions about how to use computers in the classroom.

One study found that teachers who had a chance to study computer software for use in the classroom argued for software that allowed the student to use the computer as a tool for learning rather than for software that put the computer in the dominant role, with the student pressing buttons on cue. The "teachers saw the enormous pedagogical differences between apparent user control and real user control, between answering questions and formulating them, between recognizing someone else's ideas and creating your own."[3]

Why then do so many classrooms use the computer as a manager or a drill master? One reason, of course, is that much of the pressure to install computers in schools comes from a desire to automate the classroom, to make it more "efficient." This means, in the view of the computer's proponents, that the teacher's role must be diminished and circumscribed; new management controls need to be introduced. Thus, the computer becomes a device to channel student efforts, to measure and control what students do in school. A corollary of this is that teachers are kept out of the decision-making that directly affects them and the students in their classrooms.

Some Ideas for Putting the Computer in its Place

The attempt to make computers into the shop foremen of the classroom has not been universally successful. But there is little support from the educational system or the available software, books, and articles to use computers in more creative and open-ended ways. . . . Below are some observations about how computers relate to education that might help teachers, parents, or learners redress this imbalance and put the computer in its place. . . .

The Computer's Effect on Learning

We often discuss computers in terms of their technological aspects—speed, memory size, functions, etc. and neglect to consider how they fit into a social context. Yet the biggest impact of computers in classrooms may be in terms of the ways they contribute to the social organization of a classroom rather than on how they "teach" specific concepts. For example, it is often asserted that the use of word processors by children will help them become better writers. The argument is that since good writing depends on developing revision skills, a tool which makes revision easier will encourage children to practice revision more. This may well be true, but careful observations of classrooms where word processors are in use have revealed that other factors are also at work.[4]

In a classroom in Hartford, Connecticut, a great amount of revising did occur. But the reasons were not purely technological. Because the computer was a limited resource, students tended to "mill around" the computer waiting for their turn to use it. During that waiting period they would read what others had written and decide to modify their own early drafts. Also they tended to value highly what was written on the computer and felt it was worth the effort to revise. Both of these factors—the opportunity to read others' writing and the value placed on computer writing—contributed to an increased amount of revision, which may, in the end, have helped the children become better writers. Understanding the process that was occurring in that classroom, a teacher might conclude that overall the computer had a positive impact on learning. But it would be important to remember that it was not the computer alone which brought about the changes, but rather the way the teacher and the students organized themselves for learning. . . . The major prerequisites for successful use of the computer are not characteristics of the software or hardware, *per se,* but of the classroom, the teacher, the principal, and the curriculum. . . .

The computer is a powerful educational tool. It can be used to limit children's access to information, to control the way they read and write, and to restrict their modes of learning, or it can allow children to communicate easily with others and to access information in a way that greatly expands their world. If computers are to be worthwhile tools, we must never let computer needs or faulty educational ideas embodied in computer programs come before the needs of children.

Bertram Bruce is a consultant, and has worked on a variety of studies of the prospects and potential for computers in education. He is also a member of Science for the People.

References

1. Shaull, R. Foreword to P. Friere's *Pedagogy of the Oppressed.* New York: The Seabury Press, 1970.
2. "Computers in classrooms," *Boston Globe,* Aug. 6, 1984, p. 18.
3. Olds, H. F., Jr., Schwartz, J. L., & Willie, N. A. *People and Computers: Who Teaches Whom?* Newton, MA: Education Development Center, 1980.
4. Bruce, B., Michaels, S., & Watson-Gegeo, K. "Reviewing the Black History show: How computers can change the writing process." *Language Arts,* in press.

Document 7.5

David Dickson, "Choosing Technology," *Science for the People* 19, no. 5 (September–October 1987): 5–8.

This selection is an adaptation from an address that David Dickson, then a correspondent for *Science* magazine, delivered to Science for the People members at a 1986 conference hosted by the Committee for Responsible Genetics (an SftP offshoot group). After outlining a series of critical questions related to contemporary debates over the role of science in global politics, Dickson sketched a list of "public interest criteria" for technological development that served as an alternative to the prevailing, undemocratic capitalist model of technological innovation. Dickson delivered this address after the January 28, 1986, explosion of the U.S. Challenger space shuttle and the Soviet Union's April 26, 1986, Chernobyl Nuclear Power Plant meltdown. In the aftermath of both disasters, Dickson expressed concern about the limited discussion of broader social and economic factors that may have contributed to these tragedies.

. . . A new politics of science has emerged as a direct product of broader political movements around advanced technology, and particularly around recent developments in microelectronics and biotechnology research. For since scientific knowledge provides the key to these new technologies, control over and access to this scientific knowledge therefore becomes an important goal for any group which seeks the power that these technologies can convey. It is therefore not surprising that this question of access has been highly contested in many recent debates about the social control of science and technology. Some of the key questions which have come to dominate these debates include:

Should the industrial sponsors of university research be allowed to influence the conditions under which the results of the research are published, or given exclusive rights to any patents that result?

Should the military be permitted to prevent the publication of unclassified research which it has paid for, or to choose which foreign nationals should be allowed to take part in the research?

Should government agencies be allowed to prevent foreign scientists from attending scientific conferences?

Should the patent system be revised so that control of patents awarded for publicly funded research is given to the institutions which carried out the research, rather than the public which paid for it?

Will European countries who participate in the construction of the planned space station be able to benefit from all the research that is involved, or only that which they have contributed?

Will those who carry out research projects for the Strategic Defense Initiative be allowed to use the results of that research for their own projects?

Under what conditions should Third World countries be given access to scientific results produced in key areas of strategic research?

In each case, the questions of the terms and conditions of access to scientific knowledge is one of the key points at issue. This question has therefore become central to any debate over establishing public interest criteria for technology. Indeed, we find that a new form of political discourse has been erected around the way that technological research priorities are identified, one that tends to exclude such public interest criteria. Research and development programs are not decided or presented in terms of equity or social need. Rather, they are justified as being necessary to meet two external threats: one economic—the threat of international competition—and the other military.

Supporting this strategy are two ideas which have become articles of faith for both conservative and social democratic governments alike: the "high-technology imperative," which says that if anything can be done with high technology, then it should be done; and the "high-technology fix," which says that for every problem technology causes in the modern world, high technology can guarantee to find an appropriate solution. Together, these two ideas create a mindset that blindly erects a revitalized banner of progress, the *idée fixe* of the new political discourse around science and technology.

The Enlightenment idea that rapid technological expansion was a guaranteed route to social improvement received a severe beating in the 1970s, when science and technology took much of the blame for the ills of the modern world, ranging from the horrors of the Vietnam War to the massive destruction of the natural environment and the outbreak of new work-related diseases. But the idea of science-based progress has now crept back into fashion, and its camp followers, who include most of the scientific community as well as leaders of the industrial and military communities, have done what they can to sustain and promote it.

The social consequences of technology are not ignored in this new discourse. But they are subordinated to the broader imperative of economic and military competition. Technologies are tailored to meet social needs only to the extent that these needs can be reflected in and are compatible with demand expressed through the marketplace. . . .

How does all this relate to public interest criteria for technology? I would like to suggest the following list of criteria that should be used in developing any new technological systems and technology policies:

The technology should be based on social need, and not be determined by either pressure for private profit or for the development of the technology for its own sake.

It should in principle be peace-oriented rather than war-oriented. This is a more difficult criterion than it might appear, embracing as it does the question of whether a strategy of defensive technology can be considered aggressive (as in the case of Star Wars) or nonaggressive (as in the case of several new ideas currently being developed in Europe). Nevertheless, the idea that a technology should not be primarily determined by the needs of the military remains central.

The technology should be job-creating which frequently, although not necessarily, means that it should be labor intensive—rather than job-destroying and capital intensive.

It should be a technology which is satisfying and self-fulfilling to work with, rather than one which the individual finds either personally alienating or socially fragmenting.

The technology should be one which distributes decision-making power as widely as possible in the community, rather than concentrating it in the hands of a narrow elite or powerful sectional interests.

The technology must help to increase the power of women over their lives, rather than concentrate this power in the hands of men.

In national terms, the technology must be one which encourages regional equality, rather than reproducing social and economic disparities between one region and another.

At the same time, the technology must help to enhance regional identity, rather than destroy this identity by reducing it to a single, national norm.

In ecological terms—those in which the alternative technology movements of the early 1970s first learned to express their demands—the technology must encourage a harmonious relationship between humans and the natural environment, rather than require a relationship of exploitation.

This means that the technology must be resource conserving, in the broadest sense, rather than resource intensive.

In the same way, the technology or technical systems must be energy conserving rather than energy intensive. This is not merely a question of energy resources. As the German Greens, among others, have been pointing out, the forms of energy required to meet the needs of an energy-intensive technology (and I am thinking in particular of nuclear technology) also tend to offend several of the other criteria already listed above.

The technology must not have a long-term destructive effect on the global eco-system, a criterion which could be grouped with that requiring environmental harmony, but seen from a slightly different perspective.

Finally, three criteria which will help ensure that technology meets the needs of the Third World. First, it must make maximum use of indigenous resources—including capital and labor resources—rather than import these resources from the outside. The technology must not strengthen the political power of domestic elites but must, as in the developed world, help to spread decision-making throughout the community. Thirdly, the technology must help to reduce rather than accentuate the gap between the rich and the poor countries, between the haves and the have-nots, between the North and the South. . . .

The main point that I want to end with, however, is that as public interest groups develop their strategies for the late 1980s and early 1990s, they must become aware of the way in which most all of the public interest criteria listed above are being broken in one way or another by advanced technologies currently being developed solely in the name of private profit or military power. These technologies tend to be job destroying, alienating to work with, and exploitative of the natural environment. They also tend to concentrate power in the hands of the dominant classes in society—including industrial and military elites—while removing it from women, from minority groups of all kinds, and from any attempt at community-based decision-making.

Furthermore, these technologies often actively encourage social divisions within communities, within and between regions, and between nations. Finally, not only do they drive the wedge in further between the rich and the poor nations of the world, but they also increase the power of elites within these countries and disregard the real, basic needs of large parts of the population.

In developing a public interest agenda for technology over the next few years, we must do what we can to ensure that the various criteria I have described are integrated into any strategy for technological development leading to real social progress, whether at the community, regional, national, or international level.

But we must also remain aware of the powerful political interests that remain opposed to any such strategy for a socially based technology, since this cuts directly across the economic and political goals of those representing those interests. What this means is that any strategy to incorporate public interest criteria into new technologies must be a political strategy that is prepared to confront these narrow interests and eventually supersede them. It will not be an easy task. But ensuring the proper social control of technology is essential for the future of humanity, if not for its very survival.

EDITORS' NOTES

1. Philip Bereano, "Technology and Human Freedom," *Science for the People* 16, no. 6 (November–December 1984), 17–21.
2. For examples of STS scholarship that has continued this conversation, see Edward Woodhouse et al., "Science Studies and Activism: Possibilities and Problems for Reconstructivist Agendas," *Social Studies of Science* 32, no. 2 (2002): 297–319; David J. Hess, *Alternative Pathways in Science and Industry: Activism, Innovation and the Environment in an Era of Globalization* (Cambridge, MA: MIT Press, 2007); Joseph R. Herkert, "Engineering Ethics and Its Subcultures," in *Integrating the Sciences and Society: Challenges, Practices, and Potentials*, ed. Harriet Harman, 51–69 (Bingley, UK: Emerald Group, 2008).
3. J. Carroll, "Participatory Technology," *Science* 171, no. 3972 (February 19, 1971): 647–53.
4. For a critical analysis of this movement, see Alan Irwin and Brian Wynne, eds., *Misunderstanding Science? The Public Reconstruction of Science and Technology* (Cambridge: Cambridge University Press, 1996).

What can one man do, my friend
What can one man do
To fight pollution in the air
That's closing in from everywhere?

There is one thing you can do, my friend.

SMASH CAPITALISM

FIGURE 8. In this image from *Science for the People* 6, no. 1 (January 1974), SftP clipped a photograph and text from an American Oil Company advertisement and then replaced the discussion that followed, in which the company congratulated itself for manufacturing lead-free gasoline, with the two-word answer: "Smash Capitalism." "Smash Capitalism," *Science for the People* 6, no. 1 (January 1974). For the original advertisement, see, for example, *Life*, April 10, 1970, p. 2.

CHAPTER 8

Energy and Environment

Ben Allen,
Alyssa Botelho,
and
Daniel S. Chard

Though Science for the People emerged at a time when climate change was not yet on environmental activists' radar, the organization's critiques on energy and environmental issues are highly relevant for today's climate justice movement. During the 1970s, energy and the environment became focal points for national politics, international affairs, and global resistance movements. SftP engaged in public discussions surrounding the establishment of the U.S. Environmental Protection Agency in 1970, the Organization of Arab Petroleum Exporting Countries' 1973–74 oil embargo, and the growing international anti-nuclear movement of the late 1970s. Amidst these events, SftP sought to develop a radical vision of science that could serve society's energy needs while maintaining sustainable ecosystems. While liberals typically sought technological fixes, SftP identified these problems as social and political in origin. Members argued that solutions required not only the development of sustainable solar and wind energy technology, but also fundamental political transformation—namely, the abolition of racism, sexism, militarism, and class oppression. In addition to intervening in popular debates on energy and the environment, SftP members participated in a variety of organizations seeking environmental justice and alternatives to fossil fuel and nuclear energy. Several SftP chapters also had Energy and Environment Groups that contributed articles to the magazine and reported back on activism in their local areas.

In SftP's early years—as Presidents Richard Nixon and Gerald Ford sought a massive expansion of nuclear power plants in the United States—the

organization critiqued the nuclear industry's ties to the military and sought
to expose the false narrative that nuclear power was a peaceful mode of
energy production. At the December 1970 meeting of the American Association for the Advancement of Science (AAAS), SftP members disrupted a
speech by Glenn Seaborg, trailblazing nuclear chemist and director of the
United States Atomic Energy Commission (AEC). During their mock indictment of Seaborg for the crime of "Science against the People," SftP activists
labeled the AEC as the place where "megadeath development and radiation
pollution development are directed."[1] In 1976 and 1977, SftP members joined
with the Clamshell Alliance, a New England based anti-nuclear organization,
to protest the construction of the Seabrook Station Nuclear Power Plant on
the coast of New Hampshire. On August 1, 1977, SftP members were among
more than 1,400 protestors arrested in a nonviolent sit-in at the power plant
construction site—one of the largest acts of civil disobedience in U.S. history.
Although the first reactor at Seabrook was eventually completed and opera-
tionalized, the second planned reactor never went online. Today historians
cite the protests as an important contributor to this outcome.[2]

SftP activists wrote and agitated heavily during the anti-nuclear movement, a core fight for environmentalists during the late 1970s. Two publications excerpted here exemplify the organization's intellectual intervention
on the issue. *Nuclear Power* (Document 8.1), an educational pamphlet produced by SftP's Berkeley chapter, laid out the authors' reasons for opposing nuclear energy and supporting a "yes" referendum vote on a thwarted
ballot initiative that would have required long-term safety monitoring on
all nuclear power plants in California. The pamphlet also sketched a vision
for a democratic nationalization of U.S. energy production that would
decrease the country's reliance on environmentally harmful and taxpayer-
subsidized private fossil fuel and nuclear energy corporations. In 1979, SftP
Stony Brook members Carol Cina and Ted Goldfarb wrote a *Science for the
People* magazine article "Three Mile Island and Nuclear Power" (Document
8.2), in response to the partial meltdown of a nuclear reactor in Dauphin
County, Pennsylvania, earlier that year. The disastrous release of radioactive gases from the plant into the atmosphere—the result of both technical malfunction and human error—is regarded as the worst commercial
nuclear accident in U.S. history.[3] Cina and Goldfarb focused their critique
of the nuclear power industry on the threats of accidental radiation release,
and outlined ideas for building alternative energy programs and expanding
the anti-nuclear movement.

Though the anti-nuclear movement and the Three Mile Island accident helped derail the expansion of nuclear power in the United States, SftP continued to advocate on environmental issues during the 1980s, as President Ronald Reagan and conservatives in Congress worked to undo federal environmental protection measures established during the previous decade. SftP dedicated multiple issues of their magazine to examining the industrial chemical industry's reckless exposure of communities to volatile solvents, mercury, arsenic, PCBs, pesticides, and other harmful substances.[4] *Science for the People* magazine articles also documented the negative consequences of environmental exploitation on local populations and highlighted grassroots movements in the United States and overseas that fought to protect the land against energy, mining, and chemical corporations. Importantly, SftP demonstrated that environmental catastrophes could not be undone by science alone. To succeed, scientists would have to unite with local people organizing in their communities against powerful corporations and sluggish regulatory agencies, such as the activists in Love Canal, New York, and Warren County, North Carolina, who fought for government assistance to clean up local toxic waste disasters in the 1970s and 1980s.[5] These struggles and alliances live on, most dramatically in the water crisis in Flint, Michigan, where government officials were indicted on felony charges of conspiracy and false pretense in the wake of fierce activism from scientists, healthworkers, and locals—but not before thousands of children became victims of lead poisoning.[6] The final document included in this chapter, J. Larry Brown and Deborah Allen's 1983 *Science for the People* magazine article "Toxic Waste and Citizen Action" (Document 8.3), documented the environmental and public health consequences of industrial pollutants released into the air, water, and food supply, and proposed political strategies for growing the environmental justice movement. Today, their vision for developing expertise on the ground is widely reflected in the work of activist organizations, engaged scientists and STS scholars, and even the EPA's "citizen science" program.[7] At the same time, their skepticism about the effectiveness of science alone, absent fundamental political change, also endures. During an interview with the *Chronicle of Higher Education* for example, Marc Edwards, the Virginia Tech scientist who exposed the water crisis in Flint in 2015, bemoaned the "perverse incentive structures" and political risks that prevent more scientists from allying with communities. Aptly, the interview's title paraphrased Edwards's outlook: "Public Science is Broken."[8]

Document 8.1

Science for the People, *Nuclear Power* **(Pamphlet, Berkeley, CA, March 1976), 1–21.**

Nuclear Power, one of SftP's many educational pamphlets, was produced by the Berkeley chapter to provide information about the ongoing legislative battle over California's Nuclear Safeguard Initiative (Proposition 15 in the June 1976 primary election). A "yes" vote for the Initiative, which SftP supported, would have required the state legislature to perform detailed, long-term safety monitoring of all nuclear power plants operating in California. (In the end, the initiative failed to pass—a result many attribute to the powerful nuclear energy lobby.) In addition to providing an overview of stakeholders in the California debate, the pamphlet provided detailed commentary on the benefits and risks (both financial and environmental) of harnessing nuclear technologies. This excerpt highlights the authors' concluding thoughts on the Safety Initiative and their broader vision for a democratic nationalization of U.S. energy production.

We support the use of energy in liberating people from monotonous and physically exhausting work. However, when we are not in control of these resources, energy is used primarily for other purposes. It is wasted, manipulated for profit, used to create meaningless and destructive devices; it is used to destroy our environment. If we, all of us, take control of the energy, we can insure [*sic*—eds.] employment and provide work in areas meaningful to human survival and growth.

Summing up: In this pamphlet we have exposed the scare tactics and threats put forward by the energy monopoly in their campaign to defeat the Nuclear Safeguard Initiative–Proposition 15 on the June ballot.

We see the energy problem, the escalating costs, the safety hazards, the shortage of jobs, and the pollution of our environment as all part of the general mess that the energy monopoly has created in its relentless drive for corporate profits.

We support the Initiative for two reasons:

1. It provides some needed safeguards upon any nuclear operations and may help avoid some real disasters.

2. It is an important first step in the direction of having the people take some control over the system of energy production and distribution in this country. This second item does not appear explicitly on the ballot this year but it is a subject due for much further discussion.

And looking ahead: A great many people in this country are fed up with the way the energy monopoly has been managing things:
they create phony shortages to raise prices;

they rip off the world's resources and create pollution;

they reap enormous profits even in a business recession;

they provide few jobs and tie up large amounts of capital;

they conceal or distort the truth about energy operations.

The government is powerless; the regulatory agencies in Washington protect the industry more than they protect us; and the anti-trust laws are a farce.

Even some establishment politicians have started talking about the idea of nationalizing the country's energy industry. We advocate that such a change must also be fully democratic in structure to make sure that it will be the majority of people who really benefit.

For a bad example, consider Amtrak. The government took over the railroad passenger service from the businessmen who had milked out all the profits and left a decrepit mess. Then they set up a bureaucracy, unresponsive to the public, which treats its workers and customers with as little regard as does any large corporation.

It would be presumptuous of us to try laying out a detailed plan at this time but we can indicate some general principles that we think should be the basis for democratic nationalization of the U.S. energy industry.

The kind of democratic nationalization that we advocate would mean that the industry belongs to the American people and is under their control. Profits would no longer go to the few who now own the corporations; any excess of income over expenses would be used to serve the public, by expanding and improving the industry where most needed. Decisions on energy policy would be made by a body elected democratically and accountable to the public; they would be representatives of the industry's workers and consumers, not bankers, millionaires, and the mangers of other large corporations.

Some features that we anticipate of a democratically nationalized energy industry would be:

A. *Open Information.* Full and truthful information would be given to the public about all matters—energy reserves, costs, safety questions, and all aspects of the policy choices to be considered.

B. *Rational planning.* Under democratic control, long range plans can be drawn up to meet the country's needs with a minimum of waste, duplication of facilities and "surprise" shortages.

C. *Maximum Benefits from Technology.* Released from the profit-motivated control of corporate management, science and technology could expand to create and develop the many alternative energy possibilities that are now neglected by the industry.

D. *Health and Environmental Protection.* Full recognition of the health hazards faced by workers in the industry and of the environmental hazards that affect us all would come from democratic control. Solving these problems would have a top priority.

E. *Employment.* As we, the people, gain control over where capital is to be invested for energy production and distribution, we gain control over the creation of jobs. We gain control over the type of jobs, the working conditions, and we increase the possibility that the jobs will be socially useful and rewarding to the worker.

This is a big order. Democratic nationalization of the energy industry will need a lot of careful planning and it will need a hard political fight to make it a reality. The present monopoly owners will not readily surrender their power over us. But it seems that the time is at hand when enough people in this country see what is at stake and are ready to take on this task.

Members of the S.F. Bay Area project group who worked on this pamphlet: Martin Brown, Pamela FitzGerald, Merry Goodenough, David Hollenbach, Jeff Pector, Charles Schwartz, Joel Swartz.

Document 8.2

Carol Cina and Ted Goldfarb, "Three Mile Island and Nuclear Power," *Science for the People* 11, no. 4 (July–August 1979): 10–17.

This article is an edited version of a SftP pamphlet written in response to the Three Mile Island nuclear power plant disaster in Dauphin County, Pennsylvania, on March 28, 1979. The partial meltdown, which released radioactive gases into the atmosphere, is regarded as the worst commercial nuclear accident in U.S. history. Carol Cina and Ted Goldfarb, two longtime SftP Stony Brook members, delved into the health hazards and economic myths of the nuclear power industry with particular focus on the impact of accidental radiation release, the storage of radioactive waste, and the financial costs of expanding a national nuclear program. The authors then detailed a number of alternative energy programs and articulated a plan for mobilizing a larger, stronger anti-nuclear movement. While the article expresses more optimism about the potential for "clean" coal than environmentalists now entertain, its political analysis of the power industry remains highly relevant.

Even though federal inspectors knew in the early afternoon of Wednesday, March 28 that the uranium core in the reactor at Three Mile Island (3MI) was seriously damaged, two days went by before news of the danger was made public.[1] By not ordering an immediate evacuation, corporation and government officials chose to gamble with the lives of a million people in four surrounding counties in order to protect the reputation of the nuclear power industry.

Media coverage of the 3MI disaster reflected a similar attitude. Although extensive, it generally underplayed the true magnitude of the actual and potential hazards and gave feature coverage to the Nuclear Regulatory Commission (NRC) and other government officials who showed more concern about the future of the nuclear industry than about the health and safety of the people. The nuclear industry and its government supporters are already issuing false threats of electrical blackouts and economic dislocation if the nuclear spigot is closed. Clearly, the nuclear industry will not give up without a struggle. We must be willing to engage them in that struggle. *Now* is the time to end this nuclear madness. . . . This article is designed to contribute to that process of education and to suggest an appropriate course of action.

How close the 3MI reactor came to a complete meltdown we will probably never know. Uncharacteristically, Metropolitan Edison (Met Ed) and officials of the NRC admitted that they were concerned over a period of several days that such a catastrophe might indeed occur. The extreme degree of concern and confusion is reflected in the transcripts of the NRC's secret hearing held during the emergency.[2] . . . The crucial questions in the 3MI disaster—how much radiation was released, and what will be its long-term effects—still remain unanswered.

The Radiation Release

Contaminated steam vented from the reactor containment building carried with it some of the more volatile radioactive atoms which leaked from the damaged reactor rods. The threat to health and life posed by a radioactive substance depends on several factors. These include the amount of material released, the length of time it takes for the substance to disintegrate (measured by half-life, the time required for half the atoms to decay away), the likelihood that the substance will enter the human body through inhalation or through the food we eat or drink, and the fate of the substance once inside the body.

The gases released from 3MI contained radioactive krypton and xenon.[4] These gases were primarily responsible for the high radiation levels recorded in a one to fifteen mile radius of the reactor. Another radioactive substance released was iodine-131. This substance, which can enter the body through milk, other dairy products, and seafood, was a contaminant in both the vented steam and the cooling water which was dumped into the Susquehanna River.[5] It was detected in milk produced near Harrisburg a few days after the reactor failure.[6] Iodine is concentrated by the human thyroid and poses a particularly serious threat to infants and young children. . . .

One of the most irresponsible statements featured in the media coverage of 3MI was the early assurance by HEW Secretary Califano that the radiation released would result in no injuries or deaths among the exposed workers or the two million people living within 50 miles of plant,[7] a statement which has already been modified twice by Califano as of this writing.[8]

Met Ed president Creitz admitted that the amount of radioactive material released during the first several hours of the disaster is not known, since it wasn't monitored.[9] Since then, the NRC and other official agencies which control the information have issued sporadic reports of radiation levels in the area, making it impossible to determine the total public exposure accurately. . . .

Most curious is that in all of the media coverage of the 3MI disaster there seems to have been absolutely no mention of plutonium. This is a strange omission because plutonium is present in *all* nuclear reactors. . . . Could it be that the NRC and other government officials were afraid that public panic might result from calling attention to this super-lethal substance? Surely they must know that a reactor the size of 3MI which had been operating for three months would already contain over 200 pounds of plutonium.[14]

Plutonium is one of the most lethal substances ever produced. . . . [I]f only one ten-millionth of the plutonium in the 3MI reactor core had ended up in the lungs of human beings, over 200,000 cancers would have resulted! What's more, plutonium can also get into the human body through the digestive tract. It ends up in the bones, gonads and other glands where it can cause a wide variety of cancers. Plutonium-239, the form produced in the largest amounts in reactors, remains deadly for over 200,000 years. . . .

The Radioactive Waste Problem

The failure of the nuclear industry and the NRC to take the problem of radioactive waste disposal seriously is one of the clearest examples of their criminal irresponsibility. For years the public has been assured that a safe disposal system was being developed. Recent reports by various government agencies make it clear that no such solution is anywhere in sight.[17] Indeed, a growing number of scientists believe that no acceptable solution will ever be found.

Hundreds of thousands of pounds of radioactive wastes are being produced by the nuclear industry each year. Mining and milling of uranium ore produces huge piles of waste material called tailings. These tailings release lethal radon-222 gas which threatens the lives of mine workers as well as residents of towns near the huge, dusty, windblown piles into which they are heaped. Additional wastes are generated in every other phase of the uranium fuel cycle as well as in the reactors themselves. During the reactor's operation much of the non-radioactive core materials become radioactive due either to neutron absorption or to neutron-induced splitting. Consequently reactors significantly increase the amount of radioactive material in existence. Not only is this an increase in quantity, but much of the radioactive material produced is more deadly than the U-235 with which the reactor was fueled.

So-called low-level wastes are buried in rural sites in six different states. Leakage of radiation into nearby streams has occurred in at least two of the sites.[18]

At Hanford, Washington 500,000 of the 65 million gallons of high-level wastes stored there have already leaked out into the ground only five miles from the Columbia river! . . .

The "Cheap Power" Lie

Although the 3MI disaster has seriously discredited the "safe power" assurances of the nuclear power industry, most people still seem to believe the claims of the utilities and their suppliers that nuclear power is "cheap power." Nothing could be further from the truth.

The costs of building a nuclear power plant have skyrocketed.[20] The reactor being built by the Long Island Lighting Company (LILCO) at Shoreham, New York was initially estimated to cost $262 million. Now, 10 years later, with about 80 percent of the work completed, the current price tag is $1.4 billion. And that estimate was made before 3MI, a disaster which is sure to lead to requirements for additional costly "safety" features. Shoreham may seem like an extreme example but other reactors being built or planned are experiencing similar soaring cost escalations. . . . All this has led Charles Komanoff, the leading economic expert on comparative energy costs who is not connected with the energy industry, to conclude that within the next few years electrical energy generated by nuclear power will be far more costly than electricity produced by other means.[22] He estimates that generating costs for electricity produced by new large nuclear plants will be 9 cents per kilowatt hour (a unit of electrical energy) compared to 6 cents for the same amount of energy from a coal plant equipped with highly effective "scrubbers" to reduce air pollution.

Who Benefits from Nukes

If it isn't safe and it isn't economical, why is it still being pushed? Exxon, Gulf, Getty, Kerr-McGee, General Electric and Westinghouse all have large investments in mining rights or production facilities to protect. But why are the utilities also pushing it? In most states the laws which grant utilities a monopoly over production of electricity also guarantee them a "fair" rate of profit (in some cases 14 percent per year or more!) on all their electrical generating equipment.[23] This means that the more expensive the facility they can convince their supposed regulators to let them build, the more profit they will reap. A study done by the Energy Systems Research Group has shown that New York State utilities continually resort to enormously inflated predictions of demand for electrical energy in order to justify new plant construction.[24]

But there is a catch. In order to reap the windfall profits, the utilities must be able to raise the capital to complete the project and put the plant into operation. The soaring costs are making an increasing number of utilities nervous about not being able to raise the capital to complete the job. In response to the problem of capital costs, the already heavily subsidized utilities and nuclear industry have been lobbying for even more federal and state subsidies. They also want changes in regulations, either to allow an individual utility to charge the public in advance for the full cost of building a new power plant or to permit several utility monopolies to pool their resources to help finance plant construction.

Are We Hooked?

The nuclear energy pushers would like to convince us that we are already hopelessly addicted to nukes. Since 3MI the energy industry, the utilities, and their friends in government right on up to President Carter have been telling us that all sorts of dire consequences will result if we fail to build any more nuclear power plants and shut down the ones that are now operating. They talk about electrical shortages and dim-outs, about the effect of oil supplies or fuel prices, and about potential loss of jobs. All three of these scare tactics are unjustified.

Nuclear power presently supplies about 12 percent of our electricity and about 4 percent of our total energy.[35] Nationwide there is an excess of 38 percent of electrical generating capacity.[26] Thus, for the country as a whole, if all nuclear plants were shut down, about 26 percent over-capacity would remain. . . .

As far as jobs are concerned, capital-intensive facilities like nuclear power plants have a negative long-term effect. During the building phase many jobs are created, mostly of a highly skilled nature. A large percentage of these jobs is taken by workers who move into the area rather than local laborers. Decentralized power-producing facilities using renewable energy sources and conservation measures produce many more permanent jobs.[28]

We aren't hooked yet. There is still time to break the nuclear habit!

What Are The Alternatives?

The media would have us believe that the increased use of coal is the only immediate realistic alternative to nuclear energy. They also point out that coal use even with the "scrubbers" now available to remove much of the sulfur dioxide and other atmospheric pollutants has undesirable environmental consequences. Present mining conditions are unsafe, unhealthy, and produce water pollution as well as general ecological devastation in the case of strip mines.

Much of this could be corrected by passing and enforcing new legislation. In countries like Wales, Australia, and the Soviet Union, coal mining is done much more safely and without the high incidence of crippling black lung disease which results from the dusty conditions in U.S. mines. The so-called "risk-risk" comparisons which attempt to show that coal mining is more hazardous than nuclear power production are totally invalid. They generally ignore or underestimate the considerable radiation hazards associated with every step of the uranium fuel cycle. . . .

The utilities and energy industry are fond of talking about renewable energy sources as if they were some vague hope for the distant future. This is sheer nonsense! In fact, decentralized renewable energy sources would lessen our energy and financial dependence on these huge corporations. Many of these technologies for producing electricity are available right now.[30] Aside from the direct conversion of sunlight to electricity, which admittedly requires more development before it will be cost-competitive, these include:

a. Wind power. A recent analysis shows that this one source alone has the theoretical potential for producing 75 percent of total U.S. energy consumption.[31]

b. Methane digesters, which convert organic wastes into methane gas. China is one country where people in many localities build and use these for both illumination and cooking.

c. The burning of garbage. For example, the town of Hempstead, N.Y. has recently built a plant for recycling glass and metal which will, at the same time, produce 15 percent of the town's electricity.

d. Biomass conversion, in which fast-growing plants are produced on marginal lands for use as fuel either directly or after conversion to methane or alcohol.

Most renewable energy sources are uniquely suited for decentralized use. Their development is therefore directly at odds with the interests of the utility companies and the huge energy industry companies. When Exxon or a utility does talk about developing solar energy, they talk about centrally controlled and capital-intensive schemes that will earn large profits, such as huge solar satellites beaming back dangerous microwave energy to large arrays of receivers. Such schemes can only perpetuate control of our electrical energy by those who are already in control of the energy system, as well as introduce new and unacceptable health hazards.

Federal funding for energy research is presently allocated almost entirely to the development of nuclear and coal energy technologies. Only a very small percentage of our federal energy research budget goes to solar and other renewable resources, and even these funds primarily support the inappropriate adaptation of these technologies for use in our present capital-intensive centralized delivery system.[32] For example, little money is being spent on developing low cost solar collectors which could be installed on individual homes, apartment buildings, and factories for direct production of electricity from sunlight. Many experts in this field claim that with proper funding this technology could be made cost-competitive with coal and nuclear in less than ten years.[33]

Many analysts have pointed out that our most neglected energy alternative is conservation.[24] This doesn't mean doing without present comforts, but rather changing our totally inefficient and wasteful practices, which compare very unfavorably with other countries. Both district heating (the use of waste heat from power plants to warm factories and living space—a tactic which is not compatible with nuclear power plants) and cogeneration (the use of heat produced in industrial processes to make electric power) are two methods in wide use elsewhere which are not widely used here and are frequently blocked by the legislation that gives our electrical utilities their monopoly control.

What Needs to Be Done

First we must agree on a set of goals. The following are offered as a minimal set of demands which should be supported by the entire antinuclear movement:

1. Immediately cancel all plans to build new nuclear plants and stop construction of nukes now being built.

2. Shut down all presently operating nukes in areas where sufficient alternative electrical power exists to meet essential needs.

3. Phase out as quickly as possible the few remaining nukes by construction of alternative facilities.

4. Retrain and relocate all workers deprived of employment by these actions.

5. Change the many federal and state laws which both give the utilities and energy industry giants their monopoly status and which discourage the development of decentralized, renewable energy technologies.

6. Shift our present federal and state subsidies (tax write-offs, depletion allowances, etc.) away from support of nuclear development and replace them with incentives designed to encourage the development and use of decentralized alternative energy programs.

7. Redirect our federal and state-financed energy research programs away from nuclear and fossil fuels and toward the exploitation of renewable resources.

How To Do It

The above program *can* be accomplished. It will require the building of an effective, *massive* movement to counter the well-funded opposition of the energy industry and its supporters in the Department of Energy. The movement began years ago, but the 3MI disaster has given it new impetus and urgency. *Join it today.* Here are some suggestions for getting involved:

1. Educate yourself about nuclear power and its alternatives.

2. Find out about organizations in your area that are involved in the antinuclear, pro-safe energy movement.

3. Join these organizations and convince your friends and neighbors to do likewise. If no such organization exists in your area, start one. The Long Island *Shad Alliance* has available a short organizers guide written by some Long

Island residents who got activated by the 3MI calamity (send self-addressed envelope with 28 cents postage.)

4. Set up forums, debates, living room discussions, town meetings, and film showings in your neighborhood. Put the safe energy issue on the agenda in any organization you belong to.

5. Seek media coverage for the movement.

6. Organize letter-writing campaigns to local, state, and federal legislative and other officials.

7. Be creative in efforts to organize a wide range of activities to publicize the movement.

Carol Cina and Ted Goldfarb are longstanding members of the Stony Brook chapter of Science for the People. Ted teaches chemistry and Carol is a graduate student at Stony Brook SUNY. Both are very involved in the anti-nuke movement on Long Island.

References

1. *New York Times,* May 8, 1979, p. A1.
2. *New York Times,* March 31, 1979, p. 1; April 13, 1979, p. 1; April 14, 1979, p. 9.
4. *New York Times,* April 2, 1979, p. A15.
5. *New York Times,* March 30, 1979, p. 1.
6. *New York Times,* April 3, 1979, p. C14; April 7, 1979, p. 39.
7. *New York Times,* April 5, 1979, p. 1.
8. *Energy Systems Research Group.*
9. *Time,* April 19, 1979, p. 12.
14. "Safety of Nuclear Power Reactors (Light Water Cooled) and Related Facilities," WASH-1250, Wash., D.C., U.S. Atomic Energy Commission, 1973.
17. *Time,* April 9, 1979, p. 8; *Newsday,* Feb. 10, 1979, Part II, p. 2; *Guardian,* March 21, 1979, p. 7.
18. *Critical Mass Journal,* Aug. 1978, p. 4; Nov. 1978, p. 6; Reference 29, pp. 55–63.
20. *Science for the People,* Sept. 1978, pp. 12–18.
22. *New York Times,* April 8, 1979, Business & Finance Section, p. l; *Comparison of Nuclear and Coal Costs,* Komanoff Energy Associates, N.Y., 1978.
23. *Nuclear Plants: The More They Build the More You Pay,* R. Lanoue, Center for Responsive Law, Wash., D.C., 1978.
24. *Long Range Forecasting Model: Electrical Energy and Demand in New York State,* Energy Systems Research Group, Inc., Boston, Mass., 1978.
26. *Electrical World,* Sept. 15, 1978, p. 72.
28. *Jobs and Energy,* R. Grossman and G. Daneker. Environmentalists for Full Employment, Inc., Wash., D.C., 1977.
30. *No Nukes: Everyone's Guide to Nuclear Power,* A. Gyorgy & Friends, South End Press, Boston 1979, section 3, chapter 4.
31. *Science,* April 13, 1979, p. 13.
32. *Science,* July 22, 1977, p. 353.

33. *Science,* July 29, 1977, p. 447.

35. Edward Kahn, testimony before the New Jersey Public Service Commission, 1978, p. 140.

Document 8.3

J. Larry Brown and Deborah Allen, "Toxic Waste and Citizen Action," *Science for the People* 15, no. 4 (July–August 1983): 6–12.

In this piece, *Science for the People* magazine invited two guest writers at the Harvard School of Public Health to discuss the harms that new industrial pollutants inflicted upon environmental and public health. After carefully detailing how toxic wastes entered the air, water supply, and crops, J. Larry Brown and Deborah Allen devoted much of their article to exploring the power of "citizen action" (a term many leftists today would replace with "grassroots action" so as to include undocumented people) in addressing environmental damage across American communities. The authors also identified several research questions not well understood by scientists, as well as a host of environmental laws in need of revision or stronger government enforcement.

According to the EPA, about 1,000 new chemicals are put on the market each year. Presently, of the total 50,000 different chemical compounds on the market, the EPA estimates 35,000 are definitely or potentially hazardous to human health.[1]

Today, chemical production accounts for an estimated 60 percent of hazardous waste.[2] More than 77 billion pounds of hazardous wastes are generated in the United States each year—nearly twenty pounds for each person on the face of the earth. The EPA estimates that only ten percent of it is being handled safely. Unfortunately, much of that which is considered safe is in landfills not unlike the one at Love Canal, considered safe until just a few years ago. . . .

Such wastes include metals like mercury and arsenic, volatile liquids such as solvents, synthetic organic chemicals like PCBs or halogenated hydrocarbon pesticides and industrial gases. . . . Some of the hazardous waste materials are disposed of directly into rivers and streams. Most of it, however, is disposed of on land, in wastewater impoundments called lagoons, or in industrial or municipal landfills. Once improperly disposed of, toxic wastes boomerang back into the environment.

Through wind erosion, burning and evaporation, waste gets into the air. It poisons us through direct contact or accumulation in the food chain. But the most frequent route of entry appears to be groundwater that lies a few feet to a half-mile below the earth's surface. Held in stretches of permeable rock, sand and gravel known as aquifers, these huge subterranean reservoirs hold five times as much water as flows each year in all lakes, streams and rivers. Unlike surface water, underground water is almost impossible to purify once contaminated. Once underground, chemicals are shielded from the atmosphere and not exposed to natural purification by air and sunlight which evaporate water, leaving salts, chemicals and minerals.

Chemical landfills slowly drip their contents into aquifers below. Rain and water pass through a landfill, removing soluble contents from the waste, leaving a grossly polluted substance called leachate. The EPA estimates that an average landfill of seventeen acres generates 4.6 million gallons of leachate a year for up to one hundred years. The EPA further estimates that of the 181,000 lagoons in America, 72 percent are unprotected, leaching chemicals into the pure water below.[6]

As chemicals enter our bodies through food, air and water, they affect our health. The Library of Congress, in a study of 32 chemical sites, concluded that toxic chemicals "are so long-lasting and pervasive in the environment that virtually the entire population of the nation, indeed the world, carries some burden of one or several of them."[7]

We know a fair amount about the impact of certain chemicals. Benzene, for example, has been found to cause chromosomal damage at levels less than ten parts per million. Another compound, carbon tetrachloride, is a potent carcinogen. But we know little or nothing about the effects of literally thousands of other compounds.[8]

Yet perhaps the most dismaying fact is that while we know toxic chemicals affect our health, our ability to protect ourselves or even to predict disease is minimal. Many factors contribute to disease, making it difficult to isolate any one. Often the onset of disease is delayed after exposure, limiting our ability to analyze cause and effect. The danger, according to some scientists, is that a very gradual, insidious deterioration of health might be occurring unrecognized as a result of increasing environmental chemicalization.[9]

Dr. Irving Selikoff, director of the Environmental Science Laboratory at New York Mount Sinai Hospital, states it a bit more bluntly: "We're fouling our own nest, and we can't survive if we continue.[10]

Toxics in Town: How the Problem Confronts Communities

Discovery of toxic wastes has a piercing impact on a community. So stark is the phenomenon that name symbols have come to represent the overall problem. Mention Woburn or Times Beach or Love Canal and many Americans will immediately think of environmental toxins. These symbols represent literally hundreds of communities where individuals and families have suffered dislocation of their lives through the discovery that something unnatural and potentially harmful resides in their brooks, on their playgrounds, even in their homes. . . .

Yet in virtually every community there is a common pattern to what residents experience as they confront toxins. Examination of the patterns reveals both what is wrong and, importantly, what must be done to clean up our nation.

Almost always, it is community residents themselves who discover the toxins. Seldom has the presence of a dumpsite been discovered by public officials or scientists. Only the pressure of community residents has placed toxic wastes prominently in the public mind and provided it with such political significance.

In most cases, alarmed local citizens do what they are supposed to do: they go to local officials to express their concerns and request assistance. . . . They want some action; they want at least the assurance that the problem will be investigated. Generally they do not get it. It is at this point that the initial shock of the existence of toxins takes a back seat to the outrage people experience as their officials do nothing. In some instances, local officials are simply unresponsive. They literally do not address the problem. Other officials express concern but don't know what to do. The local board of health often turns out to be a small committee appointed by the mayor with no relevant expertise. Some town officials actually become hostile because the problem was revealed and they are expected to do something about it. In a classic form of beheading the messenger, town officials may charge the citizens with being "radicals," of being "insensitive to the economic repercussions" of the issue, or even of "seeking to foster fear and turmoil in our community."

It is at this point that the town usually splits on the issue of toxins. Citizens on one side of the issue either ignore the problem by tuning out, or attack the people who exposed the problem. Sometimes, this is spurred by local industry threatening to shut down if an issue is made of pollution. Those concerned about the problem may be shunned by fellow townspeople, or labeled as troublemakers in the local newspaper. Officials say they are overstating the problem; industry charges them with jeopardizing jobs in the community. . . . On the other side of the issue, people begin to wonder if they really are overreacting. Maybe they are pushing too hard. Local officials deny the problem. Neighbors are mad. And they are told they have no "proof" that the toxins are hurting anyone. So it often happens, the people who first discovered the problem now bear the burden of proving it is a problem. The onus is on them to show that something is wrong, and to get something done to correct it. The equation has become inverted: local citizens are forced to do what public officials are paid to do.

The next stage for residents is the search for outside help. Faced with self-doubt and enormous frustration, but spurred on by concern for their families, citizens begin to look for experts. The first likely target is a state agency such as the public health or environmental agency. . . . [But] state officials, short of staff and equipment, may even be curt, asking the citizens for evidence. Even when they know what to do themselves, their actions may be constrained by their relationship with local officials or by the way the matter may be intertwined with electoral politics.

At this point, citizens often try to "get political." They have had it with run-arounds. They try other avenues, often simultaneously. They visit elected representatives, state and federal, to recount their experiences and request that pressure be placed on appropriate agencies. They go to the newspapers to politicize what previously have been descriptive stories about the local situation. And they begin to conduct their own studies: where are people ill, how many, when did they become ill, what is the diagnosis. Finally, citizens may turn to academia in the belief that science can help prove there is a problem, describe the nature of the health threat, and suggest ways to correct it.

Unfortunately, citizens usually are frustrated at this step too. Many scientists and academics have an aversion to being drawn into so-called local problems. They fear political controversy. When they are willing to help, they usually speak in the vague and hedged language of their scientific field. And when there are those who speak strongly and eloquently on behalf of community concerns, local town officials and industry can produce their own experts to counter their statements. The role of science itself becomes politicized—inevitably so, because there is no definitive, unchallengeable truth to discover.

Having gone through these stages, citizens begin to understand that they don't have a scientific or technical problem, but a political one. It is the politics of priorities, constraints and special interests which prevents action to fix their toxic waste problem. And, they begin to realize, it is the politics of citizen activism that eventually will force appropriate action. . . .

Environmental Laws: Frequently Inadequate, Often Ignored

Until the late 1960s, no laws were specifically designed to protect the public from toxins. The only recourse was private lawsuits, called damage suits, to stop one person (or company) from doing harm to another. As the scope of the toxic waste problem became more clear, it became obvious that litigation is an inadequate vehicle to protect human health: cause-and-effect is hard to prove; health hazards may be obvious to some people and more subtle to others; and it is hard to trace back to determine who was responsible for the contamination originally.

Due to public outcry, however, a body of law was developed with the intent of *preventing* harm by regulating pollutants and the sources of pollution. These laws include the National Environmental Health Policy Act, Clean Air Act, Federal Water Pollution Control Act, Toxic Substances Control Act, and the Resource and Conservation Recovery Act (RCRA). These laws, designed to prevent exposure and otherwise protect Americans from unacceptable risks, implied a promise from government: enforcement would be strong and aggressive, and resources would be available to correct the problems. Moreover, the laws promised that citizens would be part of the regulatory process through public meetings, open debate, citizen lawsuits against corporate polluters, and the right to hold government agencies accountable for carrying out their responsibilities.

In the years since their passage, none of these laws has been enforced vigorously by the federal government. . . . Nor have there been aggressive responses to violations of these laws. In July 1981, for example, the EPA announced a suit against eleven of the country's largest chemical companies for pollution of marshland and the Mississippi River in Louisana.[16]

Yet twelve years before, local landowners had sued these companies for precisely the same problem. So what did the government's suit demand? Only that the companies clean up the mess they had made. No fines were sought for their twelve-year delay. No damages were requested. The message to corporate polluters was clear: the worst that is likely to happen to you is that you may have to clean up your own mess—no penalties for not having complied all along, no punishment to you for jeopardizing the health of innocent people. So companies actually gain from dilatory delay, freeing their funds for more profitable endeavors. . . .

And, perhaps most seriously, government at no level has shown the kind of respect and openness owed to citizens concerning issues so critical to their well-being. . . . The lesson in all this is clear: laws, even laws that look strong on paper, are meaningless without citizen action. All legislation, including environmental legislation, is the starting rather that the ending point.

The Limits of Academia in Political Disputes

The presence of a toxic waste dump in a town raises a number of scientific questions for residents: what chemicals are in the dump; how do they act in the environment; what is known about their effect on human health; and what is the best means of cleaning up the site. Quite reasonably, townspeople look to science for answers to these questions. They take their concerns to experts hoping for incisive answers to what may be life and death questions. Usually they do not get them. Science, like the law, frequently is a necessary but inadequate tool.

First, it is usually difficult for community residents to find someone willing to help them. One reason is that academia usually does not reward faculty for service to the community. It is something done in one's spare time. Another problem is that many academics with expertise in a relevant field such as toxicology or epidemiology are in some way tied to industry—sometimes as part-time employees or indirectly through grants to university laboratories. Scientists dependent in this manner are unlikely to embark on work that may run counter to the interests of their funding sources. Even when willing scientists are located, money to conduct research on behalf of a group of community residents is difficult to find. And even small-scale studies cost something.

Even if scientists are found and money obtained, it is likely that little useful information can be provided by academic research—even if there is time and the desire to have it done. The issue for which communities most often seek assistance in toxic waste situations is health: have there been any effects to date, and what is the likelihood that there may be? It is almost impossible for science to answer these questions. If, for instance, two cases of an unusual cancer are discovered in a small town, should they be attributed to toxic exposure or to chance? Science has difficulty answering that question in larger populations, let alone very small ones.

Often it isn't even clear what health problems should be examined. A community may be exposed to dozens of chemicals interacting in a variety of ways under a variety of circumstances. Perhaps they cause a range of outcomes, no one of which shows up to significant excess in the population but which, collectively, are quite serious. And when both disease and toxin have been discovered, are they to be linked? If so, how? How does one measure the exposure of an affected individual if one is concerned with drinking water consumed years ago? In town after town faced with a toxic waste problem, residents facing these problems have been disappointed with the limits of science. . . .

Like good laws, good science can strengthen the impact of an organized community. But it does not replace the political power of organizing. Science alone does not make social change. . . .

The Role of Citizen Action

"I ain't an expert in nothin', but I'm gonna be an expert in gettin' rid of that company and them barrels."[20]

The widespread poisoning of American communities by industry is, by definition, a national problem. While it has been recognized as such, it largely is still being treated as a local one. Ultimately it is a problem which will only be resolved at the national level. Laws, even strong ones, will not solve it. And certainly it will not be solved by political hyperbole. Resolution of this major issue demands and requires leadership commensurate with the virtually unprecedented threat the problem poses.

The "war on waste" which this nation must fight must be comparable to a national defense alert. In fact, until it is recognized as an actual national defense threat, it will not be dealt with adequately. Little evidence exists to indicate that any administration in this country will challenge big business in the manner required, unless forced to do so. "Leadership" must be created by citizens—largely by those directly affected by toxins. Ironically, both the evidence to point to the power of citizen movements and the evidence that individual citizen efforts alone cannot remedy this national problem, lie in the experiences of those communities which already have faced the problem.

One can point easily to specific things which must happen ultimately to protect our people from toxins. Centralized planning with respect to industrial production and waste control and recovery must take place to a far greater degree than even debated in modern-day America. A strong federal role in coordinating the production of industrial waste inevitably must develop in the absence of evidence that the public health will be protected by letting industry police itself.

At both the federal and state levels, laws and responsibilities must be tightened. Responsibility must be fixed—clearly and specifically—for identifying and classifying toxic waste sites; clear responsibility must be established for responding to towns and citizens groups. Written procedures must be spelled out so citizens can know what to do, and can monitor to make sure that they get what they need, when they need it. Better data and information are needed: not only birth and cancer registries, but strong "right to know" laws that place the public interest ahead of the interest of industry to patent formulas and reap profits through secrecy, at the expense of the public's health and well-being.

Will all this happen? Not tomorrow. But it will happen. The poisoning of our environment and our citizens cuts across many of the lines which usually separate us as a people. With toxins affecting all population groups, the environmental movement is a movement waiting to happen. The nature of the problem confronting us, and the enormous power in the diversity of people affected, will help us solve this crisis. But we must not forget that this environmental health crisis is a political problem. And it must be solved politically.

This may sound peculiar to those who believe that the undue influence which industrial titans exert over America's environmental policy began under this Administration. And it may sound off-base to those who believe that science and technology hold the keys to solving our toxic waste problem. But science is uniquely incapable of altering the hold which industry has on our federal policies. Only the politics of citizens' movements can do so.

J. Larry Brown is the Director of the Community Health Improvement Program (CHIP) at the Harvard School of Public Health, where he teaches. Deborah Allen is the Senior Program Coordinator of the CHIP program.

References

1. *Time Magazine,* New York, September 22, 1980.
2. Michael Brown, *Laying Waste: The Poisoning of America by Toxic Chemicals.*
6. *Time Magazine,* New York, September 22, 1980.
7. *Time Magazine,* New York, September 22, 1980.

8. Michael Brown, *Laying Waste: The Poisoning of America by Toxic Chemicals.*
9. This position is no longer unique. Many scientists have articulated it in articles and testimony.
10. *Time Magazine,* New York, September 22, 1980.
16. Environmental Protection Agency, press releases during July, 1981.
20. Vernabelle Kastings, resident of Seymour, Indiana, quoted in *Boston Globe,* April 12, 1983, p. 60.

EDITORS' NOTES

1. "Indictment of Glenn T. Seaborg for the Crime of Science against the People," *Science for the People* 3, no. 1 (February 1971), 12. For more on this action, see Chapter 2, "Disrupting the AAA\$," and Document 2.6.
2. Michael Foley, *Front Porch Politics: The Forgotten Heyday of American Activism in the 1970s and 1980s* (New York: Hill and Wang, 2013), 145–47. Also see Robert Surbrug Jr., *Beyond Vietnam: The Politics of Protest in Massachusetts, 1974–1990* (Amherst: University of Massachusetts Press, 2009).
3. Foley, *Front Porch Politics,* 139–42. For information on the health and environmental consequences of nuclear disasters, see Kim Fortun, *Advocacy after Bhopal: Environmentalism, Disaster, New Global Orders* (Chicago: University of Chicago Press, 2001); Adriana Petryna, *Life Exposed: Biological Citizens after Chernobyl* (Princeton: Princeton University Press, 2013).
4. See for example *Science for the People* 15, no. 4 (July–August 1983).
5. For more on Love Canal and Warren County, see Foley, *Front Porch Politics,* 150–77.
6. For information on American lead regulation, see Gerald Markowitz and David Rosner, *Lead Wars: The Politics of Science and the Fate of America's Children* (Berkeley: University of California Press, 2014).
7. Pesticide Action Network, http://www.panna.org/; Jason Corburn, *Street Science: Community Knowledge and Environmental Health Justice* (Cambridge, MA: MIT Press, 2005); Giovanna Di Chiro, "'Living Is for Everyone': Border Crossings for Community, Environment, and Health," *Osiris* 19 (2004): 112–29; "Citizen Science for Envrionmental Protection," https://www.epa.gov/citizen-science.
8. On the role of scientists in such cases, see especially Steve Kolowich, "The Water Next Time: Professor Who Helped Expose Crisis in Flint Says Public Science Is Broken," *Chronicle of Higher Education,* February 2, 2016, http://www.chronicle.com/article/The-Water-Next-Time-Professor/235136.

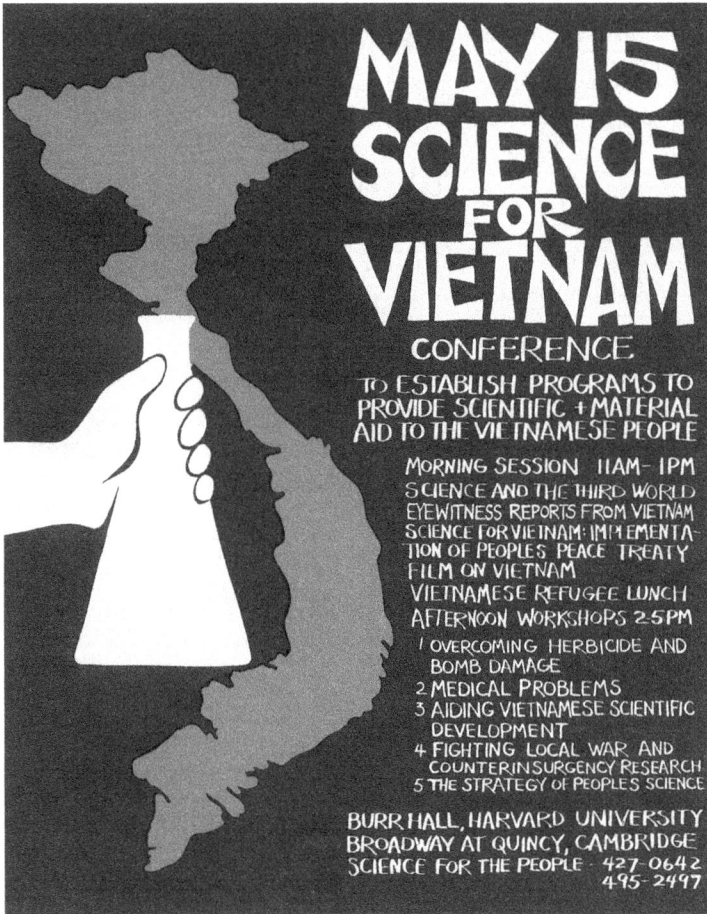

FIGURE 9. Poster, "May 15 Science for Vietnam," printed in *Science for the People* 3, no. 3 (July 1971). The poster design was by Elizabeth Fox-Wolfe, a.k.a. "Alphabet," who was an early member of Science for the People, the creator of the original "fist-and-flask" logo, and a contributor of many line drawings for the magazine. For a retrospective on Alphabet's contributions to SftP, see http://science-for-the-people.org/program/.

CHAPTER 9

Science for the People and the World

Daniel S. Chard

Throughout Science for the People's history, members of the organization acted on concerns over the critical role science played in U.S. imperialism. As *Science for the People* magazine's early managing editor Al Weinrub later recalled, SftP members recognized "science as a driving force of imperialism."[1] Like thousands of other activists in the late 1960s and early 1970s, SftP's initial members protested America's bloody war in Vietnam, and adopted the prevailing view among revolutionaries in Africa, Asia, and Latin America that the United States was the world's greatest source of violence and oppression. SftP activists believed that U.S. aims to achieve global dominance required global resistance. Seeking to disentangle the scientific profession from U.S. capitalism and military power, they built alliances throughout the world with leftist scientists and movements for national self-determination.

SftP members rejected American nationalism and the Cold War. They refused to support the U.S. government and military while the country's leaders used a range of tactics—from diplomacy and international aid to covert operations and military intervention—to force American capitalism upon the people of the world.[2] Instead they adopted identities as internationalists, and took inspiration from revolutionary movements in Cuba, Vietnam, China, Nicaragua, and elsewhere in the Third World whose leaders sought paths of socialist development independent of both U.S. and Soviet hegemony.[3] SftP activists traveled to these countries on several occasions to lend agricultural, medical, and educational expertise and to gain insights into how scientific research was funded and utilized under socialist regimes. In other acts of international solidarity, SftP protested U.S. foreign wars and raised funds for overseas scientific and educational projects. SftP was not the world's only organization of radical scientists. Others included the United Kingdom's British Society for Social Responsibility in Science, which borrowed SftP's clenched fist and Erlenmeyer flask logo and whose members regularly interacted with SftP, and India's Kerala Sasthra Sahithya Parishad (Kerala Forum for Science Literature).[4] Through their travels and organizing, SftP members ultimately hoped to forge lasting relationships with such groups, and thereby sustain a global movement for the liberation of science and humanity. It is obvious today that their efforts fell far short of this lofty goal. Nonetheless, SftP's attempts to transform the global political economy of science demonstrated an alternative approach to international relations, one that stands in stark contrast to the militarism and promotion of corporate business interests over human welfare that continue to characterize much of the U.S. relationship with the wider world.

In the early 1970s, SftP participated in the movement to end the U.S. war in Vietnam (see Chapter 3, "Militarism"). In their rowdy demonstrations inside annual meetings of the American Association for the Advancement of Science (AAAS), and in the pages of *Science for the People* magazine and other publications, SftP members also used their scientific expertise to condemn American scientists' complicity in the Vietnam War, and to propose more humane and socially beneficial uses for scientific research (see Chapter 2, "Disrupting the AAA$"). In 1971, Chicago SftP members published a report demonstrating the harmful effects of Operation Ranch Hand, the U.S. military's defoliation program, upon Vietnam's plants and animals. The same year, a series of conferences held in Berkeley, Chicago, Madison, and New York in 1971 generated SftP-affiliated "Science for Vietnam" projects throughout the United States, as well as in Canada and Europe, in which activists raised funds to ship scientific journals and other educational materials to Communist North Vietnam.[5] A 1971 article by SftP's Red Crate Collective, "Help for Scientific Education in Cuba and North Vietnam" (Document 9.1), tells of a "Science for Vietnam" effort in the Boston area, one that the organizers sought to extend to Cuba. Though the article focused on explaining U.S. science activists' efforts to assist their overseas counterparts, it explained these activities as responses to U.S. imperialism. "Scientific and technological resources of the United States should not be used to help colonize and repress people in less developed countries," the authors wrote, "but to help them improve their own economic, political and cultural position."

SftP members such as Richard Levins also visited North Vietnam.[6] Travel to North Vietnam demonstrated utmost political commitment, since commissioned flights into the country, despite their neutrality, risked being shot down by either military jets or ground-based anti-aircraft missiles. In addition, several SftP members visited Cuba with the Venceremos Brigade, an organization that led delegations of American activists to the socialist country in defiance of a U.S. travel ban. "A Scientific Visit to Hanoi" (Document 9.2) recounts an American microbiologist's visit to North Vietnam in 1971. Though the author, Mark Ptashne, was not a SftP member, his account appeared in *Science for the People* magazine, and shed important light on the lives, research interests, and political perspectives of scientists in war-torn Vietnam.

SftP members consistently denounced science and technology employed in the service of U.S. imperialism. "Toward an Anti-Imperialist Science" (Document 9.3), a leaflet written to protest a June 1973 joint meeting of the AAAS and its Mexican equivalent in Mexico City, outlined SftP's early-1970s anti-imperialist politics. The document asserted that scientific institutions such as the AAAS were integral to U.S. economic and military domination in Mexico and throughout Latin America. As evidence, they listed the U.S. corporations whose representatives dominated the conference's Executive Planning Committee, including the Rand Corporation, Riverside Research Institute, and Hudson Institute, research companies that advised the U.S. military on counterinsurgency and weapons programs. SftP members composed the declaration in collaboration with Mexican leftists, and the organization's signature appeared on the document alongside those of over twenty Mexican high school and university student groups. The manifesto concluded with an idealistic call for "a new science whose form and content form an integrated part of the struggle for human liberation." Mexican police arrested five American SftP members as they attempted to distribute the leaflet outside the conference, detaining the activists for several hours and threatening them with deportation before releasing them without charges.

Throughout the 1970s, the People's Republic of China served as a source of fascination and inspiration for SftP. The organization sent its first delegation to China on February 21, 1973, coincidentally one year to the day after Richard Nixon became the first U.S. president to visit China since its 1949 Communist Revolution. In a month-long visit carefully planned and monitored by Communist Party officials, SftP delegates toured research institutes, universities, factories, agricultural communes, and hospitals throughout the country. Activists who took part in the trip collectively wrote *China: Science Walks on Two Legs* (Document 9.4), a book that chronicled the group's favorable impressions of scientific advances achieved under China's Communist regime and offered ideas on how the Chinese socialist approach to science could benefit U.S. society. SftP's second delegation to China, in 1978, culminated in a number of articles on Chinese agriculture published in *Science for the People* magazine, but the regime change that took place in China that year left SftP, along with many other U.S. leftist organizations, deeply confused about the direction of Chinese politics and prevented the delegation from producing a second book as had been originally planned.[7]

Aside from the second China delegation, SftP participated in little organized overseas travel during the late 1970s, though *Science for the People* magazine frequently reported news from Mozambique, Cuba, Brazil, and other countries. Nicaragua's socialist 1979 Sandinista revolution against the U.S.-backed dictatorship of Anastasio Somoza, however, sparked renewed interest in international affairs among SftP members and other North American leftists. The U.S. Central Intelligence Agency sought to suppress the Sandinistas by training and funding the Contras, Nicaragua's brutal counterrevolutionary paramilitaries.

In 1982, University of Michigan biology professor and longtime SftP member John Vandermeer led the formation of the New World Agriculture Group, which organized several delegations to Nicaragua to help the country's scientists, farmers, and educators develop research programs, sustainable agriculture initiatives, and science curricula.[8] Reflecting on his experiences in Nicaragua in a 1986 *Science for the People* magazine article, Vandermeer outlined why he believed the Sandinista government had created a "new model of science and technology, clearly influenced by the kind of analyses radical scientists have been attempting for the last twenty years, but also heavily influenced by concrete Nicaraguan realities."[9] Moreover, Vandermeer explained the threat he believed Nicaragua's political self-determination and socialist agriculture posed to U.S. imperialism. Nicaragua's efforts to cease being an export-driven economy beholden to U.S. agribusiness were not substantial enough to threaten American overseas economic interests on their own, but if enough of the other countries in Latin America adopted similar programs, it would fundamentally upend U.S. relations with its southern neighbors. Thus, according to Vandermeer, "Free Nicaragua threaten[ed] the U.S. system in the same way that the ideas of abolitionists threatened the [nineteenth century] southern plantation system."[10]

In 1986, SftP activists in the Boston area also began organizing solidarity delegations to Nicaragua. "Science for Nicaragua: Cooperation in Technology and Science Education" (Document 9.5) recounts a trip to Nicaragua undertaken that year by seven Boston-based scientists who traveled there to establish a collaborative education project at the National Engineering University. The article offered a vivid account of the delegation's encounters with Nicaraguan educators and students, and of the university's expansion of scientific and technological education, particularly to young women. The delegation's solidarity across state borders exemplified SftP's commitment to internationalism and a global transformation of science and political power.

Document 9.1

Red Crate Collective, "Help for Science Education in Cuba and Vietnam," *Science for the People* 3, no. 2 (May 1971): 28.

Science for the People endeavored to make science serve the needs of humanity throughout the world, especially in countries with economic and scientific deficits that the group attributed to oppressive U.S. policies. This selection illustrates SftP's analysis of science and U.S. foreign policy in Vietnam and Cuba, and outlines the Cambridge-based Red Crate Collective's efforts to assist scientific education in those countries as part of SftP's "Science for Vietnam" initiative.

Scientific and technological resources of the United States should not be used to help colonize and repress people in less developed countries, but to help them improve their own economic, political and cultural position. That would be "Science for the People."

While the chances of official U.S. policy being changed to conform with this notion are slight as long as the U.S. government continues to be controlled by the dominant power interests, people can do something to implement such an approach. Two countries where scientific aid for the people is urgently needed are Vietnam and Cuba, where U. S. science and technology continue to be used to devastate and oppress.

In Vietnam, U.S. military strategy is designed to destroy the will of the people to resist occupation by the Saigon-Washington government. Part of this strategy is to disrupt Vietnamese society and culture by any means necessary; for example, by bombing Vietnamese villages with incendiary and antipersonnel devices such as steel needles and pellets, or by relocating a large part of the rural population in the South away from their ancestral lands. "Vietnamization" will not improve matters, since the U.S. government recently admitted that "preventive" bombing of the North will continue and intensify during the "Vietnamization" period.

This calculated disruption of civilian life, unprecedented in its severity, has not damaged the morale of the Vietnamese people, but it has hurt them in other ways. The Vietnamese value highly their intellectual tradition and system of education— aspects of their society that are practically unknown in the U.S., where most people think of the Vietnamese as tenacious but simple-minded peasants. American scientists, recent visitors with their Vietnamese colleagues, point out that U.S. bombing of the North has forced the Polytechnic University in Hanoi to decentralize and has destroyed much of the Central Scientific Library.

The Vietnamese people see scientific and technical education as extremely important. In the short run, they need it for industrial manufacturing and medical techniques to save the lives of their people. In the long run, they need it to rebuild their country and improve their living conditions.

In Cuba, U.S. policy is aimed at nothing less than starving the people into accepting the kind of government that the U.S. government believes is best for them. Not content with eliminating Cuba from the sugar quota and instituting a trade embargo that prohibits U.S. firms from exporting to Cuba, the U.S. government tries to enforce a vicious secondary boycott of European and other Western firms that sell to Cuba. Thus not only industrial articles but also food and medical supplies are very scarce, and rationing is severe.

Thirteen years ago the Revolution took power in a country that had been for half a century little more than a colony of the U.S., with its economy completely integrated into that of the mother country and almost totally dependent on one crop, sugar. Since then, despite U.S. opposition and obstruction, the Cuban people have been working to achieve stability, economic independence and control over their own political destiny.

Numerous visitors over the past few years report that the Cubans are aware of the importance of education to this endeavor, particularly in science and technology.

However, the disarray of the educational system engendered by Cuba's former colonial status has been aggravated by the departure since the revolution of the vast majority of the elite university professorial class. Thus progress in this critical area will be slow and help is needed.

In the United States "Science for the People" is not yet a reality. The corporate and military establishment controls much of scientific work, both in industrial research and development and in the universities where it is protected by "academic freedom." But American scientists can use science to help the Vietnamese and Cuban people in a significant and constructive way. These people urgently need advanced medical, scientific and technical journals and textbooks to further their educational endeavors. In addition, the Cuban people welcome American university professors, particularly in the biological and health sciences, who wish to teach for a few weeks or months in Cuban universities.

A political collective in Cambridge, Massachusetts has already collected and shipped over 3,000 pounds of books and journals to North Vietnam and Cuba, and other groups are also active. For the past two summers American professors have taught at the University of Havana, and further courses are planned for the coming summer. If you are interested in such projects, please write for more information to SESPA Science for Vietnam and Cuba, P.O. Box 59, Arlington Heights, Mass.

—Red Crate Collective

Document 9.2

Mark Ptashne, "A Scientific Visit to Hanoi," *Science for the People* 3, no. 3 (July 1971): 19–23.

Despite intense U.S. aerial bombardment of the country, several American scientists visited North Vietnam during the late 1960s and early 1970s. This personal account of a molecular biologist's visit to Hanoi in June 1971 illustrates SftP efforts to educate American activists and scientists about Vietnamese resistance to U.S. military invasion and sheds light on several aspects of science in Vietnam, including scientists' thirst for knowledge, government efforts to improve public health in the face of war, the structure of the country's scientific establishment, and research on traditional medicine. Interestingly, the author of this article was a Harvard scientist who opposed SftP on other fronts, especially on the issue of recombinant DNA.

In June of this year I spent a week in North Vietnam where I met with North Vietnamese scientists and doctors and lectured on molecular biology. Like the other scientists[1,2] I know to have visited North Vietnam—a country that is startlingly poor by American standards and yet clean and healthy by any standards—I came away with the impression of a society in which a vigorous intellectual life outruns material capacities in a unique way. And, in the face of continuing military pressures, the Vietnamese scientists and medical people I met have a firm confidence in the importance of even fundamental research for building their future society.

I confess I traveled to Hanoi doubting the usefulness of just one or two lectures on molecular biology, a science whose discoveries are not related in any simple way to the practical problems facing an underdeveloped country, particularly a country at war . . .

In fact, I found the Vietnamese to have a very lively interest in recent developments in basic science—even in molecular biology—and I was impressed by their serious efforts to develop their educational and medical programs. In attempting to convey this I should emphasize that my most vivid impressions are from direct conversations with the Vietnamese.

On a Wednesday morning at 7:30, I began a lecture to about a hundred Vietnamese students and professors in a bare room with a scratchy blackboard. My translator and I moved about a large wooden platform at the head of the room as we spoke. A microphone had been placed on the lectern, but neither of us used it. On our left, in the open doors, people who I later learned take care of the building watched, and on our right, below the open windows, oxcarts and bicycles moved by quietly. For the first few hours I reviewed a few of the basic aspects of molecular biology and described in some detail the repressor theory of Jacob and Monod. After outlining for them my own experiments, including the principal results, I paused before continuing with more recent developments in the field. At this point there was a barrage of questions. Mrs. An said:

> "We are sorry, but we do not understand. You must tell us the precise logic you
>   used in isolating the repressor." From another member of the audience:
> "Please tell us why you succeeded where others had failed. Explain to us what were
>   the scientific and historical factors which led you to choose one alternative over
>   the other at each stage."
>
> Still another questioner:
> "What did it feel like to make this scientific discovery, what precisely was that
>   experience?"

A moment earlier I had told them that the detailed methods we had used to isolate the repressors were primarily of historical interest because there now are easier ways of doing these things and besides, I had said, a detailed understanding of those methods is not absolutely necessary to understanding the overall results. They had already been listening for two hours, and I assumed they would only be bored by what seemed to me would be excessive detail. But now they were insisting that I supply them with precisely the details I had offered to omit. Moreover, they were probing for an understanding of one scientist's view of the very enterprise of doing science. And so, for the next hour or so I described our experiments step-by-step, telling them what had been hard and what had been easy.

The questions they asked me that Wednesday afternoon initiated a conversation which continued through the early evening (eleven hours in all) and into two more sessions of several hours each . . .

The Vietnamese were also interested in the organization of American science. They asked for a description of the role of the Department Chairman in American universities, and inquired whether I thought that structure was the best arrangement. Someone asked whether there was a consensus on the question of the role of competition in science, and whether science is best done individually or in groups, cooperatively. My impression was that they were trying to plan their own scientific future, and they themselves did not have any set answers to any of these questions . . .

Both at the hospital and at the Health Ministry the Vietnamese talked at length about their program to attack the health problems which faced the revolutionary government, problems greatly exacerbated by the war. An early explicit decision was made to reject the option of inviting friendly foreign governments to build modern hospitals where foreign specialists would practice and teach. Instead they concentrated on building a public health program, combining hygiene (sinking wells, building sanitary latrines, persuading people to drink only bottled water) with inoculations on a massive scale, sometimes using vaccines developed in North Vietnam. I was told the entire population is regularly vaccinated against cholera, tetanus, typhoid, and tuberculosis. For TB inoculations the Vietnamese claim to have developed an effective dead strain of BCG which is easier to transport without refrigeration than is the live strain. Children are inoculated against smallpox and polio, using for the latter a modified Sabin vaccine which the Vietnamese claim is stable for a month without refrigeration. In addition to these preventive measures, dispensaries have been established in the villages and cooperatives, and there is reportedly at least one hospital staffed by physicians in every district. Many of these hospitals were destroyed by bombing raids and now exist underground. During the bombings the Vietnamese claim deaths were minimized by massive evacuations of the cities, efficient use of air-raid shelters, and rapid on-the-spot treatment—only the most gravely wounded were transported to the better equipped centers.

Throughout North Vietnam fractures are set with light splints of bamboo using a method apparently similar to that employed in China.[5] The Vietnamese also grow and use on a large scale suspensions of the bacterium Bacillus subtilis, which they claim helps prevent intestinal infections and is an excellent healer of burns and wounds.

The Vietnamese reject "academic" procedures which restrict the practice of medicine to specialists with several years' training in medical schools. Instead, the country is covered by a network of assistant-physicians, midwives, nurses and sanitary officers. After a few years of experience, some of these sanitary officers become midwives or nurses, and with more experience, some of these ultimately become assistant-physicians. The exigencies of war demanded a large number of surgeons, and so all doctors are trained as surgeons. Even the paramedical people are often equipped to do certain types of simple surgery—for example, I was told that several thousand village workers can now perform the operation necessary to cure entropion, a frequent complication of trachoma.

The North Vietnamese claim to have essentially eliminated the major diseases which ravage the peoples of Asia—typhus, typhoid, cholera, tuberculosis, smallpox, polio, dysentery—and to have lowered the infantile mortality rate to a level comparable to that in America. I cannot verify these claims, but the general health of the people of North Vietnam contrasts sharply with that of the residents of Vientiane or Saigon.

The Vietnamese anticipate that a major post-war medical problem will be treatment of various war-induced psychiatric disorders. They feel that the collective moral discipline engendered by direct participation in the war helps their people to avoid the anguish that will surface when the war ends. A second major problem will be treatment of those disfigured by napalm and by pellets from anti-personnel bombs. There are plans to establish a plastic-surgery center in every province and,

I was told it is not impossible that they will ask for limited aid from specialists at that time.

The man most responsible for developing the health program of North Vietnam is Dr. Pham Ngoc Thach,[6] Minister of Health from 1958 until his death in 1968. In an interview[7] published in 1967, Dr. Thach described some of the obstacles to instituting these medical practices:

> We have navigated against the stream in many respects. To make physicians trained in the old faculties leave their consulting rooms or hospitals and become interested in digging wells and installation of septic tanks, in a word, in the prevention of diseases, is contrary to their deep-rooted habits. Even a medical nurse of the old school would prefer giving an injection and dislike going to verify whether a septic tank is adequately built or not. To make an injection of antibiotic which cures almost miraculously is a gesture much more captivating than to lift up the lid of a septic tank. To practice complicated surgical operations with costly ultra-modern apparatus imported from abroad gives more prestige than to lecture on hygiene in villages, or to help village cadres complete their medical education. To have toiled many long years in the faculties and now to believe that medical art can be put into the hands of the masses is not any easy matter either.

Visiting the Oriental Medicine Institute in Hanoi one afternoon, I saw that the North Vietnamese take very seriously their accumulated knowledge of traditional medicine—the treatment of various ailments with vegetal extracts and acupuncture. Here the Vietnamese are gathering traditional formulae—cures for dysentery, rheumatism, arthritis, headache, shock, bone fractures—which have been passed on through the years by word-of-mouth and in books. The workers at the institute are analyzing these traditional remedies to determine which are most useful and, if possible, how they work in physiological terms. In the meantime, throughout North Vietnam, thousands of practitioners of the ancient art are working alongside Western-type doctors, learning modern methods as they practice and teach old ones.

The Vietnamese continually emphasized their view that, subject to their severe material limitations, the practices of traditional medicine should provide a strong impetus for research in North Vietnam. And, they said, research is necessary for maintaining and improving the quality of their education and for enabling them to continue to adapt to new requirements. Although the Vietnamese have a strong interest in learning about basic research done elsewhere, their own research, according to Dr. Thach,[7] will be tied to practical problems:

> No doubt, a poor, industrially underdeveloped country has not the means that more highly developed countries possess, but shall we fold our arms in the domain of research? On the contrary, the less means a country has, the more it must develop technical and scientific research, so as to find out processes and methods appropriate to its national conditions: If we conceive research work as it is done in other places, if we only repeat and verify the works of scientists of other countries, we can only feel depressed by our powerlessness. We must carefully study what other people have

done, strive to get the latest scientific knowledge, but we must also blaze our own trail. Only by boldly taking up practical problems of our country and endeavoring to solve them, can we make our work fruitful.

At the end of the long Wednesday I spent discussing molecular biology, and more generally, how they were able to discuss and learn about abstract intellectual matters in the midst of war, I thought of America: fewer students are going into science, those who do are often plagued by misgivings, and it is not uncommon to hear young scientists complain that they find it increasingly difficult, for reasons sometimes specified and sometimes vague, to continue doing science in our society.

Dr. Nguyen Tan gi Trong, a professor of biochemistry at Hanoi Medical School rose and answered my question. He said that despite the war's destruction the Vietnamese are building a society and planning for the future which, he thought, requires knowing all these things.

References

1. Chomsky, N., *New York Review of Books*, 15, 16, 1970.
2. Schwartz, L., unpublished report.
5. Penfield, W., *Science*, 141, 1153, 1963.
6. Dr. Laurent Schwartz knew Dr. Thach and described him as "one of the most remarkable men I ever met." [2] *Le Monde,* Nov. 25, 1967, gives this biography of Dr. Thach: *After having completed his medical studies in Hanoi, then in Paris, where he specialized in phthisiology (study of tuberculosis), Dr. Pham Ngoc Thach, a native of the Mekong Delta region (South Vietnam), settled in 1936 in Saigon where he practiced general medicine and phthisiology until 1945. Very early a member of the Communist party, he was one of the founders of the Vietminh in the South and directed the resistance against the return of the French expeditionary corps in Saigon, in September 1945. Transferred shortly afterward to the North, he formed a close relationship with Ho Chi Minh and became his personal physician. Prime Minister of Health of the Provisional government, in 1945, he was later Secretary General to the Presidential Council and carried out, between 1945 and 1954, numerous missions which took him from North to South and from South to North. In 1954, he returned permanently to the North and became Minister of Health in 1958.*
7. Is North Vietnamese Medicine Facing the Trials of War, *Vietnamese Studies*, Hanoi, 1970.

Document 9.3

"Toward an Anti-Imperialist Science," *Science for the People* 5, no. 5 (September 1973): 18–19.

In June 1973, the American Association for the Advancement of Science (AAAS) held a joint conference with Mexico's National Council of Science and Technology (CONACYT) in Mexico City. Members of Science for the People traveled to Mexico to attend and protest the conference alongside leftist Mexican scientists and students. At the conference, SftP activists worked with other U.S. and Mexican students and scientists to compose "Toward an Anti-Imperialist Science." This leaflet, signed by SftP and more than twenty Mexican high school and university student groups, condemned science in the service of U.S. imperialism in Mexico and other Latin American countries. The leaflet outlined SftP's early-1970s anti-imperialist ideology and exemplifies the group's collaboration with international activists.

In the past it was possible to believe that science meant progress, that every scientific advance would better the conditions under which we all live, and at the same time would be one more step in the liberation of the human spirit. But of that dream only the rhetoric remains, and now we find that the reality is very different. Science today is property, and therefore, like all property, it is used for the benefit of those who own it. In the U.S.A. and in other imperialist nations, the major part of scientific effort is dedicated to the twin purposes of 1) extraction of profits and 2) the maintenance of the control which permits that extraction.

In imperialist countries, the scientific venture is devoted, for the most part, to the development of military technology, to mass extermination, and to fascistic control of the behavior of society as well as of the individual. The objective benefits that humankind might gain from scientific work is of secondary consideration.

For this reason, science is like a smoke-screen: while its force appears to be directed at the resolution of the most urgent problems of our peoples, it makes those problems more numerous. It covers up the social roots of "technical" problems. In the rhetoric of "harmony" it enshrouds the reality of imperialism.

This is where "Science and Man in the Americas" comes in, graced by the AAAS and the National Council on Science and Technology of Mexico.

The role of the U.S. transnational corporations in this meeting is seen clearly in the composition of the AAAS Executive Planning Committee for this event. Of the nine members of the committee, two are AAAS functionaries, while others very directly represent the bourgeois corporate interest of the U.S.A. Five members of the committee are directors of imperialist corporations or of the foundations established by corporation heads. Among the corporations represented on this committee alone are: E.I. Dupont Nemours, Rand Corporation, Riverside Research Institute, Hudson Institute (these three last are research corporations which do government consulting in the U.S.A. on questions of counterinsurgency and arms development); A.D. Little, Inc. (a corporation which investigates opportunities for investment in Mexico; also an arms developer); Mitre Corporation (arms developer); Verde Exploration (with operations in Latin America); Resources for the Future (research on how to facilitate the exploitation by the transnationals of the world's natural resources).

Three members of the committee have been government consultants in the field of foreign political and economic relations, and at least one participated in the Nixon electoral campaign.

In addition, there are ten central theme coordinators from the U.S.A. Of these ten, five are presently or were in the past, members of the Nixon Government.

In Mexico, as in the rest of the Latin American countries and other continents dominated by international monopoly capital, subjection to imperialist rule is always accompanied by the voices of nationalism, which only mask the real nature of the workings of imperialism.

In practice, the politics of those "nationalist" governments protects and encourages penetration through state organisms, which can be credit institutions, as well as cultural or scientific ones. Take the CONACYT as an example. With "harmony" they promote the imperialist interchange of capital, arms, or science and technology which serve to accentuate the domination of our peoples.

It is for this reason that now in Mexico the dominant groups need certain elements, for which they are looking in science, to develop this exploitation. And it is toward this end that the spirit of "apoliticism" and "pure research" and market-mindedness is induced and conserved in the scientist, who, without understanding of historical and class analysis, is easily made a tool of capitalist designs.

All of this we condemn: this scientific meeting is not seriously dedicated to the solving of humanity's problems, but is an imperialist maneuver which seeks to implement and perfect the dependency and the exploitation which exist in countries of the Third World. We affirm this, although the majority of the participants are there in good faith and accept the claims of the meeting organizers as beneficial fact. We affirm this although some contributions, considered separately, are valuable and interesting. We affirm that the lack of scientific and human seriousness is the fault of the meeting's administrators.

The measure of seriousness of a meeting on science and humanity is the way in which it faces the general problems which determine the technical problems. It is not serious science if one talks of the deterioration of the environment without confronting the reality of environmental imperialism: the exportation of contamination by means of the establishment of harmful industries which are not even allowed in the metropolis, the parent country; the extraction of mineral resources from dependent countries; the acquisition and cornering of their best farmlands; and the implantation of North American modes of consumption in order to acquire more markets, in spite of the fact that this destroys the environment and increases dependency.

It is not serious science if we do not confront scientific imperialism: the use of the environment and the people of dependent countries (without making an effort to integrate with the country's own scientific development) as objects of experimentation, sometimes very harmful experimentation, such as the use of Puerto Rico to test defoliants and birth control methods.

It is not serious science if it does not recognize intellectual imperialism, the exportation of North American ideology of industrialized, bureaucratized, and technocratic science; an ideology which separates feeling from thought, which sub-divides scientists, making them narrow specialists who cannot see the whole, the totality, who evince in their practice utter contempt and disregard for the people; and who promulgate attitudes of inferiority and dependency among the people.

It is not a serious scientific meeting if it is organized in a manner which essentially excludes the general discussion of fundamental questions, excludes critical people, and which is rigidly controlled by the politicians of science from the U.S.A. and Mexico.

If we do know that there exists a science which is imperialist in its uses, its organization, its method, and its ideology, there must exist, and in fact there does exist, an anti-imperialist science. It is still in its infancy, and it takes different forms, according to the conditions it is found in. In colonial countries, dependent countries, or imperialist countries, it begins by exposing and denouncing: we denounce the use of science in the service of domination and exploitation; we denounce the use of science's name in the new pseudo-scientific racism; we denounce the conversion of science into a commodity and of our universities into corporate offices. From denunciation we move to active criticism: we look for means to put our scientific knowledge at the service of the people, and therefore as an instrument of revolutionary national liberation movements.

We challenge the system of training which tries to continue producing obedient experts. We are beginning to develop a new science on behalf of the whole of technology and society—an integrated science which refuses narrow specialization and idiot realism. We repudiate hierarchical-classist structures in order to search for forms of collective work and more democratic forms in research as well as in training. We repudiate the mystification of a science reinforced by a specialized vocabulary and we will launch a campaign to popularize science. As scientists and revolutionaries we unite with anti-imperialist scientists of the world and with popular movements of our countries.

The focus of world science has to change, as it has changed in the past. But the new science which will be developed in the Third World cannot and must not copy the bourgeois science which it displaces. We will make a new science whose form and content form an integrated part of the struggle for human liberation.

Signed by Struggle Committees of UNAM schools of Architecture, Economy, Political Sciences, Chemical Sciences, Social Work, Natural Sciences, Engineering, Medicine, and Anthropology; by the Action Committee of the school of Veterinary Sciences; by the Struggle Committees of the High Schools of Science and Humanities of the South, of the West, in Vallejo, in Azcapotzalco, and by the Activists in the Naucalpan branch; by the Struggle Committees of the Popular High Schools of Poza Rica and of Tacuba, and by the Coalition of Brigades of High Schools 6 and 8; by the Struggle Committees of Vocational Schools 1 and 3; by the

UNAM Superior School of Economy; by Science for the People; and by the Union of Blue and White Collar Workers of UNAM; and by ESIQUIE.

Document 9.4

Science for the People, *China: Science Walks on Two Legs* (New York: Avon Books, 1974), 1–2, 6, 9–11.

Delegations of scientists affiliated with Science for the People organized two trips to the People's Republic of China (PRC), the first in 1973 and the second in 1978. Upon their return to the United States, members of the first delegation wrote *China: Science Walks on Two Legs,* an account of their trip and their views on science in Communist China. This excerpt from the book's introduction conveys the authors' impressions of how science functioned in Chinese society and their ideas about how American society could benefit from concepts and practices borrowed from the PRC. Although there was much that the delegates were prevented from seeing and their informants could not speak freely, the inspiration they and other visitors received had a profound significance for Leftist organizing in the United States. The delegates were: Mary Altendorf, David Aronow, John Dove, Minna Goldfarb (Barrett), Ginger Goldner, Judy Greenberg, Marvin Kalkstein, Frank Mirer, Geri Steiner, and Vinton Thompson.

China is suddenly at the center of attention in the United States. Why? For nearly twenty-five years most American were cut off from first-hand information about the People's Republic. The Chinese people, about a quarter of the world's population, were a faceless mass to us. Whatever negative image we had of China, it was mostly a blank.

Then all at once the door to travel was open and reports of travelers—reporters, scholars, and ordinary people, began to appear and were very surprising. As an image of New China formed, it was opposite to our view of the Third World as a uniform place of poverty, ignorance, exploitation, and disease. We got reports of a functioning society where food was adequate, disease limited, health care available, crime at a minimum, the children in school: a society that was making great strides in industry, agriculture, science, and military strength. A picture of the social organization of the People's Republic of China began to form and it appeared to be one of a radically different system, a developing socialist nation. And as the picture became clearer and more complete, many wondered if the Chinese experience might suggest approaches to some of the pressing problems of American society.

Why should we, authors of this book and members of an organization called Science for the People, be so interested in science in China? Think for a moment about the ways in which science and technology enter our daily lives as Americans. We read about fabulous developments in medical science, but it's hard to get emergency care no matter how much we can pay, and most of us fear the enormous cost of prolonged illness. Instead of marveling at the productivity of advanced scientific agriculture, we worry about pesticide contamination, try to cope with spiraling rises in food prices, and read about famine in the Third World. Products of industry roll out of the factories, proving the basis of our material wellbeing, but at the same time industry pollutes and degrades the environment around us and work remains repetitive and dehumanizing. Advances in transportation leave us with airport noise and traffic jams. A fuel shortage leaves us with colder houses and slower cars but little or no attention given to mass transportation. Developments in psychology result in the massive use of amphetamines to control the behavior of "hyperactive" children. The computer, touted as an almost magical thinking machine, is used to fight an absentee war in Southeast Asia, and here at home it compiles lists of hundreds of thousands of people opposed to that war. The laser, a significant scientific tool, is used to guide bombs to the targets selected by these computers, and yet a primitively armed force of guerrilla fighters is able to outfox it. Lasers and computers are popularly known for the nonmilitary uses, but the research and development of laser and computer technology had their first inspiration and initial funding within the context of military capabilities, as so most scientific and technological advances in our society. The list is endless. All around us experts with academic degrees and white coats come up with the answers, trying to force us to accept advice without understanding it, but they seem to lead us out of one crisis only to confront a new one. No wonder more and more people working in the sciences have become dissatisfied with the misuse of their own work. The Science for the People organization grew up as all kinds of scientific workers and other people affected by the results of technology began to analyze and respond to these contradictions. . . .

. . . Science "walks on two legs" in China. Her ancient traditional knowledge together with more modern advances made through regular scientific channels are one leg. The broad masses of ordinary people who had always been denied access to scientific developments have become the other leg. Basically, the idea of walking on two legs means to exercise the underdeveloped one, rather than putting all the resources into the stronger one. It does not mean cutting the stronger one off in favor of the weaker, as some western observers have implied. . . .

. . . One of our first questions as we toured scientific institutes and universities was a common one among American intellectuals trying to make sense of the Chinese experience: Wasn't it difficult for Chinese scientists to give up their research to meet scientific priorities, to be removed from their labs and reassigned to work in agriculture or industry? The response we received was generally one of great amusement. Professor Tan Chia-chen, a geneticist in Peking, told us that his work had never been as exciting as it is now. His research revolves around the theoretical genetics of crossing different plant species. When he was sent to the countryside he discovered that "the peasants were ahead of the theoreticians." Spurred by the need to increase production, they had succeeded in crossing the castor bean and the cotton plant, both oil-producing crops. Theoretical geneticists would have advised them not to waste time trying: in theory is should not have worked. Now Professor Tan spends part of each year out with the peasants learning from them so that he can take new information back to the laboratory. Sometimes peasants come back to the lab with him to teach and work with students, and students in turn go to the countryside to work with peasants. Professor Tan remains a prominent scientist, but he has developed an ability to work with practical aspects of agriculture that has made his own research more effective and beneficial.

In the Shanghai Machine Tool Factory ordinary workers study calculus at midday, so that they will eventually understand the entire production process, including the theoretical levels. Other workers set up small shops in the universities to build electronic equipment, and teach students and professors how to build it for their own research purposes.

Housewives who organized themselves into small local factories to produce paper boxes have moved on to more complex things like flashlight batteries and even transistors. Inspired by parables like "The Foolish Old Man Who Removed the Mountains," they have spurred themselves on to even greater tasks. Now there are street factories that build computers.

Peasants in Linhsien, a large, once arid valley, designed and built an enormous irrigation canal after experts had advised them against it. They built hundreds of tunnels and aqueducts along the 70-kilometer route that winds over rough mountain peaks, and it was their self-reliance and determination that pushed the task through to its completion. The Red Flag Canal serves as a monument to their efforts and an inspiration to people throughout China.

Science, in short, is being demystified in China. According to the Marxist conception, it is the summation of the laboring people's experience and properly belongs to them. The idea of science as the private property of scientists, as being something too deep for ordinary people to understand, must be abolished. In its place, a vast exercise in sharing knowledge is being carried out through the length and breadth of China, to make science a part of the mass culture.

Document 9.5

Michael Harris and Victor Lopez-Tosado, "Science for Nicaragua: Cooperation in Technology and Science Education," *Science for the People* 18, no. 3 (May–June 1986): 22–25.

In 1979 socialist Sandinista revolutionaries overthrew Nicaragua's U.S.-supported dictator Anastasio Somoza. Science for the People activists were among the hundreds of North American leftists who lent support to the Sandinistas, as the revolutionaries worked to eliminate poverty, expand education, and improve public health in their country while battling the contras, counterrevolutionary paramilitaries funded and trained by the U.S. Central Intelligence Agency. This excerpt from *Science for the People* magazine describes seven Boston-based scientists' 1986 visit to Nicaragua for the purpose of establishing a collaborative education project at the National Engineering University. The article sheds light on scientific and educational projects undertaken as part of the Sandinista revolution, and U.S. science activists' efforts to support such initiatives. The SftP activists who participated in this trip were Bill Fowler, Victor Lopez-Tosado, Marilyn Frankenstein, Robert Van Buskirk, Ann Conway, Michael Harris, and Bob Lange.

When we arrived at the UNI, the new National Engineering University, on January 3, we were not sure who would be waiting for us. We arrived during the academic vacation, which coincides with the coffee harvest. Coffee prices are up this year, and contra activity in the coffee-growing regions has been virtually eliminated. So we were told that everyone involved in Nicaraguan higher education—students, faculty, and administrators—had gone off to the mountains to pick *el rojito*, as ripe coffee beans are called.

We had gone to Nicaragua—five men and two women, all scientists from Boston-area universities—to meet with our counterparts in Nicaraguan universities in order to discuss our proposal for setting up a program of cooperation in scientific education. Our first project was to send a group of professors to teach in Nicaragua during the academic year starting March 1986. Two of our professors were engineers, so it was natural to make the UNI our first stop.

We were met by Arturo Collado, the academic vice-rector of the UNI, who launched immediately and energetically into a discussion of Nicaraguan higher education and how it had changed during the Sandinista revolution. Some statistics to start with: there are now 30,000 students and over 1,000 full-time opposed to 17,500 and 350 under Somoza. Before 1979, the medical faculty could accept at most 80 students per year; that number has gone up to 600. In the last years of Somoza's rule, women numbered only 4% of engineering students, but 56% of the 1986 entering class at the UNI are women. And there are new programs. The National Autonomous Universities (UNAN) are offering college preparatory courses to 800 students annually from disadvantaged backgrounds and remote regions. The UNI is introducing degree programs in mechanical engineering and computer science, two subjects which never were taught before in Nicaragua.

The National Engineering University

As of next August, the UNI will begin offering training in Nicaragua's new graduate program, a two-year course in environmental and sanitary engineering. It almost goes without saying that this is the only program of its kind in Central America, and the UNI already plans to accept environmental engineering students from neighboring countries. Presumably, this is an instance of "exporting revolution" that the Reagan administration is so worried about.

The UNI itself is only three years old, and is still very much in a state of flux. Housed in a former Catholic school building that still shows signs of damage from the 1972 earthquake that wiped downtown Managua off the map, the UNI looks fated to be continuously under construction for the foreseeable future. This has a positive as well as a negative side. Somoza's neglect of his country has left the Nicaraguans with an unprecedented opportunity to rebuild it from the ground up, in accordance with their goals. Anyone—Nicaraguan or foreign visitor—with enough energy to organize a new project is almost sure to be encouraged, provided the project is seen to be in the long-term interests of Nicaragua.

Nowhere is this willingness to experiment more in evidence than in the universities. The Sandinista revolution can be described as a never-ending conversation about its own future, in which everyone is invited to take part. Halfway through the first meeting, we were joined by Juan Sanchez, the Chancellor of the UNI, looking fit after a week of picking coffee, as well as visiting professors from Holland and the U.S. The purely ceremonial portion of the meeting ended soon after his arrival. For the rest of the morning, our delegation—individually and collectively—became a part of the never-ending conversation about the future of higher education in Nicaragua, and the role our project could play in fulfilling Nicaragua's goals for that future.

Sanchez and his colleagues had evidently devoted a lot of time to thinking of ways Science for the People could do useful work in Nicaragua. Before we broke for lunch we sat around the table and talked in groups of twos and threes about some of their ideas, which were later proposed to us officially as goals for the SftP Program in Cooperation in Scientific Education.

Excitement and Education

The energy and informality we felt at our first meeting are not unique to the UNI, and go a long way toward explaining why so many people from around the world have been drawn to work in Nicaragua and, in many cases, to relocate there more or less permanently. We felt this excitement again during the sightseeing part of our trip, when people on the street repeatedly came up to greet us—they had read about our visit in the newspapers—and ask us our opinions on science, education, break dancing, and on every other conceivable topic.

Uppermost in their minds was U.S. policy in Central America. Everyone assured us that the contras had been "strategically defeated," that they still caused damage in a few regions of the country but they no longer posed a serious military threat. But for this very reason Nicaraguans we spoke with were concerned more than ever about the threat of a direct intervention by U.S. troops. "How would the American people react if that happened?" We couldn't really answer that question, but our visit left us no doubt as to the Nicaraguan reaction in the event of an invasion.

When we arrived late for a scheduled meeting in Esteli, a woman who happened to be waiting in the office invited us to visit a college for elementary school teachers. Since the universities were not in session, this would be our only opportunity to witness education in Nicaragua, and two of us eagerly accepted the invitation. The director of the school apologized when we arrived, since the only classes that afternoon were in civil defense and nutrition.

Civil defense? It seems most of the students in the school were elementary school teachers from rural areas who were taking intensive courses to improve their teaching skills—a process known as *capacitacion*, which goes on at all times in all sectors of society, and which is the main method devised by Nicaraguans to overcome their historic underdevelopment. Since these teachers—95% of them women—are usually the most educated people in their villages, the government has chosen them as the vehicle to provide basic information about civil defense to remote regions. The class we visited was a methodical, matter-of-fact discussion, by a tiny woman with a powerful voice, of the relative advantages of different kinds of bomb shelters. The students took careful notes. There was much note-taking in the nutrition class as well.

At the end of our first meeting at the UNI, we were given a copy of the study on which the school's development was based. The tension between the desire to achieve technological self-sufficiency in the shortest possible time and the painful awareness of the shortage of resources—particularly of qualified technicians and scientists—is resolved through a detailed five-year development plan for the university, which takes as its starting point the country's need to develop small-scale industry based on the needs and products of the local agricultural economy.

Goals and Objectives

Nicaraguans are serious about defending their revolution, but then, they take everything having to do with the revolution seriously. Every significant reform and important new project is preceded by painstaking studies of needs and resources, and by consultations with organizations representing all sectors of society which stand to be affected by the initiative. A striking example of this is the document entitled "Fines, Objectivos y Principios de la Nueva Educacion" —Goals, Objectives and Principles of the New Education. This document, which guides Nicaragua's educational process at all academic levels, was based on the Consulta Nacional—National Consultation—of 1981. In this process, more than 50,000 representatives of different organizations, including women, labor unions, and religious groups, along with government agencies assessed the country's academic needs and gave their opinions about the type of educational reforms needed in Nicaragua. The document, approved by the Sandinista National Liberation Front, will direct Nicaragua's educators in their efforts to defeat underdevelopment and dependency. They are establishing an educational system that responds to the needs and interests of the majority of Nicaraguans, and not to those of the multinationals, oligarchs, and remnants of the *somocistas*.

Some of the problems of training students to be scientists and engineers were surprisingly familiar to us. In Leon, the second largest city in the country, we met Jilma, a leader of the student union at the National University there. Jilma is a 23-year old woman who at 14 left Leon to join the Sandinistas in the mountains and returned two years later to take part in the battle to liberate the city.

The university at Leon is Nicaragua's oldest, and apart from its famous medical school also has the longest-standing programs in basic sciences. But few students choose to follow careers in science, Jilma told us. Why? It seems the students don't like mathematics much. It makes them nervous. Given this attitude, the shortage in technical experts is likely to persist over the short run. Science for the People's project of cooperation in science education with Nicaragua hopes to address these math and science anxieties. We want to expand the program to include science teacher training and teaching science in high schools. In this component, we would be working with the School of Education at UNAN-Managua and the Ministry of Education, providing assistance in needs assessment, establishing priorities, and recruiting the needed faculty.

Nicaraguan educators expressed—correctly, in our view—that while they train scientists and technicians for industry and research, they also need to train secondary science teachers. High school science teachers are responsible for preparing Nicaraguan youth to enter science fields. They also provide the scientific knowledge needed by all citizens to assist in the building of a new Nicaragua. That will be our new task too.

Teaching vs. Terror

In March, our first group of professors began teaching Nicaraguan students courses in digital engineering, microcomputers, and statistics. The Science for Nicaragua Committee is now selecting candidates to teach next semester, starting in August. Meanwhile, in Washington, another group of U.S. citizens, with a budget about 100 million times larger than ours, is debating how much of that money should be sent to help torturers and rapists destroy the precious little Nicaragua has been able to build since 1979. Faced with such a powerful and determined adversary, the role of progressive North Americans in promoting peaceful cooperation with Nicaragua has never been so important.

We at Science for the People are planning to launch three new projects during the coming year which were suggested to us at the UNI: a program to improve Nicaraguan universities' access to library materials, in particular scientific journals; a program of short-term visits by U.S. scientists interested in working on research projects or teaching advanced seminars in Nicaragua; and a search for U.S. universities willing to provide fellowships to Nicaraguan graduate students. Nicaraguans have reminded us that it is still possible to build an independent future, even in Uncle Sam's backyard. What they have asked us to do—to teach their students science, technology, agronomy, and medicine—is meager by comparison, but we are glad the Nicaraguans are willing to make the exchange.

EDITORS' NOTES

1. Al Weinrub, email to Daniel S. Chard, January 7, 2017. Like other 1970s anti-imperialists, SftP radicals' critique of U.S. imperialism drew from contemporary theorists' elaborations on Russian revolutionary Vladimir Lenin's 1917 pamphlet *Imperialism, the Highest Stage of Capitalism*. More recently, historians and social scientists have offered new perspectives on U.S. imperialism. See Julian Go, *Patterns of Empire: The British and American Empires, 1688 to Present* (Cambridge: Cambridge University Press, 2011); Charles Pinderhughes, "Toward a New Theory of Internal Colonization," *Socialism and Democracy* 25, no. 1 (2011): 235–56; and Jane Burbank and Frederick Cooper, *Empires in World History: Power and the Politics of Difference* (Princeton, NJ: Princeton University Press, 2010). For a review of literature on U.S. imperialism, see Paul Kramer, "Power and Connection: Imperial Histories of the United States and the World," *American Historical Review* 116, no. 5 (December 2011): 1348–91.

2. On U.S. interventions in Africa, Asia, and Latin America, see Greg Grandin, *Empire's Workshop: Latin America, the United States, and the Making of the New Imperialism* (New York: Macmillan, 2006); and Odd Arne Westad, *The Global Cold War: Third World Interventions and the Making of Our Times* (Cambridge: Cambridge University Press, 2005).

3. On U.S. radicals' overseas travels and the concept of internationalism, see Judy Tzu-Chun Wu, *Radicals on the Road: Internationalism, Orientalism, and Feminism during the Vietnam Era* (Ithaca, NY: Cornell University Press, 2013). On the Third World movement, see Vijay Prashad, *The Darker Nations: A People's History of the Third World*, 2nd ed. (New York: New Press, 2013).

4. Alice Bell, "The Scientific Revolution That Wasn't: The British Society for Social Responsibility in Science," *Radical History Review* 127 (2017): 149–72; David King and Les Levidow, eds., "Forum on Contested Technologies," *Science as Culture* 25, no. 3 (August 2016): 367–446; G. Wersky, "The Marxist Critique of Capitalist Science: A History in Three Movements," *Science as Culture* 16, no. 4 (2007): 397–461; and Mathai Zachariah and R. Sooryamoorthy, *Science for Social Revolution: Achievements and Dilemmas of a Development Movement—the Kerala Sastra Sahitya Parishad* (London: Zed Books, 1994).

Also see the current organizations' websites: https://sites.google.com/site/bssrsarchive/home and http://www.kssp.in/page/about-us (accessed January 6, 2017).

5. On SftP solidarity efforts with Vietnam, see Kelly Moore, *Disrupting Science: Social Movements, American Science, and the Politics of the Military, 1945–1975* (Princeton, NJ: Princeton University Press, 2008), 180–81. On the Science for Vietnam project, see also Bill Zimmerman, *Troublemaker: A Memoir from the Front Lines of the Sixties* (New York: Knopf Doubleday, 2012), 218–20.

6. Ibid.

7. For more on this trip, see Sigrid Schmalzer, "Speaking about China, Learning about China: Amateur China Experts in 1970s America," *Journal of American-East Asia Relations* 16, no. 4 (Winter 2009): 325–31.

8. On the New World Agriculture and Ecology Group, see Ivette Perfecto, "New World Agriculture and Ecology Group: The Sandinista Years," conference presentation, "Science for the People: The 1970s and Today," April 13, 2014, Science for the People website, http://science-for-the-people.org/sftp-in-the-world/ (accessed December 9, 2016).

9. John Vandermeer, "Moving Toward Independent Agriculture: Nicaragua Struggles in the World Economy," *Science for the People* 18, no. 1 (1986), 16.

10. Ibid., 18.

Further Reading

Companion Website: http://science-for-the-people.org
This website preserves video and slideshows from the 2014 conference "Science for the People: The 1970s and Today." It also offers access to supplemental materials produced by and about SftP, including a trove of FBI documents related to SftP that were obtained through a Freedom of Information Act request by Wisconsin-based researcher Melanie McCalmont. Finally, visitors to the site can find information on the SftP "revitalization" currently unfolding around the world—a movement that is gaining strength as more and more people question liberal institutions' ability to generate the kind of populist mobilization necessary to counter anti-science, corporate, and militarist threats.

PUBLISHED WORKS

Ann Arbor Science for the People Editorial Collective. *Biology as a Social Weapon*. Minneapolis: Burgess Publishing Company, 1977.

Arditti, Rita, Pat Brennan, and Steve Cavrak, eds. *Science and Liberation*. Montreal: Black Rose Books, 1980.

Beckwith, Jonathan. *Making Genes, Making Waves: A Social Activist in Science*. Cambridge, MA: Harvard University Press, 2002.

———."The Radical Science Movement in the United States." *Monthly Review* 38, no. 3 (1986): 119–28.

Berkeley SESPA. *Science against the People: The Story of Jason*. Berkeley, CA: Berkeley SESPA, 1972.

Bernal, J. D. *Marx and Science.* London: Lawrence & Wishart, 1952.

————. *The Social Function of Science.* Cambridge, MA: MIT Press, 1967 [1939].

Boston Science for the People, Food and Nutrition Group. *Feed, Need, Greed: Food, Resources and Population.* Cambridge, MA: Science for the People, 1980.

Boucher, Doug, and Isadore Nabi. "The New World Agriculture Group: A History." *Radical Science* 17 (1985): 88–104. [Note: Isadore Nabi was a pen name for Richard Levins.]

Bridger, Sarah. *Scientists at War: The Ethics of Cold War Weapons Research.* Cambridge, MA: Harvard University Press, 2015.

Bukharin, Nikolai. *Science at the Cross Roads.* London: F. Cass, 1971.

Conner, Cliff. *A People's History of Science: Miners, Midwives, and 'Low Mechaniks.'* New York: Nation Books, 2005.

Di Chiro, Giovanna. "Living Is for Everyone: Border Crossings for Community, Environment, and Health." *Osiris* 19 (2004): 112–29.

Eglash, Ron, Jennifer L. Croissant, Giovanna Di Chiro, Rayvon Fouche, eds. *Appropriating Science: Vernacular Science and Social Power.* Minneapolis: University of Minnesota Press, 2004.

Epstein, Steven. *Impure Science: AIDS, Activism, and the Politics of Knowledge.* Berkeley: University of California Press, 1996.

Fausto-Sterling, Anne. *Myths of Gender: Biological Theories about Women and Men.* New York: Basic Books, 1985.

Foley, Michael. *Front Porch Politics: The Forgotten Heyday of American Activism in the 1970s and 1980s.* New York: Hill and Wang, 2013.

Gould, Stephen Jay. *The Mismeasure of Man.* New York: Norton, 1981.

Haraway, Donna. *Primate Visions: Gender, Race, and Nature in the World of Modern Science.* New York: Routledge, 1989.

Haraway, Donna Jeanne. "The Transformation of the Left in Science: Radical Associations in Britain in the 30's and the U.S.A. in the 60's." *Soundings* 58, no. 4 (1975): 441–62.

Harding, Sandra. *The Science Question in Feminism.* Ithaca, NY: Cornell University Press. 1986.

Hess, David J. *Alternative Pathways in Science and Industry: Activism, Innovation and the Environment in an Era of Globalization.* Cambridge, MA: MIT Press, 2007.

Hubbard, Ruth. *The Politics of Women's Biology.* New Brunswick, NJ: Rutgers University Press, 1990.

Irwin, Alan, and Brian Wynne, eds. *Misunderstanding Science?: The Public Reconstruction of Science and Technology.* Cambridge: Cambridge University Press, 1996.

Jumonville, Neil. "The Cultural Politics of the Sociobiology Debate." *Journal of the History of Biology* 35, no. 3 (2002): 569–93.

King, David, and Les Levidow, eds. "Forum on Contested Technologies." *Science as Culture*, 25, no. 3 (2016): 367–446.

Krimsky, Sheldon. *Genetic Alchemy: The Social History of the Recombinant DNA Controversy*. Cambridge, MA: MIT Press, 1982.

Levins, Richard, and Richard Lewontin. *Biology under the Influence: Dialectical Essays on Ecology, Agriculture, and Health*. New York: Monthly Review Press, 2007.

———. *The Dialectical Biologist*. Cambridge, MA: Harvard University Press, 1985.

Lewontin, Richard. *Biology as Ideology: The Doctrine of DNA*. Toronto: House of Anansi Press Ltd., 2003.

Martin, Brian. "The Critique of Science Becomes Academic." *Science, Technology, & Human Values* 18, no. 2 (1993): 247–59.

McCormick, Sabrina. *Mobilizing Science: Movements, Participation and the Remaking of Knowledge*. Philadelphia: Temple University Press, 2009.

Moore, Kelly. *Disrupting Science: Social Movements, American Scientists, and the Politics of the Military, 1945–1975*. Princeton, NJ: Princeton University Press, 2008.

———. "Organizing Identity: The Creation of Science for the People." In *Social Structure and Organizations Revisited*, ed. Marc Ventresca and Michael Lounsbury. Amsterdam: Elsevier, 1996.

———. "Organizing Integrity: American Science and the Creation of Public Interest Organizations, 1955–1975." *American Journal of Sociology* 101, no. 6 (1996): 1592–1627.

Nelkin, Dorothy. "Scientists in an Adversary Culture: The 1970s." *Newsletter on Science, Technology, & Human Values* 24 (1978): 33–39.

Nelkin, Dorothy, and M. Susan Lindee. *The DNA Mystique: The Gene as a Cultural Icon*. New York: Freeman, 1995.

Nelson, Alondra. *Body and Soul: The Black Panther Party and the Fight against Medical Discrimination*. Minneapolis: University of Minnesota Press, 2011.

Noble, David F. *America by Design: Science, Technology, and the Rise of Corporate Capitalism*. New York: Knopf, 1977.

Nowotny, Helga, and Hilary Rose, eds. *Counter-movements in the Sciences: The Sociology of the Alternatives to Big Science*. Dordrecht: D. Reidel Publishing Company, 1979.

Oreskes, Naomi, and Erik M. Conway. *Merchants of Doubt: How a Handful of Scientists Obscured the Truth on Issues from Tobacco Smoke to Global Warming*. New York: Bloomsbury Press, 2010.

Perfecto, Ivette, John Vandermeer, and Angus Wright. *Nature's Matrix: Linking Agriculture, Conservation and Food Sovereignty*. London: Earthscan Publications Limited, 2009.

Rose, Hilary, and Steven Rose, eds. *The Political Economy of Science: Ideology of/ in the Natural Sciences.* London: Macmillan, 1976.

———. *The Radicalisation of Science: Ideology of/in the Natural Sciences.* London: Macmillan, 1976.

Ross, Andrew, ed. *Science Wars.* Durham, NC: Duke University Press, 1996.

Schaffer, Simon, David Serlin, and Jennifer Tucker, eds. "Radicalizing Histories of Science and Technology." Special issue of *Radical History Review* 127 (2017).

Science for the People, Madison, Wisconsin, Collective. *The AMRC Papers: An Indictment of the Army Mathematics Research Center.* Madison, WI: Science for the People, Madison Collective, 1973.

Segerstrale, Ullica. *Defenders of the Truth: The Battle for Science in the Sociobiology Debate and Beyond.* Oxford: Oxford University Press, 2000.

Stevens, Sharon McKenzie. "Speaking out: Toward an Institutional Agenda for Refashioning STS Scholars as Public Intellectuals." *Science, Technology, & Human Values* 33, no. 6 (2008): 730–53.

Subramaniam, Banu. "Moored Metamorphoses: A Retrospective Essay on Feminist Science Studies," *Signs* 34, no. 4 (2009): 951–80.

Vandermeer, John. *Reconstructing Biology: Genetics and Ecology in the New World Order.* New York: Wiley and Sons, 1996.

Wisnioski, Matt. "Inside 'the System': Engineers, Scientists, and the Boundaries of Social Protest in the Long 1960s." *History and Technology* 19, no. 4 (2003): 313–33.

Woodhouse, Edward, David Hess, Steve Breyman, and Brian Martin. "Science Studies and Activism: Possibilities and Problems for Reconstructivist Agendas." *Social Studies of Science* 32, no. 2 (2002): 297–319.

Zimmerman, Bill. *Troublemaker: A Memoir from the Front Lines of the Sixties.* New York: Knopf Doubleday, 2012.

Zimmerman, Bill, Len Radinsky, Mel Rothenberg, and Bart Meyers. "Toward a Science for the People." Science for the People Booklet, 1972.

Contributors

BEN ALLEN is a biologist and research support staff at Oak Ridge National Laboratory, an active member of labor and progressive movements in the South, and a leading coordinator of the current revitalization of Science for the People.

ALYSSA BOTELHO is an MD/PhD candidate at Harvard Medical School and Harvard University's Department of the History of Science, where her research focuses on the history of biotechnology and biomedical activism in the twentieth-century United States.

DANIEL S. CHARD is lecturer in history at the University of Massachusetts Amherst, and author of *Nixon's War on Terrorism: The FBI, Leftist Guerrillas, and the Origins of Watergate* (University of North Carolina Press, forthcoming).

THOMAS CONNER is a PhD candidate in Communication and Science Studies at the University of California, San Diego, and is completing a dissertation about the cultural histories of hologram display technologies.

COLIN GARVEY is a PhD student in the Science & Technology Studies department at Rensselaer Polytechnic Institute, where he is completing a dissertation on the democratization of artificial intelligence.

SIGRID SCHMALZER is professor of history at the University of Massachusetts Amherst, and author, most recently, of *Red Revolution, Green Revolution: Scientific Farming in Socialist China* (University of Chicago Press, 2016).

Index

AAAS. *See* American Association for the Advancement of Science

ABM. *See* Anti-Ballistic Missile (ABM) system

Acker, Bonnie, 110

affirmative action 111, 112–13, 117–22

Africa, 5, 199

Africans, 129–31

Allen, Deborah 179, 190, 196

Alper, Joseph, xiii

Altendorf, Mary, 213

alternative energy, 178, 181, 182, 186–88

alternative technology movement, 148, 151, 173

American Association for the Advancement of Science (AAAS), 36–61; demonstrations at, 200; distribution of literature at, 137; efforts to transform, 3, 63; *Science* magazine and, 15; U.S. domination and, 201; women scientists and, 114–15

American Association for the Advancement of Science (AAAS) meetings: 1969 meeting, Boston, 3; 1970 meeting, Chicago, 4, 38–39, 43, 46–47, 49–55, 57, 178; 1971 meeting, Philadelphia, 4, 40, 55–57; 1972 meeting, Washington, DC, 40, 58–60; 1973 meeting, Mexico City, 40, 59, 201, 209–12

American Chemical Society, 38

American Friends Service Committee, 76

American Journal of Science, 43

American Oil Company, 176

American Physical Society (APS), 2, 3, 38, 40–42, 63

AMRC. *See* Army Math Research Center

Ann Arbor chapter of SftP, 3, 137, 138, 148

Anti-Ballistic Missile (ABM) system, 50, 63–64, 66–67, 81

anti-nuclear movement, 78, 177–79, 182, 189

anti-science movement, 29, 223

Apple Computer, 168

applied science, 13, 14, 18, 90, 135, 155

APS. *See* American Physical Society

Arditti, Rita 3, 85, 88, 111, 112

arms race, 37, 63, 65, 78–80, 82

Armstrong, Karl, 65, 71

Army Math Research Center (AMRC), 62, 64, 71–74

Aronow, David, 213

Ash, Arlene, xiii

Association of American Geologists and Naturalists, 43

atom bomb, 16, 70. *See also* hydrogen bomb; nuclear weapons

Atomic Energy Commission (U.S.), 39, 49, 178

Auth, Tony, 36

Bacon, Francis, 28

Barrett, Minna, xiii. *See also* Goldfarb, Minna

basic science: applied science and, 14;